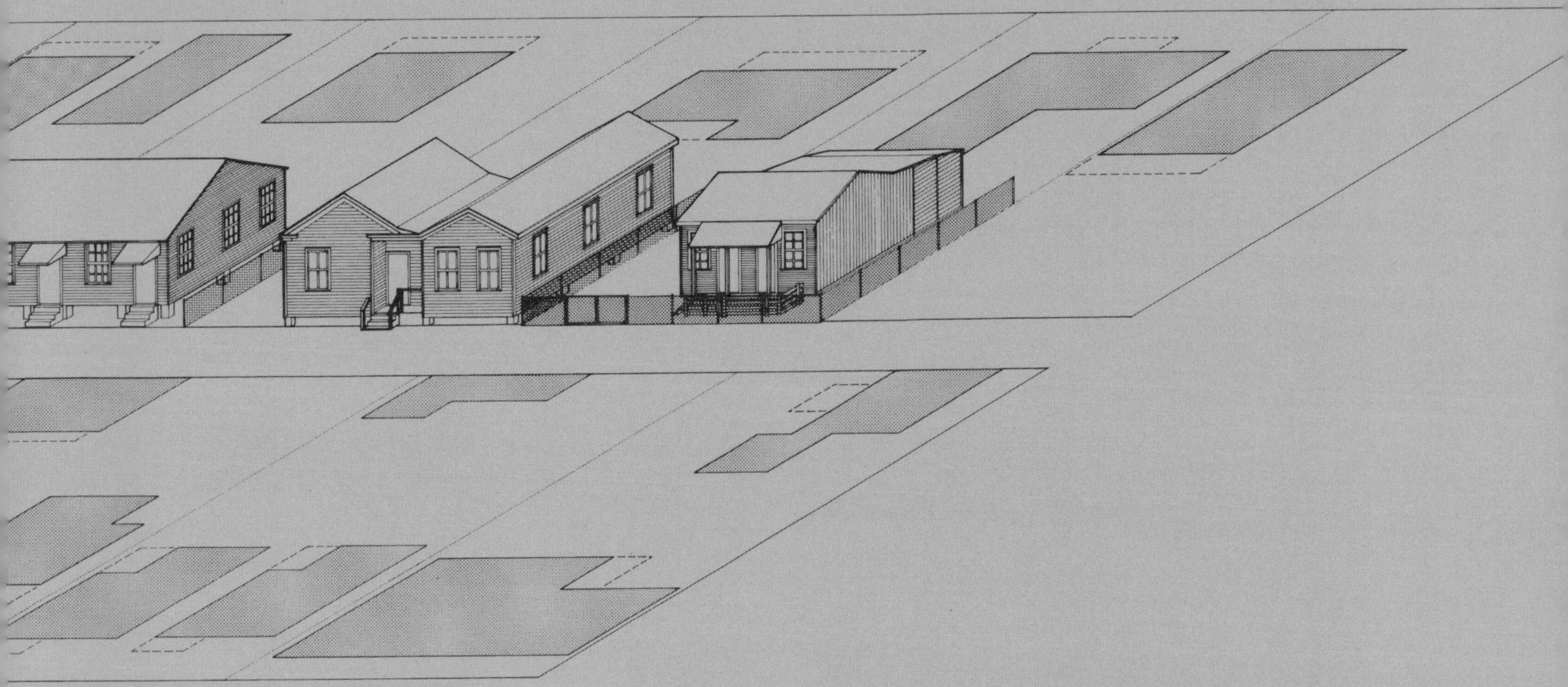

The Alleys and Back Buildings of Galveston

An Architectural and Social History

Ellen Beasley

Texas A&M University Press
College Station

Manufactured in China by
Everbest Printing Co. through
Four Colour Imports

Requests for permission to reproduce materials
from this work should be addressed to
Texas A&M University Press
4354 TAMU
College Station, TX 77843–4354

Book design by Minor Design Group, Houston
Architectural drawings by Rafael Longoria and Patrick Peters
Longoria/Peters, Houston
This edition by Texas A&M University Press

The paper used in this book
meets the minimum requirements
of the American National Standard
for Permanence of Paper for Printed
Library Materials, Z39.48-1984.
Binding materials have been chosen
for durability.
∞

LIBRARY OF CONGRESS CATALOGING-IN-PUBLICATION DATA

Beasley, Ellen.
The alleys and back buildings of Galveston : an architectural and social history / Ellen Beasley.
p. cm. — (Sara and John Lindsey series in the arts and humanities ; no. 10)
Originally published: Houston : Rice University Press, 1996.
Includes bibliographical references and index.
ISBN-13: 978-1-58544-582-0 (cloth : alk. paper)
ISBN-10: 1-58544-582-7 (cloth : alk. paper)
1. Outbuildings—Texas—Galveston. 2. Alleys—Texas—Galveston.
3. Architecture and society—Texas—Galveston—History.
4. African Americans—Texas—Galveston—History.
5. Galveston (Tex.)—History. I. Title.
NA8301.B4 2007
307.3'3621609764139—dc22
2006021631

Frontispiece: Alleyscape of alley houses on Block 375, looking west. Photographed 1990.

Contents

Preface to the New Edition

In the period between the original and new editions of *The Alleys and Back Buildings of Galveston*, some things have changed, others have not. Except for a few minor corrections, this edition duplicates the original 1996 printing. The story, along with my fervent belief that alleys are an overlooked resource in American cities and history, are among the things that have not changed. It goes without saying, however, that there have been physical changes—both good and bad, obvious and subtle—along the alleys in Galveston. That's to be expected in any urban landscape.

Galveston alleys are generally tidier and more sanitary than they were in the mid–1990s, thanks to the cooperative efforts of a growing number of neighborhood groups, the City of Galveston, and the Galveston Historical Foundation. The alleys, it should be added, are only one aspect of a concerted, ongoing clean-up program in Galveston.

Of the individual back buildings featured in the book, three have been demolished since 1996* but the larger number have been at least minimally maintained and, in some instances, renovated. There has been a continued shift in use: Back buildings, both old and new, are now even more likely to be used as guesthouses, studios, or other extensions of a front house rather than used as rental units. Most new construction along the alleys takes the form of garages.

I confess to viewing some changes with the ambivalence that is characteristic of preservationists: I welcome improvements, but lament that alley aesthetics are being altered by such things as paving and the hulky, rolling trashcans that the city now provides each household. However, whatever has been added or altered, we can all be grateful that thus far Galveston's historic scale survives, both on the front streets and the alleys of the older neighborhoods. Let's hope that the same can be said ten years from now.

The Alleys and Back Buildings of Galveston presents just one variation of an American phenomenon that continues to go begging for attention in our urban studies. I had hoped that during the last ten years, more studies of alleys and alley life in other American cities and towns would have been added to the few that do exist. The research is difficult—*far* more difficult than researching the front side of our urban spaces—but alleys and alley dwellers offer an incredibly rich return, especially on that local, individual level where any alley study must begin. Comparative studies will follow, as more in-depth local studies are available.

During recent hurricane seasons, I felt a renewed connection with the alleys and alley-dwellers of my research. Events surrounding hurricanes Katrina and Rita in fall 2005 were not-so-gentle reminders that history does indeed repeat itself and that some things take much

* *As of April 12, 2006, three alley buildings featured in the book with floor plans and contemporary photographs have been demolished: 2020 Avenue J (overleaf, Fig. 2, and page 103, Figs. 134–137); 2616 Avenue M (pages 9, 10, and 11, Figs. 8–11); and 2818 Avenue L (pages 56–57, Fig. 55, and page 110, Figs. 155 and 157). Other back buildings appearing in contemporary photographs have also been demolished since publication of the first edition, among them the row of houses in Fig. 78 (page 71) and both houses in Fig. 163 (page 113). Historic back buildings will continue to disappear—all the more reason why these buildings should be recorded photographically and, when possible, with measured drawings, not only in Galveston but also in other historic urban settings.*

too long to change. There was, of course, the obvious comparison with the 1900 storm that devastated Galveston but there were also vivid reminders that we are still challenged by our ability and willingness to provide for our most vulnerable citizens.

The people who were a part of the first edition of *The Alleys and Back Buildings of Galveston* have been no more static than the alleys themselves. This includes alley dwellers (past and present), property owners, interviewees, and supporters, both family and friends. I repeat my feeling of gratitude to everyone acknowledged in the first printing. Once again, there have been changes—some of great personal sadness.

To that first list of acknowledgements, I add a special note of appreciation to the following whose contributions made this reprint possible: Dick and Jan Coggeshall, Burke Evans, Shrub and Peaches Kempner, Robert and Susan Lynch, George P. Mitchell, Joan Richardson, John Samuels, Barbara L. Thompson, Jack and Sally Wallace, the Galveston Historical Foundation, the Old Central Cultural Center, the Trube Foundation, and the Harris and Eliza Kempner Fund.

Charles Backus and his staff at Texas A&M University Press have been a pleasure to work with, and I thank the Press for acquiring the alley book when Rice University Press closed. Friends Bill Seale and Barbara Crews have been especially supportive (and prodding) along the way.

My last and biggest thank-you goes to Burke Evans and Sally and Jack Wallace: to Burke, who ultimately made the reprint happen, and to Burke and the Wallaces, whose enthusiasm and love for Galveston and whose generosity as friends served as my introduction to this extraordinary city so many years ago.

Ellen Beasley
January 2007

Acknowledgments

"Those Alleys Again" was a headline in an 1875 Galveston newspaper. I suspect it is also a phrase that occurred more than once to many of my friends and family members who survived a project that took far longer than anticipated. My first acknowledgment, an umbrella thank-you, is extended to all those, many of whom are listed below, who endured and encouraged—and endured and encouraged.

Any study of Galveston, whatever the subject, must begin at the Rosenberg Library in Galveston. I thank the staff, most particularly archivist Casey Greene for directing me to sources that I might otherwise have missed, and photo archivist Anna Peebler. I also spent many hours reading microfilm in the Texas and Local History Department of the Houston Public Library, and especially appreciate the help of Will Howard, assistant manager, and Doris Glasser, who has since retired as manager.

I enjoyed using the records—in part because I was always welcomed by the staffs—in the Galveston County Clerk's Office, Galveston County Courthouse; the Mayor's Office, Galveston City Hall; and the Galveston offices of the Stewart Title Company.

Architects Rafael Longoria and Patrick Peters are responsible for the architectural drawings, which are so important to the book. They were assisted by H. Bellinda Osoria, Ian Sheard, Olga Vazquez, and Bev Blackwood.

The drawings also represent the graciousness of the following owners and residents who let us measure their houses and buildings and not always at the most convenient time: Kate Bluitt, Irene Caroline, Robert Clark, Willie Mae Clay, Barbara and Frank Crews, Pam Diamond, Burke Evans, Thelma Jackson, Julius W. Jockusch, Jeffrey Kilgore, Richard Melancon, Pat Quigley, Barney Rapp, Marcia Sanders, Arthur Schechter, Sally Wallace, Robert and Chris Welter, and Ann and Charles Williams.

The oral histories, which are central to the book, were a pleasure to conduct—and difficult to cut. I appreciate not only the willingness of the interviewees to be interviewed, but also their time, good humor, and thoughtfulness.

Production of the book was no small task, and I thank the staff of Rice University Press: Susan Fernandez, who, as managing editor, accepted my proposal, her successor Susan Bielstein, and consulting editor Sara Booth; and, most especially, production assistant Ryan Hess, consulting editor Mary Sieber, and consulting graphic designer Craig Minor.

Financial assistance was generously given by the Harris and Eliza Kempner Fund, the Texas Commission for the Arts, the Summerlee Foundation, George P. Mitchell, and E. Burke Evans. My experiences as a Loeb Fellow at the Harvard Graduate School of Design and a Rome Prize Fellow at the American Academy in Rome also contributed significantly to my decision to pursue this subject and write the book.

With much appreciation, I acknowledge the help and interest of the following individuals: David Bessman, Peter Brink, Kathy Burns, Al Chambers, Grady Clay and Judith McCandless, Jan Coggeshall, Margaret Culbertson, Ron Durst, Coco Eiseman, Burke Evans,

Stephen Fox, Michael Gerber, Anne Castrodale Golovin, Harrold Henck, Jean Krchnak, Elizabeth Lyon, Gwen Marcus, Sims McCutchan, Wes, Sandy, and Drew McNeely, Ross Moody, Deborah Morris, Philip Morris, Terry and Hamilton Morton, William Murtagh, Greg Nowicki, Pat Prather, Rodris Roth, William Seale, Ed Simmen, Dean Stern, John Vlach, Bob Voris, Sally and Jack Wallace, John Whiteman, Deborah Wilson, Cary Wintz, and Larry and Alice Wygant.

To these names I add a few that have a special meaning: Katharine Randall, Harris Kempner, and my father, Frank Beasley, individuals who were often in my thoughts and whose observations I missed; Joal and John Donovan, who made this book a possibility by letting me become what could be called either a latchkey visitor or an adjunct family member; James and R. L. Beasley, my brothers, who gave opinions when asked and encouragement when not; and Zula Mae Beasley, who, in so many ways, gave her unwavering support—not always certain for what but as the loving mother that she is. The first copy is for her.

Ellen Beasley
February 1996

Preface

Many American cities and towns, especially older ones, have alleys and back buildings. Galveston, in that sense, is not unusual, but what separates Galveston from many other places is how conspicuous its alleys and back buildings are. The topography is too flat, the alleyways too wide, and the vegetation too modest to ignore the long and open east-west vistas that divide most city blocks.

I knew about alleys long before I moved to Galveston. I grew up in Waterloo, Illinois, a small German community founded in the nineteenth century. Waterloo had alleys. It was the way we walked to town—out our backdoor and through the alley. It was where our milkman, Mr. Goeddel, and our grocer, Mr. Hencke, made deliveries; where we burned our trash, even some of our garbage (in a barrel); where my brother James and I played, jumped the open ditch—especially inviting after a hard rain—and fought our neighborhood wars with Dizzy Reosenmeyer, who lived across the alley. It was also how my Grandma McAllister kept a watchful eye on the neighbors on both sides of the block.

Buildings did not dominate the alleys in Waterloo, which is why, perhaps, it was the number of buildings along the alleys in Galveston that I first registered. Like most newcomers to the city, I was immediately impressed by the larger, ornamented buildings and residences, but the real reward for a lingering look about the city was discovering its minor architecture—the corner stores, the small houses, and the alley buildings. The little back buildings seemed to be everywhere and assumed a collective richness equal in size and spirit to the bigger buildings as they proudly framed the alley entrances, peered from behind the front houses, and huddled in rows along the block interiors.

What began as a casual, intermittent pursuit became a full-time commitment and curiosity, but discovering, then photographing, the back buildings was one thing, researching them another. As might be expected, the standard sources researched in the standard ways revealed more about the front houses and their inhabitants than about those along the alleys. It became obvious that I would have to research, at least in the beginning, the back buildings and their residents as I had looked at the buildings—collectively. I also realized that it was the alleys and the alley system that provided the connecting link to the mix of people and buildings found along the backside of Galveston's older residential neighborhoods.

A check of nineteenth-century Galveston city directories disclosed that they were slow to specify alley addresses, but they did document an ever-growing alley population. In 1881–82, 260 alley dwellers were listed, whereas ten years later, in 1891–92, there were 765, numbers that proved to be only a small percentage of the city's actual alley residents.

I also read selected years of nineteenth-century Galveston newspapers, the source most likely to offer a glimpse of alley life—if, indeed, there was one. I was not disappointed. The newspapers supplied a wealth of information, but at the same time left two overriding impressions: The alleys were a mess and alley life was sordid, due in large part to the sorry lot of alley dwellers. Given the present-day condition of many Galveston alleys, it was easy to accept the first impression as being fairly close to the truth.

The second impression, however, was another matter. It was hard to believe that most people living on the alleys were scoundrels, but, of course, the voice not heard in the newspapers and other written records was the voice of alley dwellers and other alley users. For this, I conducted oral interviews to balance what I suspected was a distorted, lopsided view of alley life and alley residents. Not only did the interviews confirm my suspicions, but they also documented that many aspects of daily life in Galveston and living on an alley had hardly changed since the nineteenth century.

This book, then, relies upon a mixture of written and pictorial documents, oral interviews, and the buildings and alleys themselves to tell its story. The bulk of the historical narrative covers the years from the founding of the city to the early 1890s, the period in which the distinctive characteristics of the alleys and back buildings evolved and Galvestonians cemented their attitudes toward alleys and alley dwellers. The narrative moves into the twentieth century to describe the raising of the island, a phenomenal yet little-known engineering feat far too important in the history of the city to be omitted but one that has been interpreted mostly in technological terms, never as it affected Galvestonians on a personal, individual basis—the way it affected those living on the alleys.

The historical narrative ends in 1915, with a 1920 footnote, because the early twentieth century is the period in which the written documents and oral interviews begin to overlap, providing an easy, natural transition from written to spoken sources. Moreover, with the first methodical effort to demolish alley houses and the introduction of the "auto" garage, which became the dominant type of alley service building, the years immediately prior to World War I mark the closing of one era and the opening of another in the history of Galveston's alleys and back buildings.

Although there are all kinds of back buildings along the alleys of Galveston, my primary interest has always been those associated with residential use, an interest colored, no doubt, by my preservationist's bent both to document the historical significance of the buildings and to encourage their maintenance and appreciation as a housing resource. Thus, my focus is on back buildings that are located in residential neighborhoods and that have or had a residential use, whether this was their sole use or one combined with other uses.

The buildings, small as many of them are, display an infinite architectural variety, even more than I first realized. I began my research thinking almost solely in terms of service buildings—those oriented to a front house and those whose inhabitants began their day by stepping into a yard. However, in Galveston, there is a second type of back building—the alley house—that was usually built for rental purposes and whose inhabitants began their day by stepping into an alley. It is a distinction that expanded the scope of my research, and also prolonged it.

The back buildings illustrated in the book are just a small sampling of service buildings and alley houses that can still be seen along the alleys. Although they represent some of the most common forms built in the city, they do not provide a comprehensive inventory of back buildings. That is yet another project to be done.

Over the years, living "on the alley" in Galveston has meant many things to many people, and what it meant has had a lot to do with choice—whether you were living "on the alley" because you wanted to or because you had to. In Galveston's rich and dramatic history, alley dwellers, like alley buildings, have been treated only marginally, if at all, but both the people and the buildings on the alleys have been an integral and vital part of the city since its very beginning. The city's history—and preservation—are incomplete without them.

To
Eva Lynn née Scott and Lucy Grimes
Alley sisters

The Alleys and Back Buildings of Galveston

Introduction: Views and Interviews

Everything that went on on the front streets happened in the alleys. Now, don't you think it didn't.

The Rev. James B. Thomas

In 1885, lithographer Augustus Koch published the second bird's-eye view of Galveston (fig. 1). If Galvestonians compared it with the 1871 bird's-eye view, which they surely did, they must have been impressed with what they saw. Koch's view visualized statistics that Galvestonians had read and boasts that they had made for years. It was plain to see that Galveston had grown. There could be no doubt that the port was its economic heart, that the commercial core was larger in both geographical size and building scale, and that the residential areas had expanded in all directions—to the East End Flats, toward the beach on the south, and to the west.

The number of buildings alone indicated that the population had more than doubled between 1871 and 1885. Everywhere, individual blocks were more densely developed, with a greater number of buildings on both the front streets and the alleys. Although the 1885 lithograph was not as clear as the earlier view, in part because of the number of buildings, Galvestonians could find their place of residence and work, whether it was a dormer cottage on a front street, a neighborhood corner store, a downtown commercial building, or a two-room dwelling on an alley. They also could locate—with the help of a listing on the map—sixty-one landmarks and important buildings in the city, among them St. Mary's Cathedral, the courthouse, the gasworks, the Tremont Opera House, and the Beach Hotel.

What they did not find on the list were Fat Alley and Tin Can Alley. Still, most everyone in town knew exactly where these alleys were, even though they probably were off-limits for many Galvestonians—the bird's-eye view being the closest they would ever get to the infamous alleys between Twenty-seventh and Twenty-ninth Streets and Avenues D and E.

But Galvestonians who trafficked the other alleys in town—and many did, young and old, black and white—would have been able to identify on the 1885 bird's-eye view the different types of alleyscapes and alley dwellings that had evolved in the city's residential neighborhoods. There were the back buildings that had been built as secondary or support structures and were oriented to the backyard of the property on which they were located (fig. 2). These are referred to here as *service buildings, servants quarters, secondary* or *support structures,* and *back houses.* Then there were the back buildings that were oriented to the alleys, most of which had been built as rental property after the Civil War (fig. 3). These are called *alley houses.*

On many alleys, both types of back buildings coexisted. Some alleys, however, contained only one or the other, a circumstance that Galvestonians knew was always subject to change, since buildings, both front and back, might shift in use, ownership, and sometimes even location.

There were other aspects of the city that would have escaped the uninformed viewer. The greatest concentration of prominent citizens lived between Twelfth and Nineteenth Streets on the north side of Avenue J and several blocks northward. Their properties had not only the highest monetary value in town but also the highest elevations. Domestic servants

Interpreting Sanborn Insurance Maps and Bird's-Eye Views

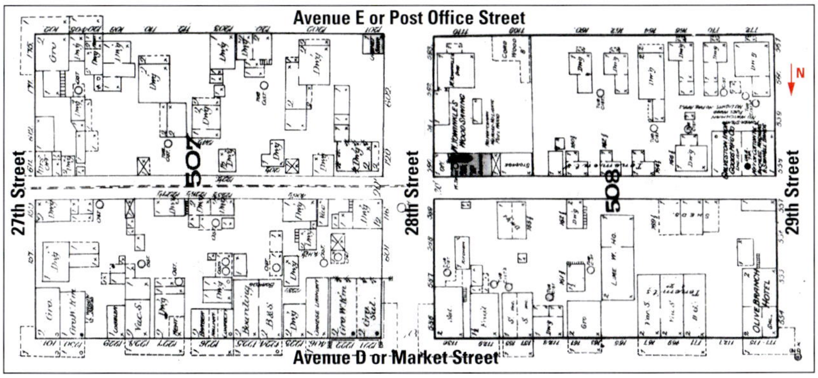

Fig. 4. Sanborn insurance map, 1885. Directional orientation matches fig. 5.

Produced for insurance purposes, the Sanborn insurance maps of Galveston and other cities provide very detailed information. In contrast, the bird's-eye views are not as exacting as the Sanborn maps, and were never intended to be because they were usually published for promotional interests, a fact that requires some caution in their use and interpretation. The coincidental arrival in Galveston in 1885 of lithographer Augustus Koch and the Sanborn Map Company allows a comparison of the two documents. If Blocks 507 and 508 are used as examples, the bird's-eye view, in this instance, proves to be a reliable and invaluable source.

The blocks containing Tin Can Alley (Block 507) and Fat Alley (Block 508) are among the blocks included on the 1885 Sanborn map. On both blocks, the Avenue D or Market Street side consists of a series of businesses and an occasional dwelling (marked "Dw'g") placed directly on the sidewalk line. All the businesses except the cobbler's shop in Block 507 have canopies extending over the sidewalk. The two-story business buildings, in all probability, accommodated residential uses on the upper floors. The Avenue E or Post Office Street side of both blocks is dominated by dwellings, with those on Block 507 being more randomly arranged than those on Block 508. The round shapes on the lot interiors are cisterns.

Block 507 is the more densely developed of the two blocks. Contributing to the density are numerous dwellings located in the middle of the lots and eight dwellings placed along Tin Can Alley. The alley dwellings include four one-story houses, three two-story houses, and one one-and-a-half-story house. Three small one-story stables (denoted by an "x") also define the alley line. The compound on the corner of Twenty-seventh Street and Avenue E is typical of properties found throughout Galveston—except in the neighborhoods with the finest residences. Securing the corner is a two-story grocery store to which three dwellings are attached, including one with a meat market on the front. Varying additions and building units extend to the back of the property and abut a three-part structure that begins with a one-story doctor's office on the alley corner.

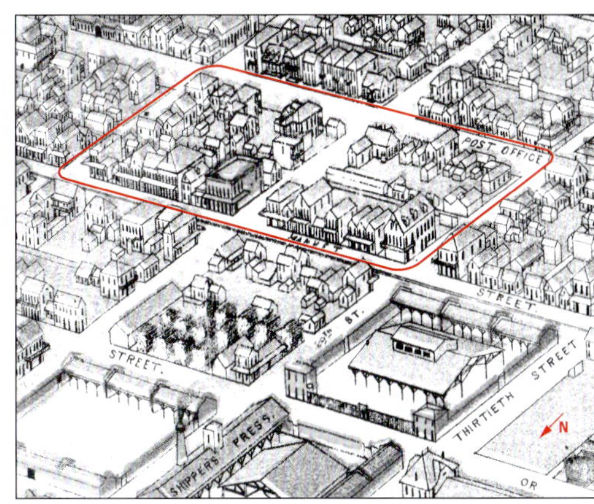

Fig. 5. Detail of 1885 bird's-eye view. The outlined blocks are 507 (on the left) and 508 (on the right).

The primary distinction between Blocks 507 and 508 is the industrial businesses situated on Block 508. Fat Alley is defined by a combination of building types and uses: a single two-story dwelling; seven one-story dwellings, includng a duplex and three "Tenements"; several sheds; and two businesses on opposite alley corners—W. Yowinkle's wood-sawing business on Twenty-eighth Street and the Galveston Iron Goods Mfg. Co. on Twenty-ninth Street. The mapmaker noted that both businesses used wood for fuel, but that neither had a watchman, fire equipment, or lights. At least Yowinkle shared the hazards of his business with his neighbors because he lived on the property—a rare notation on Sanborn maps. A lime warehouse is located in the center of the block on the Avenue D side.

Most of the buildings on the Sanborn map can be located on the bird's-eye view. As a reference point, the corner buildings on both blocks are easily matched. The bird's-eye view shows many of the small backyard and alley buildings on Block 507. On Block 508, the two businesses on the alley corners are visible, although the lime warehouse in the block interior is not. The row of dwellings on Fat Alley is partially obscured by the Olive Branch Hotel. Of course, neither the view nor the map can show all the equipage—animate and inanimate—associated with everyday activity in the backyards and along the alleys.

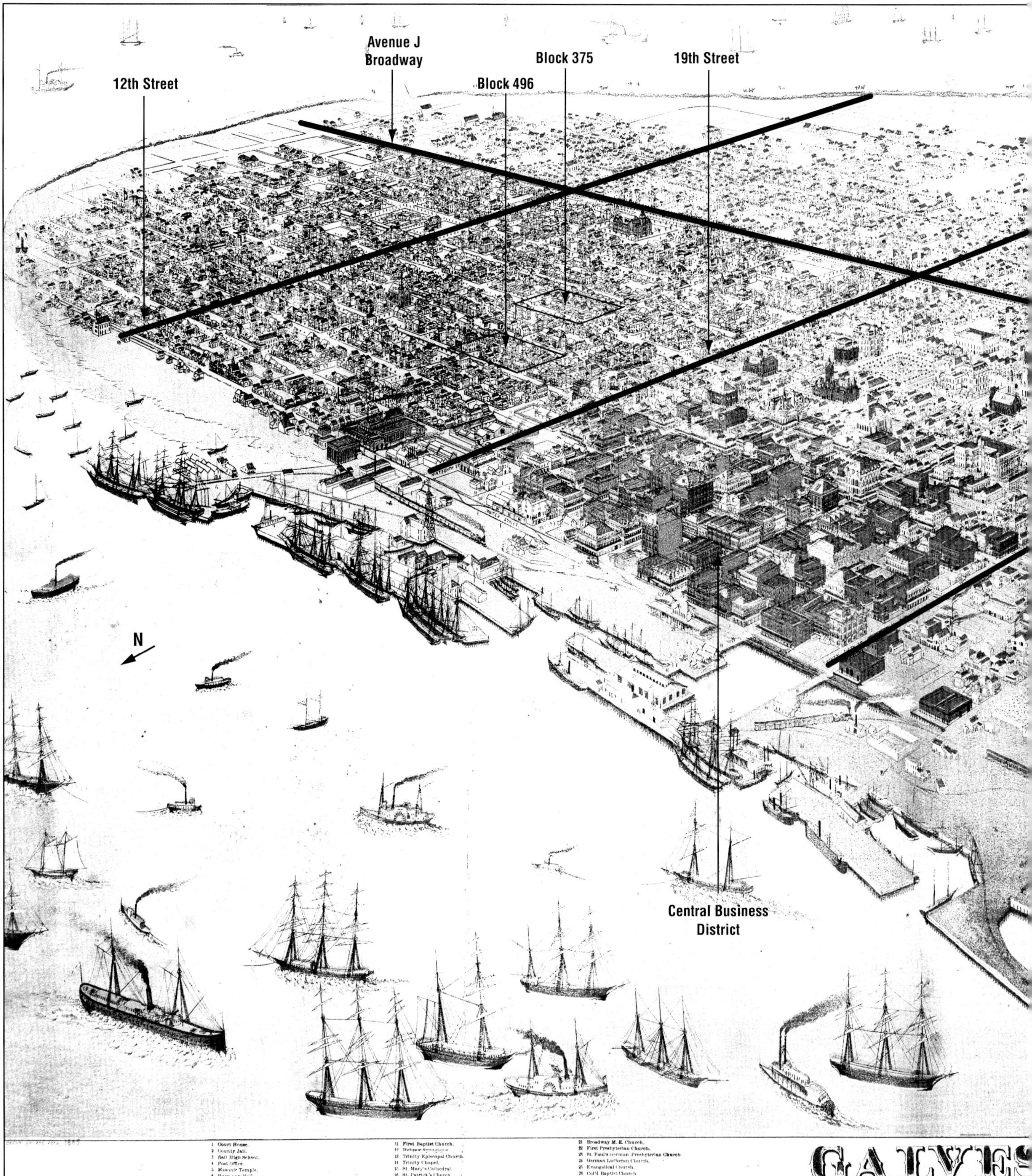

Fig. 1. 1885 bird's-eye view of Galveston. Lithograph by Augustus Koch. Drawings of eighteen buildings have been removed from across the top. To compare 1871 bird's-eye view, see fig. 23, page 27. The Gulf of Mexico is at the top of the drawing, Galveston Bay at the bottom.

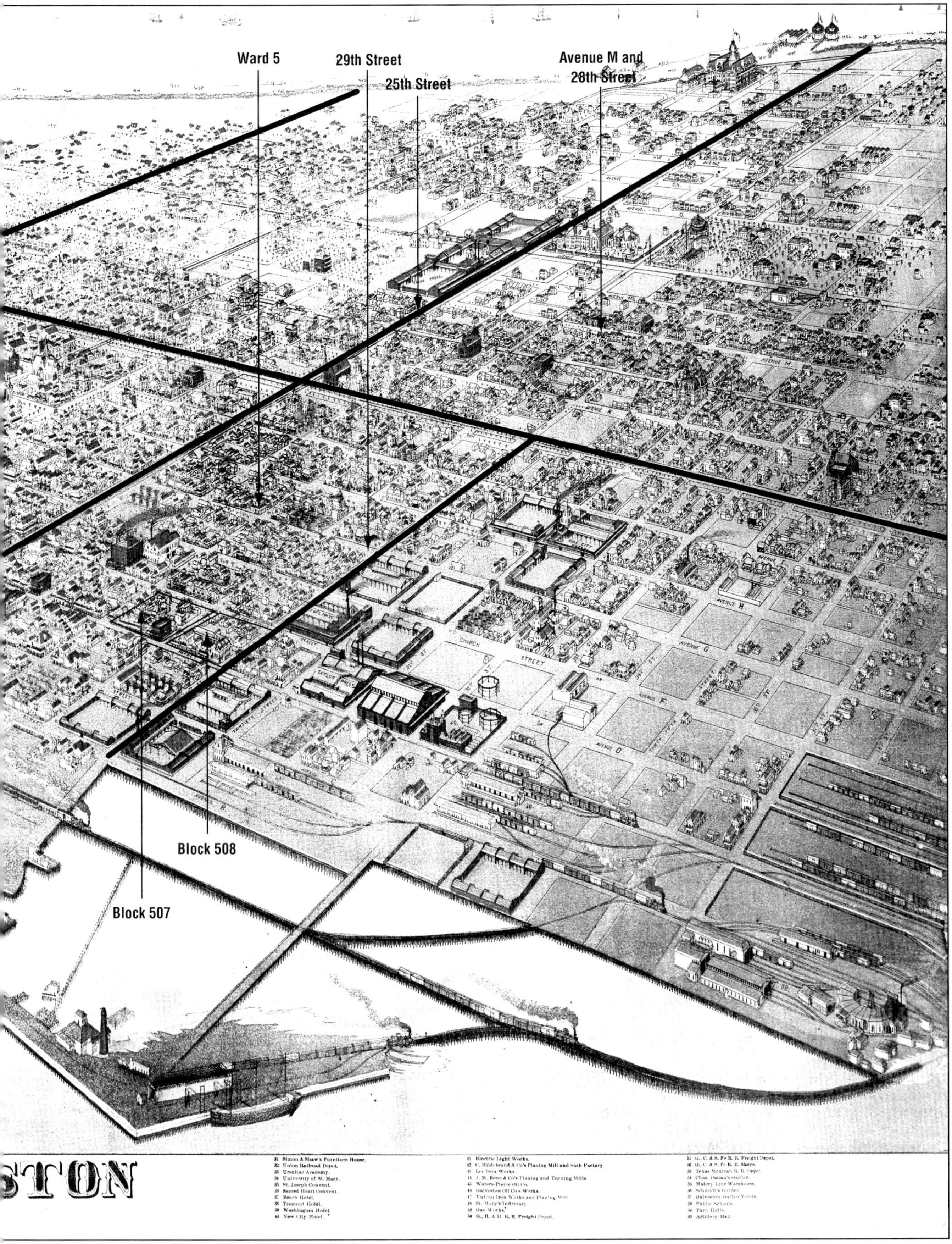
Ward 5
29th Street
25th Street
Avenue M and
28th Street
Block 508
Block 507
CHURCH
STREET
AVENUE H.
AVENUE G
AVENUE D
STON
31 Simon & Shaw's Furniture House.
32 Union Railroad Depot.
33 Ursuline Academy.
34 University of St. Mary.
35 St. Joseph Convent.
36 Sacred Heart Convent.
37 Beach Hotel.
38 Tremont Hotel.
39 Washington Hotel.
40 New City Hotel.
41 Electric Light Works.
42 C. Hildebrand & Co's Planing Mill and Sash Factory.
43 Lee Iron Works.
44 J. M. Bone & Co's Planing and Turning Mills
45 Waters-Pierce Oil Co.
46 Galveston Oil Co's Works.
47 Vulcan Iron Works and Planing Mill
48 St. Mary's Infirmary
49 Gas Works.
50 G., H. & H. R. R. Freight Depot.
51 G., C. & S. Fe R. R. Freight Depot.
52 G., C. & S. Fe R. R. Shops.
53 Texas Mexican R. R. Depot.
54 Chas. Pallan's Garden.
55 Malory Line Warehouse.
56 Schmidt's Garden.
57 Galveston Garten Verein.
58 Public Schools.
59 Turn Halle.
60 Artillery Hall

Fig. 2. 2020 Avenue J, back building. Alley side of secondary or support structure oriented to the backyard. Photographed 1990.

Fig. 3. 2621 Avenue K rear. Alley side of alley house with entrance oriented to the alley. Photographed circa 1977.

Overleaf: Fig. 1.

lived in many of the back buildings on these properties. The houses east of Twelfth Street and south of Avenue J were inhabited primarily by laborers, black and white, the poorest living closest to the water. Laborers' houses also marked the areas of recent landfill on the western and southern fringes of town.

Fat and Tin Can Alleys (figs. 4, 5) were located in Ward Five, which was bordered by Twenty-fifth and Twenty-ninth Streets and Avenue J and Galveston Bay. The blocks northward from Avenue E composed "the district," the less respectable side of Galveston's port economy, with its concentration of saloons, boardinghouses, gambling halls, and brothels. Galvestonians preferred to talk instead about the city's importance as a cotton port, second only to New Orleans, and as the port of entry for thousands of immigrants every year.

Although Galveston's black population was interspersed throughout the city, there were individual blocks and alleys, and some pockets of several blocks, that were inhabited predominantly, if not entirely, by blacks. These tended to be in the vicinity of Avenue M and Twenty-eighth Street, where the Barnes Institute (which began as the Colored Free School) was located; close to the central business core; in Ward Five; and along the city's edges.

The Sanborn Map and Publishing Company also traveled to Galveston in 1885, but unlike Augustus Koch, who printed and sold bird's-eye views for popular consumption, it recorded the city for fire-insurance purposes. The Sanborn maps document the footprints of the buildings on each block. They also show, through color codes and written notations, very specific details about individual buildings, such as the number of stories, roofing and wall materials, porches, and uses. The company made its first appearance in Galveston in 1876, then returned in 1885, in both instances recording a relatively small portion of the city. Later maps, prepared in 1889, 1899, and 1912, each with a series of updates, covered the city limits.[1]

The general public did not use the Sanborn maps, but what they documented in even greater detail than did the bird's-eye views, most Galvestonians knew about their city anyway. No two blocks—or streets—or alleys—were alike. Nor did any block or street or alley remain unchanged from document to document, a fact for which they needed no reminder when, in November 1885, more than forty blocks of the city burned. Changes and alterations could be gradual, as were those that reflected social, technological, and economic shifts, or abrupt, as were those that were caused by such catastrophes as the fire and to which Galveston seemed prone. The greatest of these, the 1900 hurricane, was yet to come.

The present-day urban historian has much in common with the Galvestonian of 1885 who was fascinated with the few pictorial records that existed of the city. For the nineteenth-century Galvestonian, the fascination may have been as much for the technique, especially of the bird's-eye view, as for the image itself. For the urban historian, it is the image and the footprint of the city, the block, and the building that hold the fascination, especially if the interest is in simpler, smaller, and rarely documented structures such as those found along the alleys. The views and maps are essential to the story of the alleys and back buildings in Galveston.

Fig. 6. Amos Sims, sitting on the steps of an alley house, probably 2223 Avenue K rear. Texas Works Administration photograph taken September 27, 1937.

Former slave Amos Sims knew firsthand the Galveston shown in the 1871 and 1885 bird's-eye views of the city. In September 1937, the eighty-six-year-old man was photographed and interviewed for the Federal Writers' Project that documented the lives of former slaves (fig. 6). He is shown sitting on the steps of a Galveston alley house, in all probability 2223 Avenue K rear, the address at which he was listed in the 1936–37 city directory.[2]

Fig. 7. North side of 2600 block Avenue M, front street, looking west. The two-story dormered house, which was originally one and a half stories, is 2616 Avenue M (the front house). Photographed 1995.

From the interview, we can learn a few facts about Sims and his family. Sims was born in 1851 in Harrison County, Texas. During his childhood, he and his parents, James and Mary Sims, were owned as a family by two slaveholders. After the Civil War, the Sims family "went to Galveston," where James Sims worked and where Amos, once he "got big . . . jus' work 'round, firs' one place an' den 'nother."[3] Unfortunately, the project accorded little importance to the lives of former slaves following the Civil War, and the interview with Sims discloses nothing more about his life between the family's arrival in Galveston and the time the photograph was taken.

Bits and pieces of information about Sims's life, however, can be gathered from other documents. City directories list him as working and living at various occupations and addresses: as a bartender living on the alley of 316 Twenty-sixth Street in 1901–2; as a laborer rooming at 819 Twenty-eighth Street in 1909–10; and as a junkman rooming at 2622 Avenue G in 1919. By 1930, he was residing at "rear 2223 Avenue K."[4]

If only the interviewer in 1937 had asked Sims about his jobs, his family, his friends and neighbors, his church, and where he lived, what he could have told us about the Galveston that is depicted in the 1871 and 1885 bird's-eye views! It was a missed opportunity. Nevertheless, the image of Sims sitting on the steps of the alley house provides a link between his generation and people like Bill Millican, whose family moved into an alley house in 1940 when Millican was seven years old and whose recollections have been recorded.

Often, oral history is a primary, if not the only, source to bridge the gaps between past and present, fact and feeling, especially for such subjects as the alley dwellers and back buildings of Galveston, where firsthand written and pictorial documentation is scarce—and always will be. There is little chance of locating a detailed account written by someone who

Fig. 8. 2600 block Avenue M, alley side, looking west. The two-story building is 2616 Avenue M rear, where Bill Millican lived. Photographed 1995.

resided in an alley house or service building, because they would have considered it of little interest or value. Pictorial records, other than documents such as the bird's-eye views, are also difficult to uncover. Most people who lived along the alleys could not afford to buy a camera. Cameras were owned by those who lived along the front streets, and few front-street residents were inclined to photograph the backside of their property.

Bill Millican's family has no visual record of the years they lived at 2616 Avenue M rear, but Millican has vivid recollections of his family's alley residence. It was located on an alley lined with rental units in what historically was a black neighborhood (figs. 7, 8). In many respects, Millican's description of alley life could have been spoken by someone living along a Galveston alley in the nineteenth century. The specific settings may differ, but many of the same themes—the alleys as a playground, the wharves as a major employer of the men, domestic work for the women—appear again and again in documents and interviews.

The recollections of Bill Millican are those of a BOI, the local term for people "born on the island." Born in 1933, Millican left Galveston to attend Prairie View A&M College where he received a bachelor of arts degree, and to serve six years in the military. Upon returning to Galveston, he taught for three years in the public schools but "found out it wasn't my calling" and began working for the city as a water meter reader in 1954. He worked in various supervisory positions and is currently Director of Sanitation.[5]

I'm a BOI. I'm very, very proud of that. I'm very proud of Galveston itself as far as the things that have happened over a period since 1933, when I was born. I think it's a very unique place.

I was raised in an alley. . . . lived in a house with the facing to the alley. I lived in the 2600 block of Avenue M directly behind old Central High School. It's a block of small front houses facing the avenue and the same amount of houses in the alley. For each house that faced the street, there was the same amount of houses that was in the alley. They were called "rears." My address was 2616 Avenue M rear and the Antones', people that lived up front, was 2616 Avenue M.[6]

A lot of people came out of those alleys to be something, and as a kid, I had a ball in them. We played mostly in the alley. We never played in the yard. The alley was bigger. We played the same as any other kids. We played stick ball, rolled old tires, played marbles—almost anything. Out of the ten families that I remember, eight of the boys that I know went to college, came out with degrees, and are teaching or preaching or lawyer or whatever.

Fig. 9

In my alley, there were three types of dwellings. There was a single house with I don't know how many bedrooms, but one family there. Then there was another type, the type where I was raised at—upstairs and downstairs. Then there was another type of apartments in the alley that had front houses, too. I mean three or four or five, six different families. Most of these houses were owned by someone else who did not even live in that particular neighborhood. I was rare to know who my landlord was—the Antones.

Our house was what they now call a duplex. It was an up and a down (figs. 9, 10). *The people who lived upstairs was my people. There was my brother and myself, my mother and my father, and downstairs was the Wallses. Mr. Walls was a yardman. He had two grandsons, his wife, and he, and his daughter that the boys belonged to. He was the only man in the house.*

We always entered through the alley. Now, my folks always came in through the gate on the side. The Wallses went right into their front door. I had to go in the gate, turn, go up the steps, and go upstairs.

In our house, when you go in the door, that was the living room. It looked out on the alley. Over on the west side was a bedroom. To the back was a kitchen. On one side was my brother's and my room, and on the other side was another bedroom. They had steps going down the back of the house into the yard so there was a front door and a back door. Same thing on the bottom.

We even had a toilet outside in the yard. We shared it with the neighbor downstairs. The people in the front house had their own inside toilet. Equal but separate—that's what they called it. But now, there were some that lived in my alley on both sides that had toilets inside.

The toilet was in the middle of the yard. It was a flush toilet. If you had to use it, you take your *toilet paper and go use it and bring* your *toilet paper back. There was a lot of togetherness during those days. And we never had problems with Mr. Walls and his family. They did the same thing. We took baths in the kitchen in a tub. A number three tub, a round tub with the handles on. At night, you had to use the slop jar.*

The alley house was heated with gas. We didn't have a ceiling fan. No air conditioning. We had a floor fan that you could raise, tighten it up, and put it in the window.

The washing was done on the back porch upstairs. We had a wringer. I don't ever remember that my folks and the Wallses had an agreement on which day one would wash, but both hung

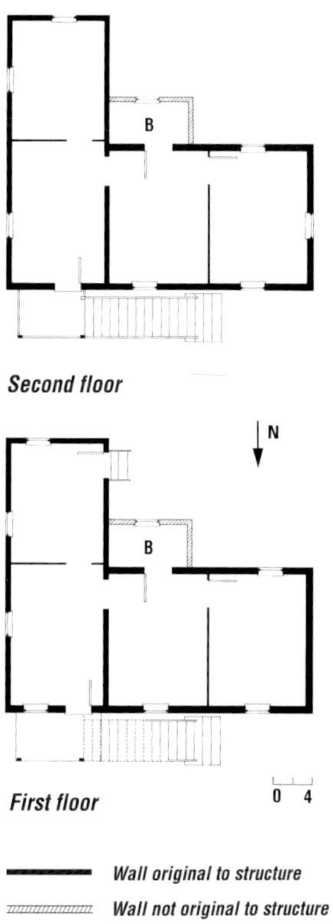

Fig. 10

Figs. 9 and 10. 2616 Avenue M rear, alley house where Bill Millican's family lived. The second-floor plan (fig. 10, top) is a conjecture based on the first floor and Bill Millican's recollection. During his family's occupancy, the space that is now a bathroom was the back porch with stairs into the backyard. Photographed 1995. The floor plans were documented in 1995.

their clothes on the line on different days. The line was in the yard with long sticks to the ground to hold it up.

I can remember when there was a horse stable in the alley. Mr. Ward had some horses and we used to ride horses up and down there.

Hey, one thing we didn't lack was love. We might have been broke as hell, but we didn't know it because there was so much love going through. And I don't mean just my family. I mean the whole stinking alley. It was like family folk.

Our alley was all black. Sure was. I think a lot of them migrated from different towns. I know there was some people from Louisiana. There were some people from East Texas. All of them weren't native Galvestonians. . . . There were more jobs to be had. . . . Ninety percent of the men were connected with the wharves—longshoremen. As a matter of fact, my father worked on the wharves for forty-six years, but he swore that he never would want me to work there. That's why he forced me to college, and screamed and fussed, "Get an education." Oh, I worked in the summer down there, worked on the boats sweeping sugar. Good job for me, man. My mother worked domestic work all her life, but she went and came back the same day. She worked almost everywhere.

We walked everywhere we went and it wasn't a problem because you looking at two miles this way and our little world didn't go thirty-two miles like it is now.[7] *Our little world went to a small area. . . . See, it was unique because I could go from my house midway to the alley, take a left, go up into what we called "the chute," and come out right in front of Avenue L. The chute was for cutting corners.*

When Mama send kids to the store that was over on Twenty-sixth and L—go to the store, go through the chute, and hurry back. Avenue L Baptist Church, our church, was one block over. I went to the Baptist Training Unit, I went to Starlight Band, I went to choir rehearsal, I went everywhere. It was a maze of stuff and in that maze there were a lot of other houses back there. Going between houses. (See fig. 11.)

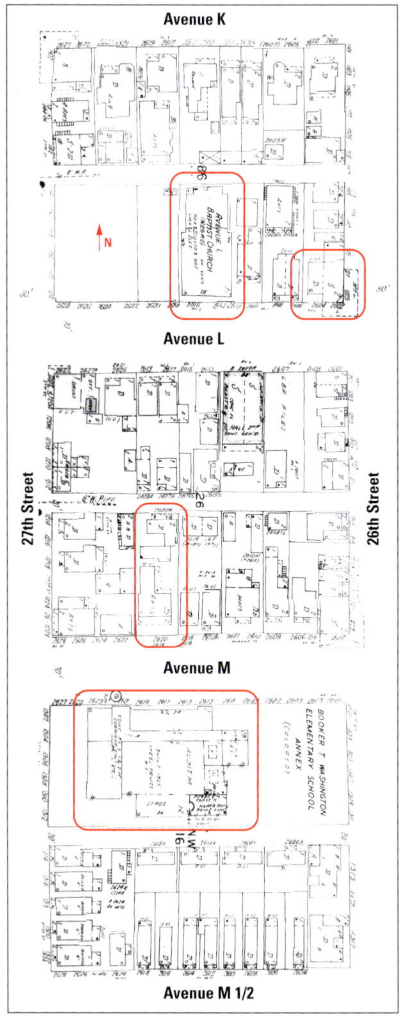

Fig. 11. Bill Millican's neighborhood. The circled areas are (top to bottom) Avenue L Baptist Church and corner store, 2616 Avenue M property, and Central High School (elementary school annex). The Sanborn insurance map is the 1912 edition with later overlays, which explains minor discrepancies between the map and Millican's account.

During the time that I was coming up, a family never moved until they started getting to the point where they could afford something else. Now, I'm speaking for my family and myself. We did the best we could with what we had, and then we started. My father got a better job. My mother started. My brother and I even got jobs. So, everything went into the pot. And, I think it was ten to twelve years before we bought a home.[8]

I can remember when it was said to us that we were getting ready to move to another place of our own. Now that was the most important thing—"of our own." My mother used to say all the time, "Well, I'll be glad when we can get something of our own," and then I was real excited. I felt like I was finally going to make a big move and then the next thought was losing my friends, because that was a strong camaraderie, relationship, that that one block had, and I'm sure that every other block had the same thing. And then, after we moved out of the alley, someone else moved in the same place where we had lived.

See, I was with a rare thing. If my best friend came to my house and lived two or three alleys down, and if something happened, we both would get a whipping. And then my mother would walk him back to his mother, and he'd get a whipping, and vice versa. One of those things. We felt comfortable.

I can remember people within the alley dying and the whole alley would get together and everybody would make food and take it to that particular place or wherever the deceased was. Everybody watched everybody's house. I can remember in the summertime going to bed with the screen door wide open. And I can remember almost everybody that came in the alley, in the neighborhood. . . . We knew basically who was and who was not a stranger and if he or she came in the alley trying to find out where somebody else lived, it wasn't like somebody out of the clear blue sky dropped in. There was a reason for it. In the summertime, we had a lot of residents in the alley. Their cousins and nieces and nephews would come to Galveston from the country to spend the summer—that type thing.

Sure, blacks resented living in the alleys, but blacks weren't the only ones living in the alleys either. I don't think it would have made any difference whether they were paved or black-topped or whatever. In my opinion, it was a situation where it was somewhere where we didn't have any choice. We had to live there. You know, when you're making a small amount of money a week, you doing the best you can with what you've got. The resentment wasn't basically living in the alleys. The resentment was because of all the other things that kept you from getting out.

Fig. 12. High school student Bill Millican and dance partner practicing the "Blue Tango" in the alley behind Central High School for Friday morning school assembly. Photograph circa 1948.

Galveston was and is a unique town as far as racial problems. We were segregated, but it wasn't as bad as other places in the state of Texas, and Galveston being a seaport town, you had all walks of life, races, creeds, colors, come in here. Oh, we had our problems, sure, but it wasn't as bad as other areas. . . . That was a unique thing about Galveston. Negroes and Caucasian people were poor and lived in the same neighborhood, ate the same food, suffered the same problems.

The alleys as I remember as a boy, there were just as many houses in the rear as there were on the curb. My idea of modern is you got more garages than dwellings. . . . There is a smaller alley population now compared to when I was in junior high school or elementary school. . . . Progress must go on. I think it's good. I've got more for good than for worse, and it's good because it's time that people who live in alleys realize that there is a curb. It is time that people who could only afford a place in an alley, which was cheaper than a place on the curb, be able to afford a place on the curb. I mean, we survived in the alleys. We had no problems with it because that was the best we could do, but there's better things that can be done.

Just as the story of the alleys and back buildings in Galveston cannot be told without the Sanborn maps and bird's-eye views, neither can it be told without the words of alley residents and alley users.

1 In View . . . on the Backside: The Pre–Civil War Years

FOR SALE. THE TWO STORY RESIDENCE. Two squares east of the Post Office, at present occupied by Dr. Jaeger—with good kitchen, carriage and negro house, cistern, etc., in good repair and desirably located.

Advertisement in The Civilian and Galveston Gazette, *December 11, 1847*

Land surveyor John D. Groesbeck's trip from Albany, New York, to Galveston Island for "health reasons" in the fall of 1837 could not have been more timely.[1] Certainly, surveyors were in short supply in the area at the time, and Groesbeck was hired by the newly organized Galveston City Company to survey and plat the proposed city. It was probably unlike any job that Groesbeck had ever had. The island was, after all, a sandbar, completely flat, less than two miles wide, and graced, according to early accounts, with tall prairie grass and only three live oak trees.

Whatever Groesbeck's own impressions about his surroundings may have been, he produced a plan (fig. 13) that gave order for future development to the shifting sands and swampy marshlands of the east end of Galveston Island. The city's physical growth would be defined by a grid pattern of rectangular blocks running primarily east-west, each with

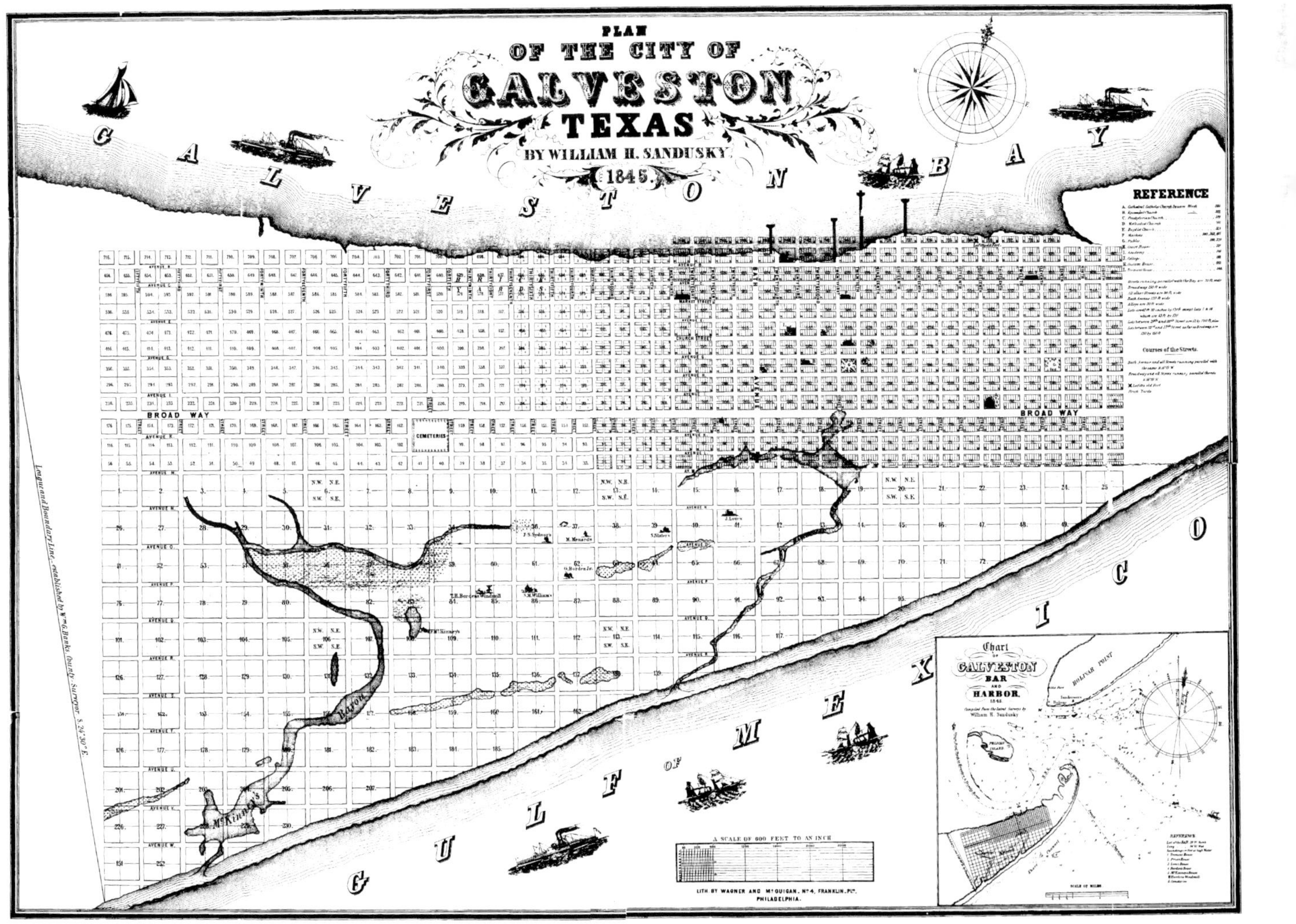

Fig. 13. *Plan of the City of Galveston, Texas,* by William H. Sandusky, 1845. Lithograph by Wagner and McGuigan, Philadelphia. The image has been slightly cropped.

fourteen narrow lots measuring 42 feet 10 inches by 120 feet, seven to a street side. Most blocks would be intersected by an alley that was twenty feet wide (fig. 14). East-west streets, referred to as avenues, were assigned alphabetical names, and north-south streets were given numerical names.[2]

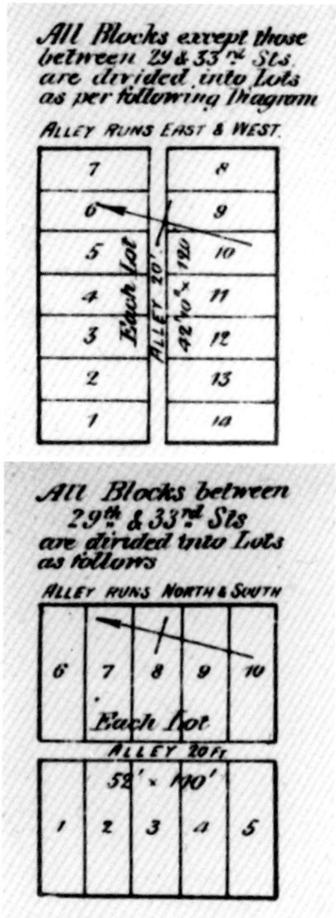

Fig. 14. Sanborn insurance map, 1885. The Sanborn maps provide the clearest explanation of block layout, which has not changed since the original Galveston plan.

Groesbeck did not record his rationale for including alleys in the city plan. Perhaps he was simply repeating other plans with which he was familiar. But then again, as he waded through what one traveler called "the oozy prairie" to conduct his survey, he would have been well aware that Galveston would be eternally plagued by land limitations in both size and topography.[3] It made sense to orient everyday household functions and city services to backyards and an alley system. Residents would be accommodating kitchens, privies, cisterns, stables, washtubs, woodpiles, chicken coops, and gardens, as well as disposing of the waste and other residues that all the related activities would produce. Many residents would also have slaves and carriages that they wanted kept in view, but on the backside of their property.

With the adoption of Groesbeck's survey in 1838 and incorporation of the city in January 1839, Galveston's future as the major port along the Texas coast was launched, and the influx of people began (fig. 15).[4] Lucy and Clark Shaw were among the early arrivals, sailing into the Galveston harbor on December 11, 1838, with their young daughter and Clark's parents. Lucy's letters to her mother back home in Maine not only disclose her particular interest in construction practices and domestic structures, but also, inadvertently, reveal patterns of development and behavior that were to characterize the back buildings and alleys of Galveston for years to come. Clark was a builder, a good trade, given the demand for houses and the speed with which they were built. If Lucy's mother had any misgivings regarding her daughter's move to Texas, she may have been reassured when Lucy wrote on February 24, 1839, that "the most money making business here now is building houses to let. I should think there had been at least one hundred built since we came. One day lately there were seven frames raised."[5]

Both the houses and the landscape seemed strange to Lucy's New England eye. When seeing a load of hay that "looked more like north than anything I have seen here," a nostalgic Lucy wrote:

Fig. 15. *Port of Galveston*, wood engraving published in the *Illustrated London News*, January 4, 1845.

There is nothing natural, familiar or homeish in the appearance of the country, the people or their dwellings. The island is perfectly flat, and though covered with beautiful flowers and this tall, tough, green grass, it looks bare in consequence of having no foliage. The houses are mostly low on account of the high winds, without any chimneys, kitchens generally little rough sheds built separate from the houses, and every dwelling has a piazza in front, at least, some at the sides, also.[6]

Upon first arrival in Galveston, living conditions were makeshift for almost everyone, and buildings, including secondary buildings, often served more than one purpose. Lucy expressed endless cheerfulness and adaptability as her family moved from one location to another. The Shaws first boarded with a Mrs. Delesdernier, and Clark immediately began building their own house on an adjoining lot, Lucy reporting that "the kitchen part is up and boarded and we cook and eat in it. . . . The frame of the other part is up and is going on very well."[7]

In mid-January 1839, Lucy observed that Galveston houses were weatherboarded on the exterior and finished with plain boards, rather than lathed and plastered, on the interior because "it is not so necessary here as at home, the weather being so warm." New residents and visitors generally agreed that the climate, at least during much of the year, demanded nothing more substantial. They often changed their minds after experiencing their first cold front or norther, as did Lucy. On February 24, she wrote that during "a dreadful easterly storm . . . our kitchen was the most comfortable place on the island. . . . People suffer here from the cold, they have such miserable houses. I have actually felt the wind move the hair on my forehead as I lay in bed at night."[8]

When English traveler and chronicler Matilda Houstoun visited the island in 1844, the characteristics that were to define Galveston's architectural landscape were obvious. She listed climate, topography, and, most especially, expediency as the factors that shaped the "paper houses," noting that they were raised one or two feet on wooden corner blocks to withstand the likelihood of high winds, as well as to keep out "the snakes, &c., to say nothing of the pigs." The resultant "faculty of locomotion" she viewed as a dubious advantage, but added that the moving of buildings was "no uncommon thing" in Galveston. In response to the argument that it took considerably longer to build brick buildings than wooden ones, Houstoun countered that they lasted considerably longer than the ten-year life span that could be expected for wooden structures in the Gulf Coast climate.[9]

Fig. 16. Twentieth Street and Avenue B (Strand), looking east, photograph 1861. In the foreground is the backyard of a property that combines commercial and residential use in the front building. The one-story structure with gabled roof is probably the kitchen and may include a small room or space for servants or slaves. Behind this is the animal yard and a small shed on the alley line. The privy is probably the tiny building, barely visible, on the east side of the shed. Galveston Bay is to the left.

As Galveston developed, the backyards quickly filled with secondary structures (figs. 16, 17). In April 1843, there was for rent "A good dwelling near the market, with five rooms all plastered, having a front and back gallery, also a good kitchen and stable, with a good Garden." Apparently, surveyor Groesbeck had found the Galveston climate enough to his liking to make investments, because in 1844 he offered for sale a "DWELLING HOUSE WITH carriage house, stable and other outhouses." In the same year, William M. Hudson recorded a mortgage for the purchase of three lots on Avenue G between Tenth and Eleventh Streets, "with the dwelling House, Stable, Cistern, Cowpen, Shed, Chicken Coop and all other improvements thereon erected."[10]

In December 1847, auctioneer A. F. James advertised a "Two story house, very spacious, and finished in *modern style*—Kitchen, servants rooms, store rooms, wash house, stable and carriage house, brick cistern, etc. etc. Terms $2000 cash, balance at 6 and 12 months with interest." Kitchens, stables, carriage houses, and servants quarters are the larger outbuildings most frequently named in advertisements, but other terminology and building types, including "out offices" and "carriage and negro house," occasionally surface.[11]

Specific references in advertisements to alley buildings are rare because most back buildings provided support services to a primary, front-street structure. There were exceptions. Auctioneer James advertised that he had for sale a store and dwelling on the front of a lot, as well as "THE STORY AND HALF BUILDING in rear of the above on the alley—to be removed by the purchaser within 5 days after the sale. Terms cash."[12]

James's advertisement suggests several characteristics that typified Galveston real estate from the beginning. The purchaser had to move the alley structure, and in all likelihood would move it to a leased lot. In fact, the building may have been situated on leased land in its alley location, because it was not uncommon for buildings, especially residential structures, to be moved from one leased parcel to another. The building was also, in all probability, a rent house. Just how much rental property was located along the alleys at that time—or at any time, for that matter—cannot be determined, but it did exist. In 1854, real estate investor John L. Darragh credited John Morgan in his ledger with $10 "for 2 months of lett[ing] Hous on the Aley."[13] Unfortunately, Darragh's records do not identify who Morgan was, or why or for whom he was renting the house in this specific instance. There are, however, several possibilities regarding the inhabitants of rental alley housing in Galveston prior to the Civil War.

Houses were rented for slaves. In July 1851, a local newspaper reported that the ordinance allowing slaveholders to rent houses for their slaves was "the cause of no little trouble," there being "upwards of forty houses in town occupied exclusively by negroes, and it is next to impossible, with the limited police of the city, to prevent occasional disorders among them."[14] Although the locations of the forty houses were not specified, most, if not all, would have been located on the back or alley side of properties.

During the 1850s, city officials enacted a series of stricter ordinances in an attempt to curtail the movement and residency of the slaves in the city. In 1854, it became unlawful "for any person to rent or lease any house or building to any slave," indicating that houses were rented not only for slaves but also by slaves. A year later, the aldermen determined that slaves could live apart from their owners only if they resided on the property of white employers who hired them as domestic or household servants. The maximum punishment for violating the ordinance was raised to a $50 fine for anyone renting to a slave and for the slave's owner or legal manager, and to "thirty-nine stripes" for the slave.[15]

Galveston was no more successful in its efforts to totally control slave activity than were other southern cities and, as was also true in other cities, some leniency was still permitted.[16] Former slave Josephine Ryles related in a 1937 interview that James Sultry owned both her parents until her father was sold "to Mr. Schwoebel in de day time an' [he] come back to his

Fig. 17. Twentieth Street and Avenue B (Strand), looking south towards the Gulf of Mexico, photograph 1861. In contrast to the view in fig. 16, the blocks shown here, including the backsides, are more densely developed. The building with the tower on the left is the city hall and market.

family at Mr. Sultry's at night. Lots of folks did dat way when dey was sold here." On July 14, 1857, a newspaper article credited the discovery of a fire in a bookstore to "some negroes living in the adjoining yard." The vagueness of the phrase, especially the absence of a slaveowner's name, invites conjecture about both the status of the blacks and the ownership of their living quarters.[17]

Free blacks may have been among the renters of alley housing, but their numbers were nominal in Galveston: thirty in the 1850 census; two in 1860. Galveston was too young to have developed a free black population comparable in size to those living in older and larger southern cities such as Charleston, Savannah, and Mobile. But the city's age is not the only explanation for the limited number of free blacks. Their immigration had been discouraged, in some cases prohibited, by another set of laws enacted when the city was incorporated.[18]

Alley renters would have included some of the city's sizeable white transient population, the people Lucy Shaw described in the account of her first exposure to yellow fever in 1839. All 205 people who died in the epidemic lived or worked in the vicinity of the "perfect mud hole, never dry" that ran through the middle of town. The majority of them were "carpenters and mechanics who lived in sheds and cooked, ate and slept in them, or very likely many in the open air, as many do here in hot weather."[19] Some of the sheds, no doubt, were located along the alleyways, although at this point in Galveston's development, it may have been difficult to always distinguish between a main street and an alley.

Alley inhabitants also included permanent residents of the city. The first Galveston city directory, published in 1856–57, does not include an alley address, but the second directory, published in 1859–60, lists three alley residents, including one carpenter who owned his property.[20]

Galveston had a substantial nonrenting alley population—the slaves who lived in housing that was located almost exclusively at the rear of their owners' property. In April 1841, after Clark Shaw became manager of the Tremont House, the largest hotel in town, Lucy wrote her mother that the hotel had sixteen servants, of which "one of the dining room servants is white and the second cook is white, one of the servants (the head waiter) is an Indian, the head cook is a free black, all the rest are slaves." Most, if not all, of the servants lived on the third story of the main building, but Lucy noted that "we are going to have a house put up in the backyard for the blacks to sleep in, that is the way in this country."[21]

Reminiscences of Galveston families recorded in the 1930s relate that the McLeods "were very wealthy people owning many slaves and also the entire block of land, between 25th and 26th street, on Broadway and Ave. I (Sealy Ave). . . . The negroes living in small huts on the far end of the block." A similar source describes the Frosch family household as also commanding a full block: "At the north east of the property were the servants quarters. There were eighteen servants. Nearby were the sheds and stables for the stock; the chicken run; the hog pen."[22]

By using the 1850 and 1860 census records for Galveston, it is possible to ascertain the approximate number of slaves who lived within the city limits, and, in 1860, the number of slave houses. The first official census of Galveston, taken in 1850, lists a population of 4,177, including 678 slaves and 30 free blacks. By 1860, the total population of the city had grown to 7,307, of whom 1,178 were slaves. The number of free blacks had dwindled to two.[23]

In addition, the 1860 census included a separate Slave Schedule that lists 261 slaveholders by name and their slaves by age and sex but not by name. It also enumerates the "Slave houses" on each slaveowner's property in two of the three wards in the city. These numbers suggest there were at least 321 slave houses in the three wards sheltering the 1,178 slaves, who composed almost one-sixth of the city's population.[24]

The census offers no description of the slave houses and their condition, nor does it indicate whether the census takers only counted structures that were physically separate from a primary building. Some slaves would have lived in a wing attached to the main house or in the main house itself. Most, however, lived in separate quarters that ranged from "small huts" and other minimal, primitive shelters, such as those on the McLeod property, to more style-conscious and finished buildings that often combined uses.

Fig. 18. Henry Rosenberg house, northwest corner Thirteenth Street and Avenue D, built 1859. The carriage house is on the right. In the background, on the left, is the stable, which was demolished. The property, including the carriage house and a second outbuilding, has been restored by the present owner, the University of Texas Medical Branch. Historic American Buildings Survey photograph by Harry L. Starnes, 1937.

When merchant Henry Rosenberg built his fashionable brick Italianate residence in 1859 (fig.18), he also built two complementary outbuildings, a slave house and a carriage house, and perhaps a third, a stable, although the latter may have been built at a later date. According to the 1860 Slave Schedule, Rosenberg had two slaves, an eighteen-year-old mulatto male and a fourteen-year-old black female, and one slave house, which was probably the two-story brick structure situated along the alley line on the interior of his property.[25]

Laborer Eugene Marshall arrived in Galveston in mid-December 1859, just when Henry Rosenberg was completing his house. Marshall typifies many of the journeymen mechanics who passed through Galveston for short periods of time—in his case, forty-four days—and worked at whatever jobs were available. Most of these people remain nameless in the history of the city, as would Marshall, had he not kept a diary that offers a rare description of his boardinghouse complex, including the back buildings.[26] Beginning with the main house, Marshall omitted few details.

> *On the West & north are streets crossing at right angles & on the south an alley paralel to the street in front The lot on the corner some 100 by 120 fet has considerable shrubery amongst which are two large Orange trees now unhapily killed by the front several fig trees which appear to be in good condition in it is a small two storied house white with green Venetian blinds and a portico in the rear. The front is occupied by two rooms conceled by folding doors. The one being the living & sleeping room of the family & the other a parlor with sofa centre table chairs & an old Piano this room opens to a small open porch in front and to the portico in the rear At each end of the portico is a small room just large enough for a bed each Upstairs is whooly devoted to sleeping rooms from the East side of the house extends the dining room some twelve feet wide & thirty feet long whooly unfinished save a coat of whitewash*

Marshall then described the buildings in the backyard:

> *In the rear of this is the kitchen where all the cooking is done which is about ten feet square At the rear of the lot is a low shed or stable some fifty feet long which appears to be unoccupied save for the storage of old lumber. The main house is finished by nailing cloth to the studing & papering it over the ceiling being merely whitewashed To this house is a large concrete cistern sunk in the ground and next to it on the east is a small building used as a servants room & storehouse.*

He concluded with a description of the buildings on the adjoining lot that was part of the same parcel. Because it was a boardinghouse, there were more people than usual living on the property, but the mix of buildings and uses in the backyard was typical of properties throughout the city.

> *On the next lot twenty five feet wide is a small house divided into five rooms & containing nine beds this is well finished & is the best house of the three Next [to] this is another lot of the same size on which is one of the patent portable houses 16 x 24 with kitchen in the rear & in this are lodged nine persons in the rear of each of these are large woden cisterns The whole of the houses are raised from the ground about three feet on brick piers The lots are separated by fences & the whole surrounded by a good substantial fence. This property with the furniture which is of the cheapest & roughest is valued at $5000 & has been sold for that amount.*

Marshall saw his boardinghouse proprietor as "a little dried up old man of about sixty" who "looked upon his boarders as a sort of turnep [sic] from which he was trying to extract the blood," and who was "living for convenience with the old lady who is perhaps fifty." Completing the household was their nine-year-old daughter, four black female servants, and two black children. The six blacks would have lived in the "small building used as a servants room & storehouse."

It is a safe assumption that in 1860 all the occupants of Marshall's boardinghouse and most of the other seven thousand Galveston residents, free and slave, engaged in some activity in their backyard or alleyway on a daily basis. In the two decades following Galveston's incorporation, the alleys had become increasingly busy, if for no other reason than the growing number of people who used them. In 1876, Galveston historian Charles W. Hayes wrote that during the period of rapid development in 1839, houses were built "on the low, marshy grounds, without any attention to filling or drainage." As a result, standing water, poor drainage or, more correctly, no drainage, and the "mud and mire," as Matilda Houstoun called it, were problems from the very beginning.[27]

It was the responsibility of city officials to adopt and revise regulations pertaining to the streets and alleys as well as to such related issues as garbage removal, privy placement, and animal control. Disease prevention was a primary motivation for many ordinances. The 1839 yellow fever epidemic prompted passage of one of the first ordinances requiring property owners to fill their lots and the areas beneath their buildings with sand. In 1840, the city hired a contractor to "remove all garbage, filth or offal" from the markets and from every household within the corporate limits between June 10 and December 1. Each household was required to put out its "garbage buckets or barrels" by nine o'clock every morning, subject to stiff fines for noncompliance.[28]

In 1857, the city published the *Charter and Revised Code of Ordinances . . . Passed in the Years 1856–57.* As stated in the document, the purpose of the alleys was very clear. They were to be used for deliveries and services, but not as thoroughfares. Privies and necessary houses were to be placed at least three feet from an adjoining lot, street, or alley, and were to be used and kept in such a manner that would "not be offensive." Contents were not to be removed at any time between June 1 and October 1 without permission, nor at any other time of the year except between the hours of eleven o'clock at night and four o'clock in the morning.[29]

Although citizens could keep animals on their premises (and most did), they could not harbor "the carcass of any dead animal, or any carrion, putrid meat, fish, entrails, or any filth, putrid or putrescent matter, or other unwholesome substance." Citizens were responsible for depositing these materials at a location designated by the mayor and for burying their dead animals.[30]

Fire was always a fear in this town of "paper houses," and fire along the alleyways, where Galvestonians threw their trash and garbage, was a constant danger. Building a fire in a yard, alley, or street was forbidden. Regulations regarding the installation and placement of stoves, connecting pipes, and chimneys were very explicit, and everyone was required to have at least one two-and-a-half-gallon fire bucket for every room in which a fire was kept. People were not permitted to use firearms or fireworks within the city limits nor to carry burning coals or brands in streets and alleys except in covered vessels.[31]

In essence, the 1857 *Charter and Revised Code of Ordinances,* and subsequent documents like it, serve as both a summation of the city's rules and regulations and a reflection of its development. As the city grew, so did the need for regulating services, public health, and public safety, including many of the activities and functions relegated to the alleys and the backyards. A growing population meant not only more people and more buildings but also more animals, more traffic, more waste, and more smoke.

2 Independent of the Front House: The Post–Civil War Years

The alleys were where the integration of the city was, not only because the children, black and white, played together in the alleys, but also because it was where the black people had their little houses next to the main houses all over town.

George P. Mitchell

Although Galveston was the site of only minor skirmishes during the Civil War, the city was in shambles in June 1865. The population had dropped to 3,500, one-half the number listed in the 1860 census. "Everyone knew," wrote contemporary historian Charles W. Hayes, "that Galveston was an entrenched camp during the war. No effort had been made to cleanse and purify the city, the garbage and compost had not been removed for years, there was realy [sic] no drainage, the island being almost level, stagnant pools of green slimy water that gave forth a horribls [sic] stench, were allowed to stand under public and private buildings." In addition, "hundreds of houses and squares of fences have disappeared since the war commenced, and hundreds have been reduced by the soldiers to a condition worse than horse stables." It was a situation, lamented the *Galveston Daily News,* made even more "mortifying to the patriot to reflect that all this wasteful desolation has been the work of our own troops."[1]

The "ingress of strange and old citizens" began in the summer of 1865. By January 1866, the city's population equaled its pre–Civil War number of 7,000, and that was just the beginning. When the 1870 census was taken, the population had once again almost doubled to 13,818 residents, of whom 3,007 were black.[2]

The "old" citizens were residents, both black and white, free and slave, who had left Galveston during the war. The "strange" citizens were those arriving in the city for the first

CUSTOM-HOUSE, GALVESTON, TEXAS.—Sketched by Theodore R. Davis.—[See Page 686.]

Fig. 19. Galveston scene, published in *Harper's Weekly,* October 27, 1866. In the background is the city hall and market; to the right of the Custom House and on the alley corner is a back building belonging to a residential property.

time. Some were enticed by claims that there was "plenty of Work . . . for Every one Who Wanted Work at good Wages." Many simply had no other place to go. They included soldiers from both armies, "crowds of men whose clothing was in taters [sic], many of them sick and worn, without money, property, occupation or home." They also included "negroes, most of whom come from Houston. Among these . . . many children 12, 15, and 18 years of age, who seem to be going about without any home."[3]

Pseudonymous columnist Don José exclaimed that the lack of accommodations should not discourage "the mania for emigrating to Texas," because "we have room and to spare, for all honest, sober, industrious settlers. . . . Galveston is destined to be the principal port of entry—in fact, the commercial emporium of the South West."[4]

Everyone was scrambling for a place to live. It was, at first, a question of utilizing what was already available, whatever the condition. Even those who owned property were not guaranteed a shelter because "very few, if any . . . have more than the means to make their

Fig. 20. Looking northeast and across the backyards of the 2400 block of Avenue G. Photograph published in 1870 city directory. The Eclipse Livery & Sale Stables were located on Twenty-third Street between Avenues E and F. The mastheads of ships docked in the Galveston harbor are visible in the background.

former residences tenantable, and hundreds have not the means even for that." If an owner had the means, materials were "scarce and dear" until the end of the summer. There were rent houses, boardinghouses, and tenements for those who did not own property, but given the number of people entering the city, their financial situation, and the condition of existing buildings, "overcrowding in houses and tenements" quickly became a problem. Many people had no choice but to live in abandoned buildings or in the open air.[5]

For the first time, blacks were among those competing in the housing market. In late July 1865, *Galveston Daily News* editor Willard Richardson wrote that he saw "poor white people almost every day looking for some small houses to rent. They say a large portion of such houses are occupied by negroes, who have left their former homes." Two months later Richardson noted that "nearly all the freedmen and women of Houston and Galveston are living by themselves," by which he probably meant that many blacks were renting houses rather than occupying living quarters provided by an employer.[6]

Horace Scull and his family were among those former slaves who took their chances, moved to a new location, and also took what they could get for housing. Immediately after the war, Scull moved his family to Galveston, where he plied his skills as a carpenter and cabinetmaker, eventually operating his own business and purchasing a house. Scull's son, Ralph Albert Scull, remembered that the family first "lived on Tremont between H and I," probably the same house to which he referred when writing that "the ex slaves rented several rundown houses about the town. One at Tremont and Ave H where several families lived. Others lived in backyard stables etc."[7]

It took little time for alley houses—those structures that were oriented towards the alleys and functionally independent of a front house—to become a primary housing source, especially for blacks. In 1866, Dr. Greensville Dowell, editor of the *Galveston Medical Journal,* wrote, "The negroes are generally living in crowded huts, upon the alleys or in the outskirts of the city."[8] Some of the "crowded huts," converted stables, and alley houses were structures that had survived the Civil War. Others, perhaps most, were built in response to the postwar housing demand.

Most alley housing was rental property. Writing from Savannah, widow Rebecca McLeod, an absentee property owner and former slaveholder, instructed her Galveston real estate agent, Jonathan Sturges Beers, to consider moving an existing house "on the alley" for one of her former slaves to rent. She also inquired about the cost of building "a house with two rooms 15 by 16 . . . of boards," a description that applied to hundreds of rental alley houses in the city.[9]

Some alley houses were owner-occupied and located on leased land, but finding documentation for these rental agreements is difficult. Most land-lease transactions probably were verbal or, if recorded, recorded in private papers. According to Ralph Albert Scull, "In the early days of freedom H. Scull carpentered and built many houses for the ex slaves, nearly all on leased ground." Although Scull did not record the locations of his father's houses, no doubt they were built along the alleys as well as on the front streets. In August 1870, Lucian Minor wrote his cousin and real estate partner, H. M. Trueheart, that "a respectable looking old negro, who says he can give good testimonials, as to character &c. wants to lease lot 10—[Block] 371. owned by Mrs. D. White, the lot you agreed to let Jasper Rhodes (col'd) have just before you left, who has not taken it. The terms you offered J. R. were, $5. a month, 3 months in advance, and you give him a lease for one year at a time. Please instruct me."[10]

The 1870 census shows that many black Galvestonians owned personal property of limited value, but no real estate. Since personal property was defined as movable property, and real estate as immovable property, the census listings suggest that a substantial number of blacks may have owned their houses and leased the land on which they were situated.

After the Civil War, some blacks were given property by their former owners, but finding a record of these transactions is even more difficult than finding references to land-lease agreements. In 1867, Edward A. Burk, for "a sum of $1.00 & in further consideration of faithful and [blank] services," deeded Hannah Ashe, "a free woman of color . . . [a] One story frame Building, with two rooms built and erected by me situated on the premises of Mrs.

Fig. 21

Fig. 22

Figs. 21 and 22. Front and back views of Turner Hall or the Alberts house, 2015 Avenue I, built 1858. The backside of the property was typical of many residences during the nineteenth and twentieth centuries (although considerably tidier in this photograph). Demolished. Historic American Buildings Survey photographs by Harry L. Starnes, 1937.

Ebenezer Allen, in the City of Galveston, being the same connected with her residence, and now used as a dining room and kitchen."[11] Records do not reveal whether Ashe moved her house or left it on the Allen property, or if she paid ground rent wherever it was located. Given its size, original use, and the financial circumstances of its inhabitants, the house was probably never moved to a front street. It may have graced more than one alley location, as would have been the case for some houses built by Horace Scull.

If Ashe was living in the same two-room house at the time of the 1870 census, there were nine people in the household: Hannah and Tena Ash[e], fifty- and seventy-five-year-old women, both of whom were washerwomen; Alford James, a forty-two-year-old laborer; James's thirty-two-year-old wife, Penny, a washerwoman; and their five children, who ranged in age from seven months to twelve years. No one in the household could read or write. According to the census, Hannah Ashe did not own any personal or real property, which suggests that either she lost the house because she could not pay the taxes or the census taker felt the value was not worth recording.[12]

While ever-increasing numbers of people were living in rental alley housing, many domestic servants lived in back buildings provided by their employers. (See figs. 21, 22.) However, the number of blacks who stayed where they had lived as slaves is virtually impossible to determine. The Slave Schedule for the 1860 census does not list slaves by name, and their listed age is unreliable, so a comparison with the 1870 census is of limited value. Galveston city directories also are of little help in the years immediately following the Civil War, because they list very few, if any, blacks until the 1872 edition.

The question of where black domestic servants should reside was an issue that elicited strong opinions. Author Amelia Barr moved to Galveston with her husband, three daughters, and two sons in fall 1866. In March 1867, she wrote a friend that she had employed "a half white/half Indian girl," but her washing and ironing was done twice weekly by another woman who had moved half a mile away and wanted a carriage sent for her, to which Barr replied that it was against her principles "to send carriages for washwomen." By June, the Barrs had rented a larger house and employed another servant:

We have said 'Good Bye' to Negro service   I have a splendid white girl who does all my washing Ironing & cooking for $20 specie a month   I have not been so comfortable for 14 years in this respect   There are no dearth of white servants here now   The Negroes are becoming Insufferable & actually demand a Bedroom in the House & a seat at your Dining Table   of course we can expect no better when we see prominent Politicians Lawyers & soldiers courting them for their miserable votes.[13]

Rebecca McLeod viewed the situation somewhat differently. Writing to her real estate agent, she lamented not having a house in Savannah where two of her older former slaves "could live on the lot with me and in the same house," although she acknowledged that they would not be satisfied because "they have friends and associations in Texas dearer to them than they ever can have here." She asked her agent to place the youngest of her former slaves with "a very pious" family where she could work as a domestic servant in exchange for board and schooling. Mrs. McLeod added: "I of course would wish her to sleep in the house but occupy the position of a servant."[14]

Most domestic servants, especially those who were black, continued to live in separate quarters, but finding documentation that describes the buildings is difficult. In July 1869, the *News* reported an inquest into the death of a black servant who "did not make her appearance at the usual time." Her employers related "going to a window" of her separate living quarters where they saw "a little child of the woman, who was sleeping in the bed with her . . . trying to wake her." In fall 1870, the *News* claimed that, for the first time since the Civil War, there were more servants than servants' positions, adding that employers were "no longer required to furnish servants' apartments with marble-top dressing tables and tapestry carpets."[15]

There were, no doubt, servants who lived in relatively comfortable surroundings, but many, perhaps most, lived in considerably reduced, even primitive, circumstances. Lucian Minor wrote his cousin that renter James Owen wanted to have "battens put on the stable, and a door and window put in to make it a servants' room. Mr. O. has laid a floor there. There is but one servants' room, very inconveniently situated in the house." Assuming that the request was accommodated, the first inhabitant of the Owens' newly converted stable was probably Mary Richardson, a fifty-year-old, Virginia-born black woman who could not read or write and whose occupation, according to the 1870 census, was "Washing" for printer Owen, his wife, and their four children.[16]

Following the Civil War, building activity along the alleys was a backside version of what was happening throughout the city. When property began selling in the fall of 1865, the rapid rate of new construction demanded more mechanics. In 1866, carpenter John Burbank moved from Cincinnati to join his brother Nelson, also a carpenter, and a cousin, James Codling, a painter and paperhanger, both of whom had been in Galveston since 1865. Burbank was able to save money while working for his brother at $6 a day because "times were good—2000 houses were built in Galveston within two years," which means that a substantial number of back buildings also were built.[17]

With Galveston's alleys already in dire condition at the end of the war, they only worsened with the addition of more people and more buildings. In May 1866, the *News* issued its annual spring scolding to citizens regarding the condition of their properties, reminding them that warmer weather brought with it yellow fever and other diseases.

The alleys were central to any clean-up campaign because the habit "of depositing the filth and slop of their backyards in the street, gutters and alleys is a sure prescription for inducing cholera." Dr. Dowell linked specific diseases not only to the environment but also to the houses that people inhabited: "Typhoid fevers are always likely to prevail from the people living in small rooms, and by reason of the constant influx of emigrants. Plurisy [sic] and pneumonia will continue until we have better built houses."[18]

In spring 1867, the *News* was calling, once again, for garbage carts "to remove the offal now generally thrown out into the streets and back alleys." Add to the garbage the one or more animals that most households kept for transportation, food, or income, and on any walk through the alleys, Dr. Dowell wrote, "your nose is greeted with effluvia arising from filth, the decaying carcasses of dogs, hogs, cats, rats, mice, old bones, fish and fowls." The city health officer began an inspection of "back yards and filthy resorts," which the editor of the *News* predicted would take all summer to complete. In early July, the mayor urged citizens "to cleanse their premises by the use of cheap and ready disinfectants, in view of the possibility of a visit from the yellow fever," even though he claimed the fears of an epidemic were "groundless."[19]

The mayor was wrong. By August, Galveston was experiencing the worst yellow fever epidemic of its history. "Everything About Galveston," wrote Tim Finn, a house painter who had immigrated from Boston, "had the appearance of a grave Yard no Buissnis of any Kind but to Attend the Sick and Buiry the dead."[20] By the time the epidemic was over, 1,171 people had died, among them Amelia Barr's husband and two sons, and John Burbank's brother Nelson and cousin James Codling.[21] Finn survived the fever because of "good Attendance and a Strong Constitution With the help of God," but his boardinghouse roommate "Died alongside of Me on the Same Bed." The Scull family temporarily fled the island and escaped the illness. John Burbank believed that the epidemic "put Galveston back for years," and returned to Cincinnati.[22]

Galveston had been terrorized by the epidemic. Everyone agreed that sanitary conditions had to be improved, but residents quickly resorted to their old habits. The following spring, the *Galveston Republican*, decrying the "deplorably filthy condition" of the streets and alleys, demanded that they be filled, repaired, and cleaned by the city and suggested that citizens use charcoal to keep their cisterns "sweet" and wood ashes to deodorize their privies.[23]

The 1867 epidemic proved to be only a temporary interruption in the growth of the city. In July 1869, the *News* claimed that there were more "expensive improvements" under construction than at any other time in Galveston's history, and that a sure sign of progress was the razing of buildings, "often nearly as good as new," to make way for others of "a superior style of architecture." In spring 1870, the paper reported that it was the chronic scarcity of building materials that retarded housing construction and also repeated a plea for reduced rents to meet the "demand for comfortable houses such as men of modest means require."[24]

Newspaper accounts describing construction and real estate activities in Galveston divulge little or nothing about alley buildings. Fortunately, lithographer C. Drie documented the expanding city in his bird's-eye view published in 1871 (fig. 23). The alleys are shown populated with an array of buildings, although surely someone must have pointed out that their pristine appearance, as well as that of the city as a whole, was hardly true to life.

The view also must have prompted at least some comments about the drastic changes that Galvestonians had witnessed along the alleys in the few short years since the Civil War.

Fig. 23. ***Bird's Eye View of the City of Galveston, Texas 1871,*** **drawn by C. Drie.**

Before the war, the back buildings in Galveston were predominantly secondary or support structures that serviced a front house, and if residential, were most likely inhabited by slaves. Few of these back buildings and their occupants functioned independently of a front building. Following the war, there was still the need for back buildings such as stables, carriage houses, kitchens, and servants quarters. Many of these buildings—new and old— continued to be used for housing, as did makeshift structures along the alleys, whatever their previous use and condition.

But with the overwhelming influx of people beginning in June 1865, and the desperate need for housing, Galveston experienced an enormous volume of new construction, primitive as some of it may have been, along the alleys as well as on the front streets. The alley housing that emerged immediately after the war and set the pattern for years to come was predominantly rental and oriented to the alleys. Not only were these buildings physically independent of a front structure; so were their occupants.

3 From Privies to Prostitution: The 1870s and 1880s

I come to Texas in 1877, an' come on here to Galveston. Galveston was a little pen den, nothing but a little mess.

Pierce Harper, Texas Narratives

For many Galvestonians, the pattern of daily life in the 1870s—whether they were living in a front house or a back building— differed little from the years before the Civil War. Certainly this was true for the household of wholesale grocer Harris Kempner. Although the family's resources were greater than most, the Kempners' routine, as described by Kempner's son I. H., was duplicated in manner and in varying degrees throughout the city.

> *The management or operation of our household at 20th and M was typical of the times (1873 to about 1882). All the mule teams, drays and trucks of the wholesale grocery firm of Marx & Kempner were quartered on the rear of our residence property (which comprised at least seven city lots). The Negro drivers or hostlers, most of them recently freed from slavery or children of those emancipated (though father had never owned any slaves), would assemble at daylight to water, feed and harness the stock. Our cook would serve father coffee and toast and the coachman would drive him to the store shortly after daylight—never later than 6 A.M. He would return for breakfast between 9:30 and 10 o'clock. This arrangement lasted until, as far as I remember, about 1880 or 1882. The 9:30 breakfast was for the entire family, but did not affect school attendance. I was taught by a governess until we had moved our residence and I was sent to school. Dinner was supposed to be served at 5 P.M. though frequently it was nearer 7 o'clock before we sat down. If we ate at 5 or 5:30, father would often return to the store afterward.*

The daily meals in the Kempner household were no small production. They always included "soup and soup meat (boiled beef) . . . besides fish or any roast, steaks or fowl," and were cooked on wood-burning stoves in the kitchen, which was located off the back gallery of the house. The servants quarters were also on the backside of the property.

> *The current wages for household servants were $10.00 a month for women, $15.00 for men. But the coachman, the cook, the housemaid were furnished living quarters on the place and were bountifully fed. Their numerous children, whether legitimate or "source unknown," crowded into the quarters assigned their mothers and were fed by our household without question. In turn they ran errands for mother, her friends or neighbors and my first governess repeatedly asserted they were more tractable than me. My governesses tried to teach the Negro children to read; there were no schools for colored. Mother also tried but found dual difficulties between birth of her babies and the irregularities of time available for scholastic instruction. I recall the fidelity to my parents of my old Negro mammy, Aunt Eveline, and of another valued aid, a colored midwife, Aunt Isabel, who officiated with the doctor at the birth of several of my brothers.*[1]

The backyard and alley-side activities and relationships of the Kempner household represent those with which the majority of Galvestonians were most comfortable and tolerant. But changes were taking place along the alleys in Galveston, as signaled by the gradual inclusion

Fig. 24. 1602 Avenue E, Landes carriage house, viewed from the front sidewalk looking north. The Landes house, built in 1887, is to the right. Photographed 1991.

Fig. 25. Captain Henry Grenrood house, built early 1870s. Watercolor circa 1886 by Galveston artist Julius Stockfleth. The Grenrood property was located on the northeast corner of Thirteenth Street and Avenue G. The four-room dormer cottage, like many houses in Galveston, was actually quite small, but many household functions and services were performed in rear additions and separate back buildings. The house and the residence on the alley corner have been maintained.

of both alley addresses and black residents in the city directories and by the number of alley happenings reported in the local newspapers.

Although still woefully incomplete, the 1875–76 Galveston city directory had forty-four entries for residences that included the word "alley," a significant increase when compared with previous editions. Twenty-six of the alley addressees (twenty-four men and two women) were white, and eighteen (all men) were black, for which the abbreviation was "c" or "col'd." The listing for Robert Ennis, a black drayman, is typical: "Ennis, Robert, (col'd) drayman, r. alley, near cor. av. L and 25th." The forty-four alley addressees were scattered among twenty-seven alleys in the city. The directory also listed one business with an alley address, that of Cullen and Gleich, horseshoers and farriers.[2]

The alley population also included some, and perhaps most, of the seventy-one individuals who were listed in the directory as servants. The listing for Alford Jones is typical: "Jones Alford, servt. Col. Anderson, av. H, bet 21st and 22d." Fifty of the seventy-one servant listings were black. Forty-eight were concentrated in the area north of Avenue J and east of Twenty-fifth Street. No one was listed as a Kempner servant.[3]

By 1875–76, Galvestonians who had been reading their local newspapers would have been well aware of the expanding alley population. The happenings, conditions, and residents along the alleys were increasingly popular subjects if the number of newspaper stories is any indication. But the stories were more than just a simple reflection of a growing alley population. They were an acknowledgment that the alleys and an alley life were emerging—or had emerged—with an identity that was independent of the people and buildings on the front streets. References to someone living "in the alley" began to appear in the newspapers in the 1870s; by the 1880s, such references were common.

The newspapers may be the richest source of information about the alleys and alley life in Galveston, but they also give a selective and distorted view. Galvestonians were not interested in reading about the majority of individuals, black and white, who quietly lived and worked in back buildings throughout the city. Rather, alley news was dominated by the alleys in which the density was highest, the housing rental, the activity illegal, and the occupants were black. Nevertheless, if the prejudices are sifted out, the articles offer glimpses of everyday life in an alley network that was full of people, buildings, and movement.

By 1870, articles about the alleys were appearing in the newspapers with some regularity. There was the "row in the alleyway, between Winnie and Church Streets, leading out of Tremont [Avenues G and F, and Twenty-third Street]" that resulted in the arrest of a man and a woman who were each fined $10 plus costs "for the privilege of giving pugilistic exhibitions." French Mary, who "had only come up to see the fun," was sentenced to three days in jail so that she could "become acquainted with all the funny things belonging to the machinery of municipal justice." The newspaper demanded that either the city or the military remove "the negro prostitutes that nightly prowl about our streets," most notably in the alley behind Trinity Episcopal Church (figs. 27–29). In Recorder's Court, "James Kane and George Cleveland, the former white and drunk, the latter black and crazy," were fined for being found "in an alley locked in a tight embrace," the court "not having sufficient appreciation of this illustration of social equality."[4]

In May 1875, the *News* reported that "numerous complaints come in from the residents in the neighborhood of Avenue H and Twenty-eighth street concerning the disturbances in that quarter. It appears that an alley contains an overplus of colored population, who seem to have agreed to disagree on all subjects, at all hours." The "overplus" of residents, however, is not documented by the 1875–76 directory. Only one alley resident, black laborer Pat Harris, was listed in the vicinity.[5]

By 1880, at least three alleys in the city were known by name and location. The two most notorious alleys were located in Ward Five: Fat Alley was between Avenues D and E and Twenty-eighth and Twenty-ninth Streets; Tin Can Alley, or Can Alley, was immediately to the east of Fat Alley between Avenues D and E and Twenty-seventh and Twenty-eighth Streets. (See figs. 4, 5.) Howard's Alley, also referred to as "Alley No. 8," was described in 1880 as "one of the hard spots of the city in days gone by" and probably was in a block that bordered Eighth Street.[6]

Fat Alley winds its way in and out of news reports throughout the 1880s and the 1890s. In October 1880, Mollie Waters's Saratoga trunk was stolen from her brothel on Twenty-fifth Street. Police were led "to a house in the alley . . . the notorious Fat alley," where they arrested two black thieves. In February 1886, George Raines, "while visiting a place commonly known as Fat alley," became violently ill, probably from the morphine he had purchased from neighborhood druggist Albert Hesse. Luckily for Raines, a doctor who "chanced to be in the vicinity" administered aid.[7]

In fall 1885, "a white woman, named Eva Lynn, but better known as Eva Scott, who resides in a little 10 x 12 shanty in what is known as the Can alley" (fig. 26), purchased poison from the same Hesse, then joined friends at a saloon across the street. As she lost consciousness, she was taken on a dray down the alley to her house, where she died several hours later. Friends stated at the inquest that Scott "was merely tired of the wretched life she was living," to which the newspaper added that "the world loses one more unfortunate and both are probably better off." Just fifteen days later, Scott's sixty-three-year-old black neighbor, Lucy Grimes, died "from the effects of a fit" at her house in an alley. According

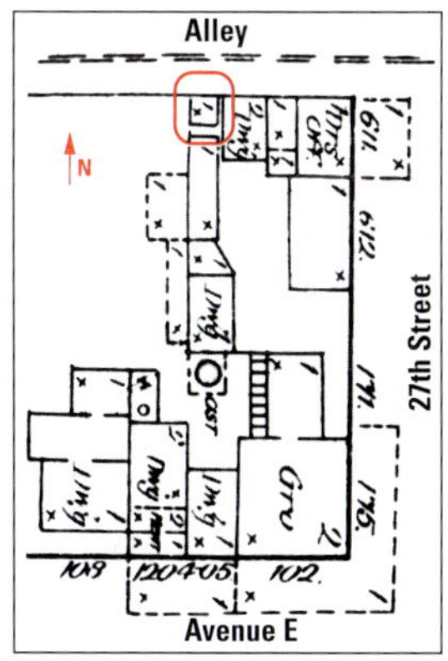

Fig. 26. Circle denotes what was probably Eva Lynn née Scott's "little 10 x 12 shanty" in Tin Can Alley. Sanborn insurance map, 1885.

There was a lot of gambling in the alleys. It was a favorite recreation and they used to keep fighting chickens. They'd fight those poor things and gamble on them. It was not uncommon at all. This is the 1950s and '60s. . . . The alley behind the Episcopal church was a gamblers' hangout . . . up until fairly recently. When the Episcopal church bought the Tartt property that faced on Twenty-third Street, we did away with the alley on purpose, because it had been the scene of so many fights and even murders. As late as the '60s, it was a bad alley. It was a business area on Twenty-third Street. The Tartt building was a hardware store and it was the last surviving business on that street. ***Inez R. Lasell***

Fat Alley must have been the same alley when you used to talk years ago about Bleich's Alley. There was a grocery store on the corner. There was a lot of activity and they always said, "If you go down to Bleich's Alley, you can get whatever you're looking for." It was down on West Market about Twenty-eighth and Twenty-ninth between Market and Postoffice [Avenues D and E]. ***Oscar T. Ekelund Jr.***

Fig. 27. Detail of 1871 bird's-eye view. The three circled blocks match the paired photographs and Sanborn maps in figs. 28–33. The circled buildings are the Custom House (far left) and St. Mary's Cathedral, both landmarks in fig. 32.

Fig. 28

Fig. 30

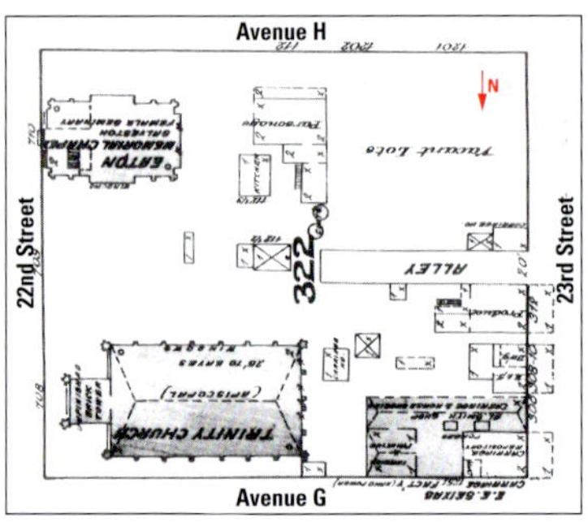

Fig. 29

Figs. 28 and 29. Block 322. Photograph circa 1875. Trinity Episcopal Church is the large building. Although activities in the alley behind the church may have been of great interest to nineteenth-century Galvestonians, the block and alley to the north had a far greater variety of buildings (as would be noted by an architectural historian). The block with the church on the 1885 Sanborn insurance map closely matches the photograph.

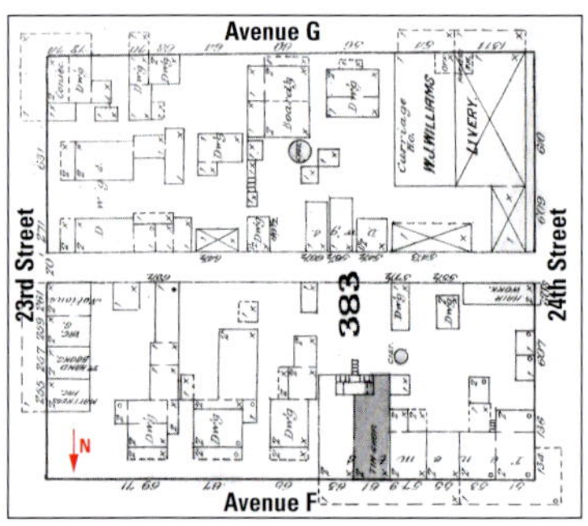

Fig. 31

Figs. 30 and 31. Block 383. Photograph, early 1880s. The backyards and alley buildings of Block 383 are seen in the foreground. The photograph can be matched with the 1885 Sanborn insurance map for the block. The large roof surface in the upper right of the photograph is the W. J. Williams Livery business.

Note: The Sanborn maps on this page and the next are oriented to match the photographs, as is generally the case throughout the book. When there is no pictorial documentation to match, the maps are oriented with north pointing up. Architectural floor plans are shown with north up unless noted otherwise either on the drawing or on an accompanying map.

Fig. 32

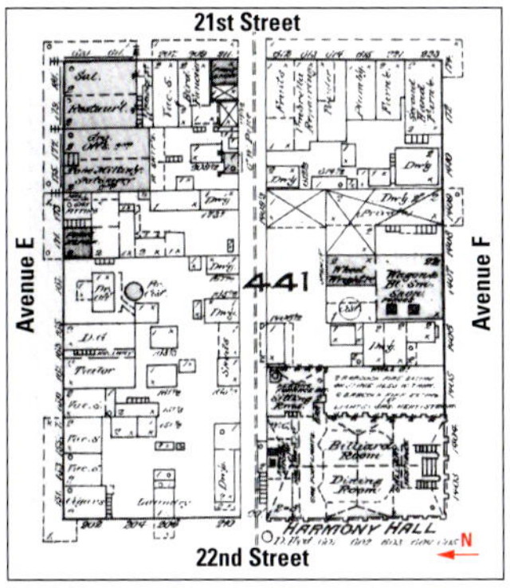

Figs. 32 and 33. Block 441. Circa 1881 stereoscopic view, looking east from Tremont House Observatory, by Blessing & Brother. The cross street at the bottom is Twenty-second Street. The alley on the left is on Block 441. The north half of the alley is a continuous line of dwellings and sheds. The Custom House is in the background. Avenue F is on the right with St. Mary's Cathedral at the corner of Twenty-first Street. The 1885 Sanborn insurance map shows that the major change on Block 441 since 1881 was the construction of Harmony Hall, a social hall, that replaced the house and church fronting Twenty-second Street.

Fig. 33

to mortuary records, thirty-two-year-old Lynn died of suicide, Grimes of epilepsy, and both women were buried in Potter's Field, the burial ground for destitute citizens.[8]

In June 1887, the police launched a raid on "women of disreputable character, corralling some twenty-five or thirty of the residents of Tin-can and Fat alleys." Charged with vagrancy, a euphemism for a variety of activities, seven of the women were sentenced to fines of $10 or ten days in jail, with the rest receiving $5 fines or five days in jail. Of the thirty-one women named in the article, seven white and nine black women were listed in either the 1886–87 or the 1888–89 city directories as living in the vicinity, but not necessarily in Fat or Tin Can Alley.[9]

Fat Alley had lost neither its name nor its reputation as late as May 1899, when police answered an emergency call from "Fat alley" for a black woman being assaulted by a black man with brass knuckles. On the same trip, they picked up a "dead man" lying in the alley and took him to the hospital, where he died of morphine poisoning.[10]

Alley reports were not confined to Ward Five. For ten days in September 1885, readers followed the drama of Louise Berry, who was found in "a house of ill repute on Winnie street [Avenue G]," having been enticed there by Joe Martin, her family's boarder. Martin was arrested "while in bed in a house kept by a negro woman named Mary Walker, in the alley" between Avenues G and F and Twenty-second and Twenty-third Streets, and was charged with rape. At the trial, it was disclosed that on the night of her disappearance, Louise "went into the backyard, and [the] defendant was at the back gate, and, catching her in his arms, took her away," obviously through the alley. The final ruling was seduction, not rape, and Martin offered to marry Louise, who was soon to be eighteen years old.[11]

The alleys and their network of back buildings provided cover for other misdemeanors and mischief, some of it injurious. A house at the corner of Nineteenth Street and Avenue F was "mysteriously assailed by brickbats" hurled by a party that "appeared to be concealed on the other side of the alley in the rear of the house. One of the bricks thrown struck a colored woman, who was coming out of the premises after wood, in the breast, injuring her quite seriously."[12]

Not everyone escaped detection. James Lindsley was jailed and fined $1 for sleeping "in a back alley," and Fannie Miller was fined $5 for "disorderly conduct, and using abusive and indecent language in alleys." George Harris was ordered to pay a $2.50 fine or spend five days in jail for "depositing filthy water in the alley," but charges that Henry Williams had removed sod from an alley were dismissed. People were arrested regularly for using the alleys as thoroughfares.[13]

Other articles about the city's alleys described the kinds of incidents that could be expected from everyday use. Accidents were bound to happen with the alleys accommodating all kinds of traffic, including deliveries and vendors, the collection of garbage and waste, the stabling of work and pleasure animals, and the keeping of carriages and wagons. Typical was the collision between two wagons when Mr. Klockenbrink's horse, "coming out of the stable . . . took fright, and ran at a fearful rate up the alley."[14]

Dead as well as live animals were always a problem. There was the dead pig in the alley between Avenues J and K and Eighteenth and Nineteenth Streets, the removal of which "should be attended to immediately." Apparently, the latter was not always accomplished in a timely manner:

Defunct Canines. Several pet dorgs [sic] of late paused in alleys for want of breath, and still remain there. Any hash-house can be supplied in the alley on Nineteenth and Postoffice streets, [Avenue E] while the great objection to the one in the alley near Bath Avenue [Twenty-fifth Street] and Avenue I is that decay will probably set in in less than ten days more.[15]

Water shortages caused confrontations in backyards and alleys, especially among those who shared cisterns. In anticipation of such problems, some lease agreements defined the terms for cistern access and use. One citizen recommended that underground cisterns be placed in the alleys to provide fresh water both for fighting fires and for the health of citizens, since many landlords were "culpably negligent as to rent property with inadequate cistern accommodations."[16]

The alleys were a favorite and usually a safe place for children to play, and perhaps for some children, the only place to play. But alleys, children, and fire could be a dangerous mix. When children ignited a pile of rubbish in one alley, disaster was averted by "the unexcitable presence of mind of surrounding parties," who emptied their washtubs on the fire and extinguished it. Sam Blessing and a friend were burned, but not seriously, when they were

---

We didn't do any playing in the alleys. We played on the sidewalk. We used the alleys for horses and buggies to go through and for deliveries. Mother had to order groceries so the man always came to the back door and then we had an icebox . . . They would bring the ice twice a week and put it in the icebox. The groceries would come once a week. We had a regular dairyman. Everything came to the back and was delivered in a horse-drawn wagon. **Helen O'Rourke**

The alleys were used more, mainly because the trucks and wagons were not as wide. Most deliveries are from the front side now. A lot of the deliveries were from the back. Certainly, the peddlers all went through the back side. That's the thing I remember most of all—the peddling, and the scrap pickups, and things like that, and bottle pickups. . . . I'd pick up, make my money for little odds and ends, by gathering bottles and scrap steel for Mr. Levy. He had a little ridge wagon with his horse, and I can see that gentleman today, heavy-set person, sitting on top of the little board on top there and calling, "Junk today," or something like that, going down the alley. I remember because that's where I got a little money. **George P. Mitchell**

---

playing "in an alley" with explosive powder. Other children were not so fortunate. One "little negro boy living in the alley between Thirty-second and Thirty-third streets, on Avenue I, crawled under a bed in the paternal mansion and deliberately inserted a brand of fire into an oil can." The can exploded and the child died; neither he nor his family was identified by name in the newspaper. Interment records tell us, however, that the victim was Alf Jackson, seven years old, born in Texas, and buried in Potter's Field.[17]

Fires along the alleys were always a danger, but even more so during the dry hot months of summer and the stove-burning months of winter. If newspaper stories are any indication, alley dwellers were burned more often than alley buildings. The story about Jennie Coleman, a ten-year-old black girl, was not unusual. She died an excruciating death after being burned when lighting a fire with kerosene in "a house occupying the alley between Market and Postoffice [Avenues D and E], on Ninth street."[18]

Sometimes an alley served simply as the backdrop for a story, but even these articles can reveal details about alley life and alley houses. In one account, a white woman left her three-week-old infant with Jane Gains, a black woman who lived in the alley between Avenues F and G and Thirty-first and Thirty-second Streets. A reporter visiting Gains's house after she was given temporary custody of the child "found the infant in a deep slumber on a double bed, under a mosquito bar, being watched over with the tenderest solicitude." The newspaper added the postscript that the child's mother, who had left for Lake Charles on a schooner, "was said to be a fine-looking woman, and stated that her husband was an old frontiersman."[19]

Alley life and alley dwellers were popular subjects for newspaper articles except during times of disaster and emergency, when they were relegated to an almost invisible status. Following a major storm in September 1875, for example, and the devastating fire in November 1885, the newspapers only indirectly reported losses along the alleys.

The 1875 storm caused the greatest damage on the Gulf side of the island in an area of laborers' cottages where the backyards were full of outbuildings, animals, and some alley houses. On September 15, residents east of Eleventh Street and along the Gulf shore were forced to leave their houses when water began to rise and the recently filled streets "seemed to be rivers and the alleys were veritable lakes." In just one ten-block radius, an estimated 150 houses were damaged and 30 houses, "including negro cabins," destroyed. On one corner were four houses "occupied by colored people, all more or less damaged, their sheds and outhouses almost totally destroyed." One reporter noted that "the losses of the poorer classes will bear harder on them, for they lost their cows, pigs, poultry and nearly all except their furniture and clothes, for their poverty in a majority of instances compelled them to live near the beach where rents were low."[20]

Once Galveston had recovered from the initial shock of the storm, relief efforts were organized and damages assessed. One of the most urgent requests for donations was to provide "women with tubs, sewing machines, and other articles by which they could be enabled to earn their own support." Presumably, the many washerwomen who were alley dwellers were among the washtub recipients, but the newspaper never described how the items were collected nor where they were distributed.[21]

By early October, Galveston apparently had returned to normal, at least for most citizens, because the newspaper was back to complaining about the general condition of the alleys, which was "anything but pleasant, to either the optical or olfactory nerves." The "vailiant [sic] police" arrested "eleven little newsboys for gambling in a back alley," five of whom were discharged; the other six each paid $2 and costs or spent three days in jail. By the end of the month, the houses had "been rebuilt, the old landmarks restored," and evidence of the storm was almost entirely gone, much to the disappointment of tourists.[22]

In 1885, lithographer Augustus Koch recorded the city in his bird's-eye view, a document that quickly became obsolete, if not more valuable, in mid-November when fire destroyed more than forty blocks that extended "almost from bay to gulf" between Sixteenth and Twenty-first Streets (fig. 34). As the *Galveston Daily News* went to press on November 13, the editor inserted a short notice that "the fire bells have sounded the alarm. At this hour, 2:15 a.m., the conflagration has spread from Strand to Mechanic street [Avenues B and C], in the neighborhood of Seventeenth street. The wind is blowing very stiff from the north, causing the flames to spread rapidly." The fire was discovered in the alley behind the Vulcan Iron Foundry on Avenue B between Sixteenth and Seventeenth Streets, an area with a sizeable alley population. Delay in sounding the general alarm, defective waterworks, a small fire-fighting force, and a thirty-mile-an-hour wind allowed the fire to get out of control once it had ignited a lumberyard across the street.[23]

By the time the newspapers were on the street, many Galvestonians had lost their homes as the fire moved toward the beach. Sparks skipping from one wooden roof to the next did not discriminate between the larger two-story dwellings of the more well-to-do professionals and businessmen and the one- to three-room dwellings of servants and laborers. Neither the buildings lining the alleys nor those along the front streets were spared. The Kempner family's house, now located at Eighteenth Street and Avenue E, was destroyed. When interviewed in 1937, Ella Washington remembered running home from her domestic job "to look for my things an' found my house was burn down to de ground an' everything I had burned up but what I had on my back."[24]

Fig. 34. Area burned by the fire on November 13, 1885.

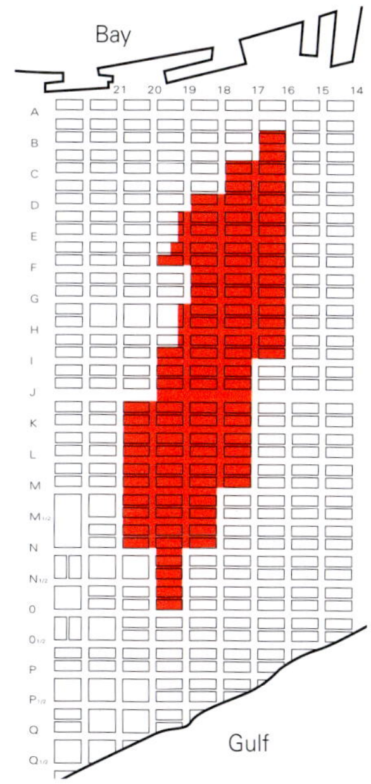

With daylight, the city grasped the magnitude of the disaster (fig. 35). According to news accounts, in five hours, an estimated five hundred houses had burned, a number that included "some of the most elegant residences of Galveston" but excluded back buildings and alley residences. One report acknowledged only that the fire had consumed "general improvements, accessories to every well appointed household in the way of stables, outhouses, fences, cisterns, etc." Property loss was estimated to be $2,500,000, or more than one-eighth of the taxable value of the city.[25]

A massive relief effort was organized to help the estimated five thousand citizens left homeless. The original list of those who suffered losses was composed of owners of taxable property. It includes two identifiable alley dwellers: Peter Brantigan, a cabinetmaker, whose shop and residence were located on the alley between Avenues H and I and Eighteenth and Nineteenth Streets; and Mrs. Johanna Toebleman, who lived on the alley between Avenues K and L and Eighteenth and Nineteenth Streets. The final accounting of sufferers listed householders by name, but made only a cursory reference to "lodgers, servants, etc., who lost by the fire," many of whom would have lived in back buildings.[26]

Rebuilding efforts began immediately. Many of the first structures were built as temporary housing, with the intent that they would eventually be adapted for use as outbuildings. Building permits published in the *News* reported the construction of stables, outhouses, and one chicken house, and although servants quarters, back houses, and probably rental alley houses were also built, they were not specified by name. Within five months, the newspaper claimed that every new house in the "burnt district" was an improvement on the old, and that the area in which the fire originated had been "wonderfully improved." Some of the rebuilding took the form of elaborate residences, such as the house that merchant Jacob Sonnentheil built on the corner property next door to cabinetmaker Peter Brantigan (figs. 36–38).[27]

Fig. 35. Photograph of the "burnt district," looking toward the Gulf.

During the 1870s and 1880s, Galveston was coping with the pressures of rapid growth, which, in turn, meant a heavier use of the alleys. Not only were there increasing numbers of people living directly on the alleys, but Galveston's ever-fluctuating, ever-expanding population was also becoming more demanding of services and conveniences that depended on the alley system. In addition, the extension of the city limits and the rising population meant that there were more alleys to maintain and more garbage to collect. By September 1885, Galvestonians were producing, on

Fig. 36

Fig. 37

Jacob Sonnentheil house, 1828 Avenue I, built 1886–87. Fig. 36. Circa 1890 photograph shows the carriage house in the background. The edge of cabinetmaker Peter Brantigan's property is visible on the right. Fig. 37. Sonnentheil carriage house, looking east from Nineteenth Street. Photographed circa 1987.

a monthly basis, thirteen hundred loads of garbage, refuse, and scrapings, which had to be removed by drays and carts, mostly via the alleys.[28]

Trash and garbage pickup was always a problem, some citizens complaining that the garbage carts never found their way on their daily routes to "those little hillocks of trash" in some sections of the city. During one house-to-house inspection period, a resident accused the city of collecting trash only in the business district, "while every alley from the Strand [Avenue B] to the beach is filled (almost its entire length) with the worst filth in the city."[29]

Fear of disease remained a primary motivator for alley improvements. Any rumor of yellow fever along the Gulf Coast prompted the Galveston City Council to appropriate monies "to thoroughly scavenger the city" and to clean up the "greenish yellow putrid mass of death-dealing filth" that could be found in the drains of even some of "the best portions of the city." Adequate drainage was a seemingly unsolvable problem. Although the city considered paving some alleys and actually experimented with the installation of a wooden drainage system, the Council concluded that filling and grading the alleys to a proper level was the most efficient and economical solution. The grading system, however, was never evenly enforced, and some of the areas with the poorest drainage continued to be in the most populous parts of the city, including Ward Five.[30]

Cleaning the privies was yet another problem for which there seemed to be no satisfactory solution. At one point, the Board of Health recommended that all privy vaults be cemented, but the city attorney declared that the city lacked the authority to enforce such an ordinance. The Board found this difficult to understand, because lawyers "have such little quibbles when, if there was a conflagration raging whole blocks of buildings could be torn down to check the flames."[31] The advent of indoor plumbing provided part of the solution, but there were many residents—especially along the alleys in rental property and, once again, in the most populous parts of town—for whom indoor plumbing was not a reality until well into the twentieth century.

At least there were fewer animals on the loose, which meant some improvement to the alleys. Hogs could no longer be kept in the inhabited sections of the city "because the filth of their pens poisons the atmosphere and breeds pestilence." Citizens could still keep horses and cows, and chicken coops were common to many backyards.[32]

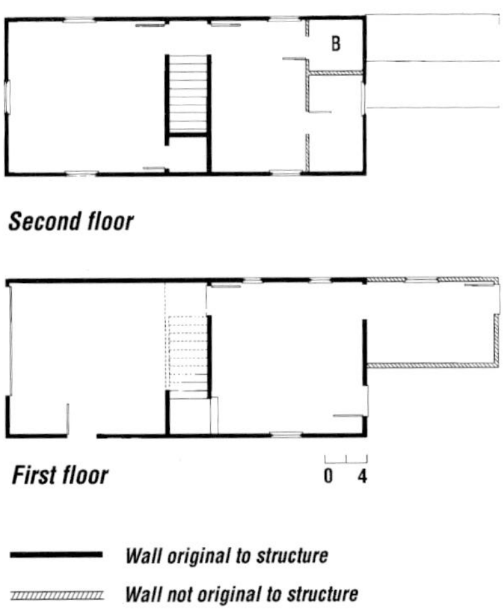

Fig. 38. Floor plans of the Sonnentheil carriage house. Documented 1990.

In 1887, the City Council was criticized for not allocating adequate budgets for the City Engineer and the City Health Officer to fulfill their responsibilities in a city that was "located in a semi-tropical climate, devoid of natural drainage, possessing not a yard of sewerage nor a gallon of continuous water supply." The City Engineer pointed out that the city's reliance on individual action for maintenance of the alleys had proven to be an unsatisfactory policy, and yet the public was unwilling to grant adequate powers to the Board of Health. The Engineer and the Health Officer submitted a long list of sanitation priorities: institute a better system to remove "the accumulation of filth"; prohibit the use of open gutters for waste; disinfect polluted soil; move the dumping ground farther away from the central portion of the city, or use a garbage incinerator; install a proper drainage system; and enforce existing ordinances more stringently.[33]

Fig. 39. Typical backside view of small house with multiple additions, cistern, and buildings on adjacent property. Photograph taken in 1911 but representative of Galveston backyards during the nineteenth century. Copied from *The Housing Problem in Texas: A Study of Physical Conditions under which the Other Half Lives* by George Waverly Briggs (*The Galveston-Dallas News*: 1911), p. 39.

As Galvestonians entered the 1890s, their interest in alley activities and alley dwellers tapered off. Instead, they were "Caught on the Curb," as one popular column was called, discussing and debating how to resolve and pay for major municipal improvements, including the paving of all streets, a proper sewer system, and a waterworks. Some changes would have a greater impact on the alleys than others—such as the installation of a sewer system, which, detractors claimed, would require that every alley be paved. Perhaps most importantly, technological advances offered the possibility for real relief from some of the sanitation problems that had seemed insurmountable since the city was incorporated. Galvestonians, however, were not quite ready to address the living conditions along the alleys, even though the number of alley dwellers had steadily increased.

4 Living "in the Rear"

A lot of good people lived in the alleys. . . . Lot of the people were on low income, doing the best job they could, had to live where they could afford to live, and that's where the cheap rent houses were, in the alleys.

Oscar T. Ekelund Jr.

Richard Johnson, a twenty-three-year-old black laborer from Louisiana, and his family were typical alley dwellers in Galveston in 1880. Johnson's wife, Nettie, was twenty years old, a washerwoman by occupation, and a Texan by birth, as was their only child, three-year-old Susie. Nettie could read and write, but Richard could only read. Charles and Lena Wilkman, immigrants from Finland, were also typical. Charles was a forty-year-old laborer. Lena was thirty-nine and "keeping house" for the couple and their four children, nine-year-old Mary, born in Alabama, and three sons, ages two, four, and six, all born in Texas. Mary attended school.[1]

In December 1880, when names were collected for the 1881–82 Galveston city directory, both families were living at alley addresses—the Johnsons at "rear 426 Church [Avenue F] cor 16th" and the Wilkmans at "al. bet 15th, 16th, Water and Strand [Avenues A and B]."[2] Six months earlier, when Ward Two was canvassed for the 1880 census, both families were living in the same blocks, presumably at the same locations. (See appendix B.)

Richard Johnson and Charles Wilkman are among the alley residents whose names can be found in both the 1881–82 Galveston city directory and the 1880 census, important documents in the history of Galveston's alleys. City directories are the primary source for a listing of alley residents and their occupations, and an indication of their numbers and mobility. Census records provide more complete information about an individual's age, sex, race, occupation, literacy, birthplace, and household position. When the two documents can be matched for a comparable date, as in 1880, characteristics of alley residents and households begin to evolve.

But both documents, as central as they are to a study of Galveston alleys, have their limitations. For starters, not everyone was listed in the directories. As the editor of the 1868–69 directory observed, the city's population as a whole, not just its alley dwellers, was "as changeable as the sands upon our beach."[3] The first serious attempt to include blacks in the directories was not made until the 1872 edition, and then was not repeated until 1875–76.[4] Directory entries listed mostly heads of households and working adults and did not reflect the number of people actually living at each address; to estimate the city's total population, directory editors multiplied each entry by three.

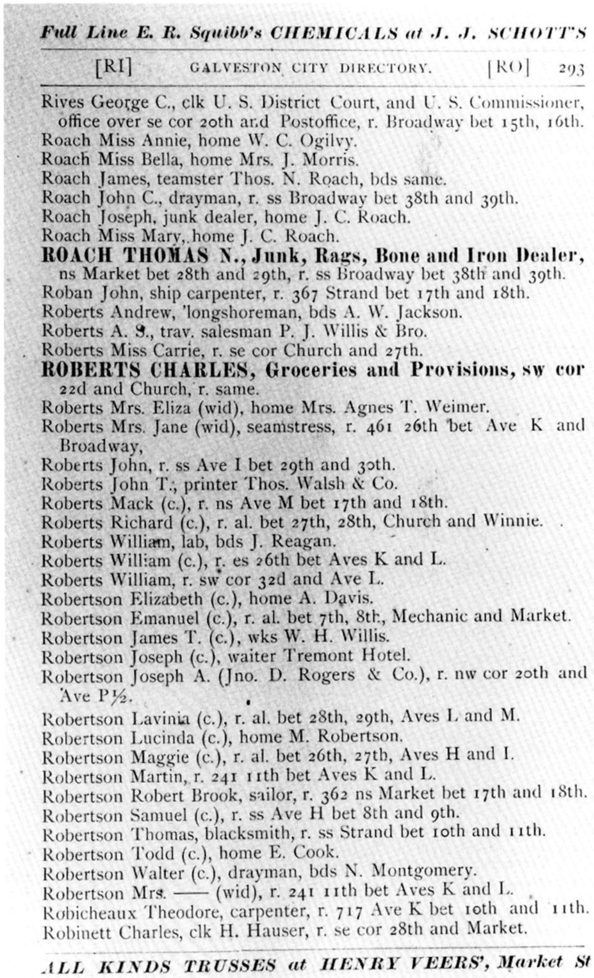

Full Line E. R. Squibb's CHEMICALS at J. J. SCHOTT'S

[RI] GALVESTON CITY DIRECTORY. [RO] 293

Rives George C., clk U. S. District Court, and U. S. Commissioner, office over se cor 20th and Postoffice, r. Broadway bet 15th, 16th.
Roach Miss Annie, home W. C. Ogilvy.
Roach Miss Bella, home Mrs. J. Morris.
Roach James, teamster Thos. N. Roach, bds same.
Roach John C., drayman, r. ss Broadway bet 38th and 39th.
Roach Joseph, junk dealer, home J. C. Roach.
Roach Miss Mary, home J. C. Roach.
ROACH THOMAS N., Junk, Rags, Bone and Iron Dealer, ns Market bet 28th and 29th, r. ss Broadway bet 38th and 39th.
Roban John, ship carpenter, r. 367 Strand bet 17th and 18th.
Roberts Andrew, 'longshoreman, bds A. W. Jackson.
Roberts A. S., trav. salesman P. J. Willis & Bro.
Roberts Miss Carrie, r. se cor Church and 27th.
ROBERTS CHARLES, Groceries and Provisions, sw cor 22d and Church, r. same.
Roberts Mrs. Eliza (wid), home Mrs. Agnes T. Weimer.
Roberts Mrs. Jane (wid), seamstress, r. 461 26th bet Ave K and Broadway,
Roberts John, r. ss Ave I bet 29th and 30th.
Roberts John T., printer Thos. Walsh & Co.
Roberts Mack (c.), r. ns Ave M bet 17th and 18th.
Roberts Richard (c.), r. al. bet 27th, 28th, Church and Winnie.
Roberts William, lab, bds J. Reagan.
Roberts William (c.), r. es 26th bet Aves K and L.
Roberts William, r. sw cor 32d and Ave L.
Robertson Elizabeth (c.), home A. Davis.
Robertson Emanuel (c.), r. al. bet 7th, 8th, Mechanic and Market.
Robertson James T. (c.), wks W. H. Willis.
Robertson Joseph (c.), waiter Tremont Hotel.
Robertson Joseph A. (Jno. D. Rogers & Co.), r. nw cor 20th and Ave P½.
Robertson Lavinia (c.), r. al. bet 28th, 29th, Aves L and M.
Robertson Lucinda (c.), home M. Robertson.
Robertson Maggie (c.), r. al. bet 26th, 27th, Aves H and I.
Robertson Martin, r. 241 11th bet Aves K and L.
Robertson Robert Brook, sailor, r. 362 ns Market bet 17th and 18th.
Robertson Samuel (c.), r. ss Ave H bet 8th and 9th.
Robertson Thomas, blacksmith, r. ss Strand bet 10th and 11th.
Robertson Todd (c.), home E. Cook.
Robertson Walter (c.), drayman, bds N. Montgomery.
Robertson Mrs. —— (wid), r. 241 11th bet Aves K and L.
Robicheaux Theodore, carpenter, r. 717 Ave K bet 10th and 11th.
Robinett Charles, clk H. Hauser, r. se cor 28th and Market.

ALL KINDS TRUSSES at HENRY VEERS', Market St

Fig. 41. Page from the 1881–82 Galveston city directory.

Fig. 40. Woman identified as "Aunt Harriet" shown washing clothes in a typical washhouse structure. Photograph circa 1892.

Alley Addresses

Mail went anywhere that you lived. . . . Most mailboxes on the alley were on the fence or you had to walk up on the porch to deliver. We never had any large rural-type mailboxes. We always had the little envelope-type mailboxes. They did have a little wire rack at the bottom to hang a magazine, but there were very few magazines. **The Rev. James B. Thomas**

Fig. 42. Mail box on alley house.

If it was a mailing address, it was "so and so in the rear." But if you knew somebody—was telling somebody how to get to somebody's house—it was "back of such and such a house." **Robert M. Tucker**

I've never heard the term "in the rear" anywhere else and I always think of it rather humorously when I hear it today. I think of living in the alley when someone says, "You might have to go to the rear." We always thought of it as alley dwelling space of some sort. You would hear it as an address. "So-and-so lives at 2602 N 1/2 rear" or "I live at 1122 Avenue E rear," and the envelopes were addressed "rear." **Danny Lasell**

Back houses were always referred to as "in the rear," not "on the alley." Being behind somebody was like being behind somebody in real life. The person behind always felt inferior to the person up front. You got more recognition in the front house. **Leon M. Banks Sr.**

Occupational listings and residential locations in the directories can be unclear, especially for those in servant positions who were listed merely as working for a specific individual, like the black man James T. Robertson whose listing read: "Robertson James T. (c.), wks [works] W.H. Willis." Addresses were not always given in such instances, but many of these people added to the alley population, because they frequently resided in separate servants quarters on their employer's property.

Directory listings also reflect social, racial, and economic biases. Occupations were more likely to be listed for whites than blacks, a disparity that became more pronounced with time. The 1872 directory listed a considerably wider range of specific occupations and trades for black men than did later editions, in which the majority were listed as laborers or with no occupation. Denying blacks the recognition associated with a specific job or skill contributed to their being relegated to the lowest paying, lowest status jobs as day laborers and domestics.

With rare exceptions, black women were not addressed or identified as "Miss," "Mrs.," or "widow," giving the impression there were no married, much less widowed, black women in the city. Honorific distinctions were accorded white women only, including those whose profession was not acknowledged—the prostitutes. These omissions, combined with the similarity of many names among the black population, often make it difficult to determine the relationships among black household members and their place of residence. Before and after widowhood, a black woman would be listed, for example, as "Caldwell Sarah." Any marital relationship remains unknown unless discovered in another document, such as the 1880 census or marriage records. In contrast, it is usually easy to determine when a white woman was widowed because she would be listed, for example, as "Coffey Mrs. Kate (wid)." A check of addresses in previous directories will indicate whether Mrs. Coffey continued living at the same address after her husband's death or if she moved.

The 1881–82 Galveston city directory lists 9,052 people. Of these, 260 have an alley or rear address, a number that should be interpreted as only a rough indication of the alley population, even if multiplied by three. Of the 185 blacks with an alley address, 108 are men and 77 are women. The 75 whites include 55 men and 20 women, 14 of whom are widows.

Fig. 43. Distribution of 260 alley addressees listed in 1881–82 Galveston city directory. The map is based on a 1904 map that was a compilation of a series of earlier maps and surveys, which is why some blocks showing alley addressees on this and subsequent schematic maps do not always show an alley. The alleys in some blocks were cut through or closed at various times. The twelve city wards are indicated on the map.

The 260 listings are dispersed among ninety-five alleys, with some clusterings of alley listings. (See fig. 43.) Most alleys with multiple listings are racially mixed, but of the seventeen alleys with five or more listings, two are all white and seven are all black.

The occupations of only 20 of the 108 black men are identified. (See table 4.1.) All are laborers, including Wiley Peterson, who is listed as both a pastor and a drayman. Richard Johnson is among the 88 black men whose occupations are unspecified. In contrast, the occupations of 52 of the 55 white men are recorded, including that of laborer Charles Wilkman. None of the women, black or white, has a listed occupation.

Also listed in the directory are 254 "wks" [works] entries, the majority of whom would have been servants. Because only 62 of the 254 are black, it is obvious that the listings for servants are far from complete.

The 1880 census enumerates 22,248 Galvestonians. Not all of the 260 alley addressees listed in the 1881–82 directory can be found in the census, for which the fluidity of the population is only a partial explanation.[5] Some census takers were careless about the legibility and accuracy of their listings, especially in Ward Five, which had the highest alley population in the city. All the census takers were lax in designating alley locations and signifying households that were in separate buildings but on the same property. It was a habit that creates

Table 4.1
Male alley residents, 1881–82, by race and occupation

Occupation	Black	White
Drayman	7	3
Laborer	4	16
Cook	3	2
"Works"	2	-
Longshoreman	-	9
Screwman	-	3
Cabinetmaker	-	2
Oyster dealer	-	2
Saloon proprietor	-	2
Miscellaneous	4[a]	13[b]
No occupation	88	3
TOTAL	**108**	**55**

Source: Data from *Morrison & Fourmy's Directory, 1881–82.*

[a]Cooper, cotton sampler, hostler, and pastor/drayman.
[b]Clerk, dairyman, driver, oyster fisherman, night watchman, oyster opener, painter, peddler, porter, printer, sailmaker, ship carpenter, and "works depot."

some confusion when interpreting the census records for a city like Galveston, with its transient, seasonal population; its households of related and unrelated families, boarders, servants, employees, and relatives; and its jumbling of multiple units and separate buildings on a single parcel. And certainly, there must have been those citizens who had their reasons for not wanting to be counted or interviewed. But even with all these qualifications, a portrait of Galveston's alley residents in the last quarter of the nineteenth century can be pieced together by using the 1881–82 city directory and the 1880 census and supplementing them with other documents.[6]

In 1880, Nathaniel Hornsberry and Lewis Cole were typical alley dwellers except in one respect: both were centenarians. Both resided in rental alley housing in neighborhoods with a clustering of alley listings in the 1881–82 directory. Hornsberry lived in the northeast corner of town, on the alley bordered by Seventh and Eighth Streets and Avenues C and D. First listed at the address in 1876–77, Hornsberry lived with black laborer Manuel Robinson, his wife India, who was a washerwoman, and six children. None of the adults in the household could read or write.

Unlike Hornsberry, who is typical of those alley residents who stayed in one location, Cole moved with some frequency. Between his first listing in the 1875–76 directory and his last in 1886–87, Cole moved four times, including two moves to alleys. In 1876–77, he was living on an alley in Ward Five. By 1881–82, he had made his fourth move, which was to his second alley address, the alley bordered by Avenues L and M and Twenty-ninth and Thirtieth Streets. According to the 1880 census, the hundred-and-five-year-old Cole lived with his sixty-five-year-old wife, Esther, who could read.

Just how long Lewis Cole and Nat Hornsberry lived in Galveston is unknown. Esther Cole's death record states that she arrived in Galveston in 1855, in all probability as a slave. The marriage of "Nat Hornsby" and "Matilde Johnson" was entered twice in Galveston County records—November 1868 and September 1870—but neither the Hornsberrys nor the Coles can be found in the 1870 Texas census. All four were born in Virginia, including Matilda Hornsberry, whose birthplace was recorded when she died at age eighty on October 14, 1876.

Both men died of "old age," Hornsberry on December 24, 1884, and Cole on January 14, 1887. Prior to his death, Cole had moved back to Ward Five, probably to "rear 2620 Winnie" [Avenue G], where his widow remained throughout the 1890s. When Esther Cole died in 1905, she was buried in Potter's Field, as were her husband and the Hornsberrys.[7]

Sarah Bennett, another alley resident, was one of many domestic servants who, during their lifetime, worked for a number of families while living in a series of servants quarters and rental alley houses. Bennett migrated from Alabama to Galveston in 1870, when she was seventeen years old. Her first Galveston residence was probably a rental alley house that she shared with another black woman who was from Kentucky. Both women were washerwomen; neither could read or write.

When the 1875–76 directory was published, Bennett was working as a "servt" for Christopher Dart, Clerk of the United States District Court, who lived on the corner of Avenue E and Tenth Street. By 1882–83, her work location and probably her residence had moved one block west, where she was the cook for M. H. Royston, Clerk of the Criminal Court, a job she held at least through 1888–89. The next three directories find her working for three different people, all in the same neighborhood, and in two instances definitely living on her employer's property (fig. 45).

Bennett may not have worked for a sole employer after 1895–96. She is listed in 1898 as a "laundress" living at "rear 501 9th Street," the same location where she was "Living alone" and working as a "Day laborer," according to the 1900 census. Following the 1900 hurricane, Bennett moved to "rear 1508 Winnie" [Avenue G] in Block 375, which was her address when a teenage nephew, Henry Hudson, began boarding with her. According to the 1910 census, Hudson was Texas-born, earned his living at "odd jobs," could neither read nor write, and was only seventeen years old, but he had assumed the care of his aunt. Bennett moved

Fig. 44. "Backyards and Lafitte House," drawing by E. M. "Buck" Schiwetz, 1949.

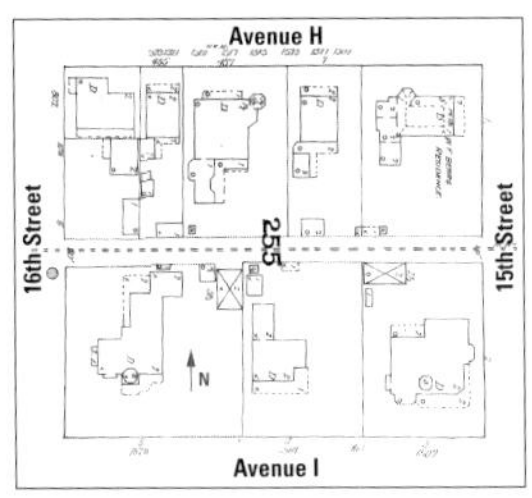

Fig. 45. One of the blocks on which Sarah Bennett worked and lived during the early 1890s. Houses are generous in size with attached wings and separate support buildings. Sanborn maps do not always indicate uses: no doubt there were living quarters on the second floor of both stable buildings (marked "X") as well as in other one- and two-story buildings along the alley. Sanborn insurance map, 1889.

with Hudson and his growing family to various front-street addresses. When she died of "Paralysis" on November 29, 1920, they were living at 1802 Nineteenth Street. She was buried in the New Pottersfield Cemetery.[8]

Sarah Bennett lived most of her Galveston life in the part of town where there was the greatest concentration of servants working for individual households. Many servants lived in separate structures on their employer's property, but their numerical impact on the alley population is difficult to determine. For example, we know from the 1881–82 directory that Richard Johnson and his family, whom we met at the beginning of the chapter, shared their alley with two other black families. They probably also shared the alley with fourteen other individuals, thirteen of whom, according to the 1880 census, were working as servants in eight households on the same block. Only two of the servants, however, are listed in the 1881–82 directory. (See appendix B.)

Charles and Ophelia Pettit lived just one block north of the Johnsons in the servants quarters at "rear 451 Mechanic [Avenue C] cor 16th." The Pettits are listed separately in the 1881-82 directory: Charles Pettit as a laborer and Ophelia Pettit as "wks W. B. Hance." According to the census, Pettit was forty-five years old and born in England, whereas Mrs. Pettit was thirty-eight, a Texan by birth, and the cook for the Hance family. Hance was a ship's captain who owned his property and whose household consisted of his wife, three children, and his paralytic English mother-in-law.

The Pettits typify many of the couples who occupied servants quarters, with one person, usually the woman, working in the front house and the other working elsewhere. The Pettits also illustrate that white as well as black servants lived in separate quarters, and that multiple directory listings do exist for the same household, thereby affecting any estimation of the alley population.[9]

Many businesses operated from alley locations, but few are listed in city directories. One exception in 1881–82 was oyster-opener Mariano Jalousey's shop on the "al. bet 21st, 22d, Postoffice and Church [Avenues E and F]." It was the first year in which the thirty-two-year-old Austrian immigrant was listed in a directory, and the only year at an alley address.[10]

Certain occupations, such as washerwoman and drayman, were associated with an alley location; both terms float in and out of directory listings and frequently appear in census records for people known to be alley residents. In the 1880 census, Richard Johnson's wife Nettie and her neighbor Emma Davis were among thirty-three women in Ward Two whose occupation was "Washing & I" or "Washerwoman." (See figs. 40, 44.) Of these, twenty-five were black, seven mulatto, and one white. Nineteen were married. We can assume that many of the women lived on an alley because they tend to be listed consecutively and in small clusters. Although "washing" was the primary means of income for many women, the 1881–82 directory does not acknowledge "washerwoman" as an occupation except to list a few women who worked in commercial laundries.[11]

Once in a while, we would have a laundress and take the laundry to her, and that was always in an alley. And I can remember—I'm a little vague whether it happened here or whether this happened in Birmingham because I was a very young child—but I remember my mother saying to my father that she was going to go over to colored town—you know, as though it were a place, a definable area—and she was going to find someone to do our laundry. I went with her. It was just about dusk and I remember my mother letting me roll down the window (so it must have been in the winter) and asking those women—just kind of to the world: "Do you know anyone who will do my laundry? Will anyone do my laundry?" and someone came out and said she would. So my mother said, "I'll be back next week," and drove off.

Irene Ayers

Many black and immigrant white men worked as draymen (fig. 49). For some, like Hermann Ackermann, an alley address was a temporary residence. Ackermann, a twenty-seven-year-old blacksmith from Germany, wasted little time after his arrival in Galveston on June 2, 1870. Three weeks later, he was recorded in the 1870 census as working in a store and living in a boardinghouse managed by twenty-four-year-old Christina Schmish, whom he married on October 7, 1870. Ackermann is first listed in a directory in 1876–77, when he was working for a furniture business. By the next directory, he had become a drayman whose residence, and in all probability his business, was located on the alley between Avenues N and N 1/2 and Seventeenth and Eighteenth Streets, in a neighborhood of workers' cottages.

In 1884, Ackermann purchased a lot for $200 on Sixteenth Street between Avenues N 1/2 and O. Tax records and directory listings indicate that the family did not move to the front-street address until 1886. In June 1900, Ackermann was recorded in his fourth American census as a drayman living at 2601 Fortieth Street, another property he had bought in a developing part of town near the beach. It proved to be a vulnerable location during the hurricane that devastated the city on September 8. The names of Ackermann, his wife, their daughter, and one son are first on the list of thousands killed.[12]

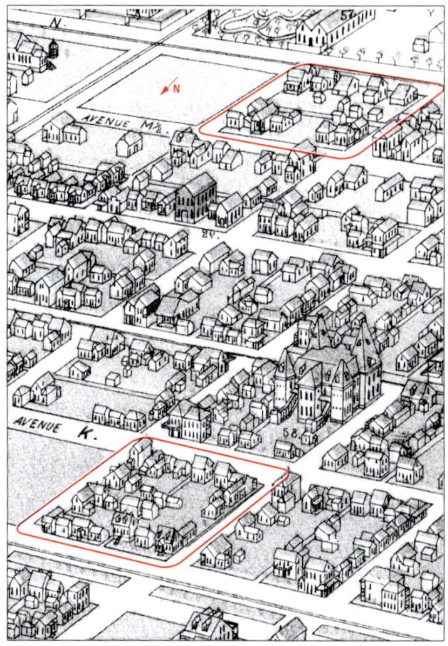

Fig. 46. 1885 bird's-eye view showing blocks in which the Griffin (top) and the Jackson (bottom) families lived.

Some alley dwellers stayed at the same alley location for years. Amelia and Mitchell Jackson lived at least twenty years in a house on the alley bordered by Thirtieth and Thirty-first Streets and Avenues J and K (figs. 46, 47). They may have been among the residents of their neighborhood who, in June 1875, were "crying for immediate relief from the stench and filth" of the alley just one block south. The Jacksons' one-story house probably had been two smaller units that were joined to make a four-room house (figs. 47, 48). Their alley house, three front houses, and two lots on the block belonged to Harold Marwitz, a wholesale and retail grocer who owned rental property throughout the city and lived at the corner of Avenue O and Thirty-first Street.

Although city directories list Jackson as a laborer, he specified his skill as plasterer in the 1880 census. The thirty-eight-year-old Mississippian had been unemployed for three months during the census year. Amelia Jackson was a housewife, thirty-seven years old, and born in Maryland. Neither of them could read or write. Their two children were born in Texas: a five-year-old son and a seventeen-year-old daughter who attended school, probably the school for black children two blocks away.

Jackson died of stomach cancer in August 1896 and was buried in Potter's Field. As often happened, Mrs. Jackson began moving from one location to another after her husband's death. By 1906–7, she was rooming at her fourth change of address, two of her

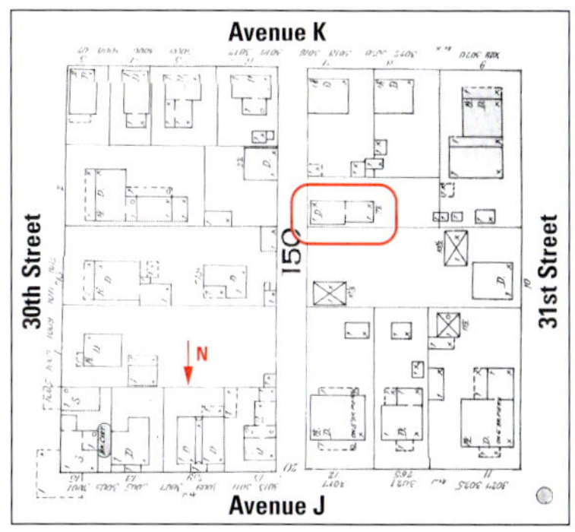

Fig. 47. For over twenty years, the Jackson family rented the house that is circled. The alley runs north-south in this block. Sanborn insurance map, 1889.

Fig. 48. 1315 Avenue K rear. Building type very similar to the house rented by the Jackson family. Photographed 1987.

addresses being places where she had worked as a servant. In both instances, she probably lived on the second story of a back building that doubled as a stable on the first floor.[13]

For Amelia Jackson, widowhood meant losing the security of an alley residence where she and her family had lived uninterrupted for at least twenty years. For other women, often white women, widowhood meant moving from a front house to an alley residence. Many white women living on the alleys were married to first-generation immigrants or were immigrants themselves, as was Kate Coffey. In 1866, the fifteen-year-old Irish immigrant married Thomas Coffey, a twenty-eight-year-old longshoreman and laborer from South Carolina. Mrs. Coffey apparently lived a turbulent life on the north side of Avenue K between Eighth and Ninth Streets, for in 1877, Coffey was fined $25 and required to execute a $100 peace bond for "disorderly conduct, abusing, striking and badly treating" his wife.

Thomas Coffey drowned in a boating accident in May 1881. Shortly thereafter, his widow moved to an alley address on the same block, which was probably on the same property where she is listed in the 1882–83 directory as "Coffey Kate Mrs. (wid), al. bet 8th, 9th, e Broadway and Ave K." She and her son John, a waiter, lived at the address at least until 1893–94. Their disappearance from the directories and their absence from other documents after that time suggest that they may have left Galveston.[14]

Although there were alley residents who lived for long periods of time at one address, it is far easier to find documentation for those who frequently moved. Andrew Thompson was a black stableman who, between 1875–76 and 1895–96, worked for the major livery businesses in Galveston and lived at seven different locations, including four alley residences. At the time of the 1900 census, the Thompson household of five was living at "rear 314 26th Street," on a property they shared with six other rental households and ten people.[15]

Thompson's directory listings, with their inclusion of specific employers' names—all long-standing businesses—suggest that he had steady employment. But the family's frequent changes of address also suggest that paying the rent was a constant struggle, as it was for many laborers, whether they lived on an alley or a front street and whether they were black or white.

Fig. 49. During the nineteenth century and well into the twentieth, many men living on the alleys worked as draymen. Photograph taken in 1920 during a massive alley cleanup in response to an outbreak of bubonic plague.

Galveston was not immune to the labor unrest that erupted throughout the country in the late 1870s. Among the demonstrators and strikers in Galveston were draymen, wharf workers, day laborers, laundresses, and newsboys—people whose occupations were well represented among the alley population. Occasionally, an alley dweller like Louis Griffin can be identified in newspaper accounts of the demonstrations. In late July and early August 1877, Galveston laborers demanded a fixed daily wage of $2.00, protesting that the current $1.00 to $1.50 was not a living wage, nor was the

50 cents or $1.00 paid their wives. At one public meeting attended by some three hundred strikers, mostly black, the *Galveston Daily News* quoted Griffin as stating that he "was a representative man of his race, and as such was ready to say that the colored men do not desire to do anything that was contrary to law. He said that he had been a worker on the Narrow Gauge road, but when the strikers came around and asked for his shovel he had given it to them because he thought his labor was worth more than he was getting."[16]

In conjunction with the strike, the newspaper reported "What it Costs to Live" for "a laboring man" in Galveston. The source, a married man with two small children, calculated that the monthly cost of living was $38.25 for food, wood, medicine, and rent ($10). If a man worked twenty-six full days at $1.50 a day, his total earnings of $39.00 left 75 cents per month, or $9.00 per year, to buy clothing and pay for doctors' visits, which cost $2.50 each. Most laborers actually averaged only twenty working days each month because of "sickness, bad weather, and loss of time between jobs."[17]

Believing they had been guaranteed an increased wage, demonstrators returned to their jobs only to discover that some contractors would be paying the old wage of $1.50 per day. Workers acquiesced, stating that they realized their only options were to accept the wage or "beset themselves to hunting up another job." Whereas the strike resulted in higher wages for at least some male laborers, it apparently had little impact on the wages of female domestic workers. Rather than pay $2.00 per day for washerwomen and $20.00 per month for cooks, "some of the first ladies of this city . . . announced themselves as ready to carry their accomplishments into the kitchen rather than yield to the unjust demands of those who are clamoring for increased wages."[18]

Just how the strike affected individuals, especially outspoken or quoted ones like Louis Griffin, is unknown. At the time of the strikes, Griffin was a laborer living on the alley bordered by Twenty-eighth and Twenty-ninth Streets and Avenues M 1/2 and N, an address he maintained at least from 1876–77 through 1886–87, although his occupation changed to porter (figs. 46, 50). In 1880, he and his wife Mina, a washerwoman, were supporting four children. Some time in the late 1880s, the family moved to a front-street rental house in the same neighborhood, which is where they were living when Griffin died in June 1890 and where Mrs. Griffin continued to live before moving to another address by 1893–94.[19]

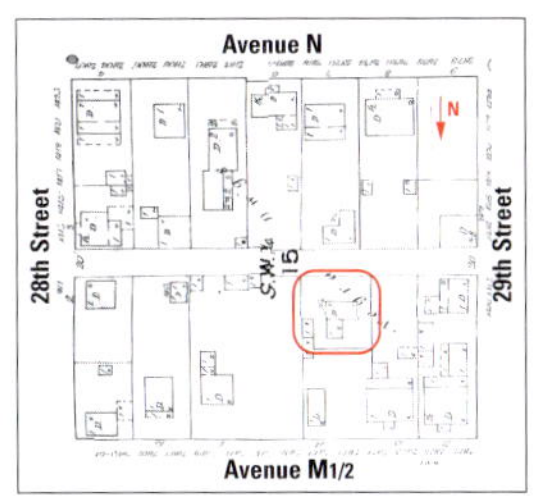

Fig. 50. During the 1870s and 1880s, the Griffin family rented a house on the alley of this block, perhaps the one that is circled. The block is one of those labeled "Negro Dw'gs" on the Sanborn insurance map in 1889. Orientation of this figure matches the 1885 view, fig. 46.

For those living on the alleys, as well as those on the front streets, taking in boarders (who were often relatives) was one way to help pay the rent. When the census taker interviewed Isaac Robinson in June 1880, his household included his wife Linda and a daughter. Six months later, the family had a boarder, William Green, a cook, living with them at "rear 105 C between 27th, 28th" in Ward Five.

Events between visits to the Robinson household by the census taker and the directory tabulator provide us with one of the few physical descriptions we have of an alley resident. On October 27, when Mollie Waters's Saratoga trunk was stolen from "her house," a well-known brothel on Twenty-fifth Street, police followed "clews" to "the notorious Fat alley," where they arrested two men—Isaac Robinson and a Bill Green, obviously the Robinsons' boarder, William Green. During his confinement, Robinson attempted to escape from the county jail with the help of "a negro woman, Melinda Mason," who supplied him not only with food and clothing on a daily basis but also with a file and two small keyhole saws, one of which he broke. When a reporter questioned Robinson, this "bold, bad man . . . some 5 feet 6 inches in height and heavily built . . . [he] could only glean from him that he 'had swallowed the remaining parts of the broken saw with his lunch.'"

In all probability, the various women listed in the Robinson accounts (Melinda Mason,

Fig. 51. Squeeze Inn, 3915 Avenue G. Opened in 1948, the restaurant was one of the last alley businesses. The building and restaurant were owned by the same person. Photographed 1987.

Alley Businesses

I associate the alleys of my childhood with beauty shops, because every time I went to a beauty shop to get my hair pressed, they usually used a little back room. People often would go underneath their house for a beauty parlor or back in the kitchen. . . . Those were flourishing businesses. We had things done, as I can remember as a child, where we were often going up somebody's backstairs. It wasn't hidden. That's just the only room or place they had for it and so they operated on the back of their homes sometimes. **Izola Fedford Collins**

There weren't real businesses on the alleys. Just businesses like a lady made tamales or a lady baked bread or something like that. Probably didn't have to have health certificates. You'd find your best tamales in some place in the alley and you'd go get them. An old black lady made stuffed crabs and we used to go there and buy stuffed crabs--between K and L, Sixteenth and Seventeenth Streets. **Robert M. Tucker**

I remember taking one of our maids to the voodoo man in the alley. That was his business, where black candles made of monkey blood were sold. He had an alley house. . . . It was rather a dark place with drapes hanging here and there and beads on the wall and stashes of stuff. I remember the candles and powder in little jars. **Danny Lasell**

A lot of places were in the alleys after I returned from the war. Cafes . . . there's a famous one right now, the Squeeze Inn. . . . Dean's used to have a bar in the alley right down from the Squeeze Inn. . . . People just started opening up. You didn't have to have a license to cook or the health inspector didn't have to come around. Or somebody was selling pies out of their house. . . . Anything could spring up in an alley because there were just no restrictions.

The Rev. James B. Thomas

---

the Linda Robinson who is listed as Robinson's wife in the 1880 census, the Melinda Robinson who is listed on Fat Alley in the 1882–83 city directory, and the Melinda Battles who married Robinson on February 23, 1883) were the same person. The use of different names for the same person in census records and city directories, whether deliberate on the part of the individual or careless on the part of the recorder, is not unusual.

After Isaac Robinson was released from jail, his family began its gradual migration to a front-street address. In 1886–87, they were living at Avenue F between Thirty-third and Thirty-fourth Streets in a service building on property owned by George Parker, an engineer with the Gulf City Cotton Press and Mrs. Robinson's employer. Robinson worked as a drayman, then as a laborer in an iron foundry. When Parker sold his property in 1895, the Robinsons apparently had to move. In 1899–1900, they were living in a rental alley house at "rear 2917 H" on Burnett's Alley, which is where they were living at the time of the 1900 census. Their two children had died. Once again, they had a boarder—John Adams, a forty-year-old black man from Mississippi, who was a fireman.

The couple then moved to a shotgun house at a front-street address on the same block, which is where they were living when Isaac Robinson died at age fifty-nine of "Organic Heart Disease" on October 13, 1907. Robinson had been a Galveston resident for thirty years. He was buried in Lake View Cemetery, an indication that his widow could afford his burial.[20]

Every alley resident has a different history, but generalizations about those who lived along the alleys in Galveston in the last quarter of the nineteenth century can nevertheless be made on the basis of the 1880 census, the 1881–82 city directory, and other documents. Most alley dwellers were black. Many of them were former slaves, but determining the number of those who had lived in Galveston before the Civil War and those who had migrated to the city later is impossible. Alley residents also represented a mix of nationalities, including a substantial number of first-generation immigrants.

Most alley dwellers were domestic workers and laborers who rented their house or lived in servants quarters. Their financial resources were limited. Many were buried in Potter's Field. House-sharing was as common among those who lived in back buildings, especially rental alley housing, as among those who lived in front houses. The tax assessor's records substantiate that few alley dwellers could afford to become property owners, but home ownership was more a possibility for white than black alley residents.

Alley dwellers were frequently on the move for reasons of economics, employment, building condition, health, or choice. The possibility of moving from an alley location to a front-street address seemed to be far greater for whites than blacks—or it may be more accurate to say that the probability of living on an alley seemed far greater for blacks than whites.

The alleys with the highest density were usually those with rental housing and were located in blocks where the density was high on both the front streets and the alley. These were the alleys in which the buildings were oriented to the alley. But alleys in blocks inhabited primarily by domestic servants who lived in service buildings or back houses on their employer's property could also have a substantial population.

Some alleys were crowded—very crowded. Exact numbers are virtually impossible to determine, but obviously there were far more alley dwellers than directory listings indicate. If we apply the directory standard of calculating the city's population by multiplying each directory entry by three, the combined total of 260 alley addressees and the 259 "wks" listings in the 1881–82 directory represents an alley population of 1,557. Duplications and the uncertainty of the "wks" entries are balanced by what is suspected to be a sizeable but indeterminate number of omissions and a highly transient population. In fact, the 1881–82 numbers are probably truer to the alley population in 1875–76, when the directory listed 44 alley addressees.

In the next decade, Galveston alleys only became more crowded. Judging by the 765 entries with an alley or rear address in the 1891–92 Galveston city directory, the alley population had tripled in a ten-year period. The number of blacks living on the alleys had also grown. Of the 765 alley entries in the 1891–92 directory, 530 are black (312 men and 218 women), and 235 are white (163 men and 72 women).[21]

The 1891–92 directory offers the alley researcher a convenient ten-year period since publication of the 1881–82 directory. It is also the first directory to list addresses—16,074, to be exact—according to a new numbering system adopted after years of discussion and debate (it is still in use today). Loss of the 1890 census, however, makes it impossible to reconstruct alley households as thoroughly for this period as for the earlier years.[22]

Table 4.2
Male alley residents, 1891–92, by race and occupation

Occupation	Black	White
Factories, cotton mill	-	37
Laborer [a]	107	20
Wharf-related	36 [b]	6
Service	24	19
Drayman	18	1
"Works"/ laborer [c]	11	5
Building trades	9 [d]	13
Cotton industry	9	16
Stable/livery	9	-
Woodyard/wood sawyer	8	-
Oil mill	6	-
Railroads	3	7
Commercial fishing	-	7
Gas and waterworks	-	4
Miscellaneous	6	14
No occupation	66	14
TOTAL	**312**	**163**

Source: Data from *Morrison & Fourmy's Directory, 1891–92.*

[a] Employer unspecified.
[b] Sixteen were employed by the Mallory Steamship Line.
[c] Employer specified.
[d] Four carpenters, three plasterers, one glazier, one brickmason.

During the decade between the two directories, the alley population was highly mobile. Only twelve people—nine blacks and three whites—are definitely listed at the same alley address in the 1881–82 and the 1891–92 directories. Mitchell Jackson was among them. Twenty individuals, all black, had moved from one alley to another, including Andrew Thompson and Bill Green. At the same time, the number of people who remained at one alley address for relatively long periods was probably much greater, but the inconsistent and ofttimes unclear directory listings make it difficult to document those numbers.

Almost all alley dwellers continued to earn their living and pay their rent from laboring or service positions, although there were a few exceptions among both blacks and whites. (See table 4.2.) In 1891–92, black entrepreneurs included Henry Johnson, whose restaurant at 1005 Thirtieth Street was just around the corner from his alley residence, and James Clark, whose residence and clubroom on the alley between Twenty-fifth and Twenty-sixth Streets and Avenues L and M was one of the few businesses listed on an alley. Two engineers, a sculptor, and a "real estate owner" were among the whites living on an alley.

Of the 218 listings for black women in the 1891–92 directory, 198 do not indicate an occupation. Seventeen black women are identified as domestic servants working for specified employers but living elsewhere on an alley. For example, Sarah Caldwell lived at rear 2620 Avenue G and worked for A. F. French, the bookkeeper of a banking and commission merchant firm, who lived at 2425 Avenue F, less than two blocks away. To go to work, Caldwell, no doubt, left her rear dwelling, turned east, and walked through the alley, crossing Twenty-sixth, then Twenty-fifth Street, to enter the back entrance of the Frenches' house.

Of the 35 white women with a listed occupation, 29 were employed by the mills and factories, which collectively had become the major employers of white alley dwellers of both sexes.[23]

The 765 alley addressees in the 1891–92 directory are spread throughout 221 blocks (fig. 52), a major increase over the 95 blocks with alley addresses in 1881–82. The alleys with the highest densities tend to be in the same sections where there had been clusterings of inhabited alleys in 1881-82, while the growing number of alley addresses to the south of Avenue L and west of Twenty-ninth Street reflects the direction in which the city was expanding. (See fig. 53.)

Many alleys continued to have a racial mix, but the number of high-density alleys that had only black residents, or all black residents except for a single white, was increasing. The greatest concentration of alley listings, once again, was in Ward Five, where there were 130 alley dwellers, of whom 105 were black. (See appendices C and E for a comparison of the 1881–82 and 1891–92 directories.)

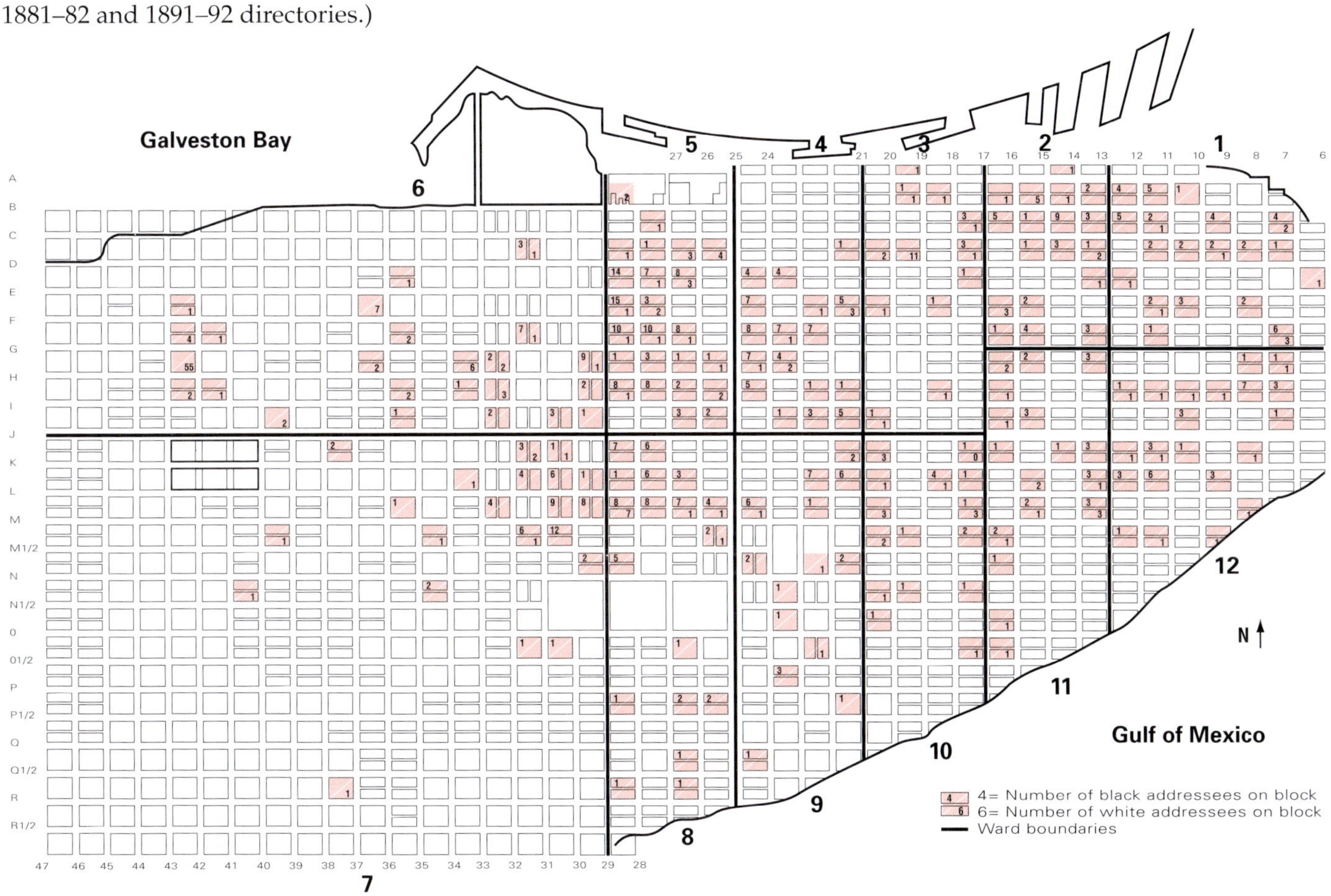

Fig. 52. Distribution of 765 alley addressees listed in 1891–92 Galveston city directory. One block with an alley listing is outside the map area. The twelve city wards are indicated on the map.

In addition to the 765 alley or rear addressees in the 1891–92 directory, there are 719 individuals listed as working and residing at the same location. Of these, 448 are black and 271 are white. The majority would have been domestic servants, probably living in a back building.[24]

And what had happened to Charles Wilkman and Richard Johnson between 1881–82 and 1891–92? The Wilkmans' tenure at their 1881–82 alley address between Fifteenth and Sixteenth Streets and Avenues A and B was short-lived. In each of the three directories after 1881–82, the family is listed at a different location. By 1888–89, they had returned to their old neighborhood, specifically to the front-street side of Avenue C between Sixteenth and Seventeenth Streets. Charles Wilkman died on January 14, 1892, from an "Accidental Injury on Ship." Lena Wilkman was unsuccessful in her attempt to buy the property on Avenue C, and by the 1905 city directory, the family had moved to another location.[25]

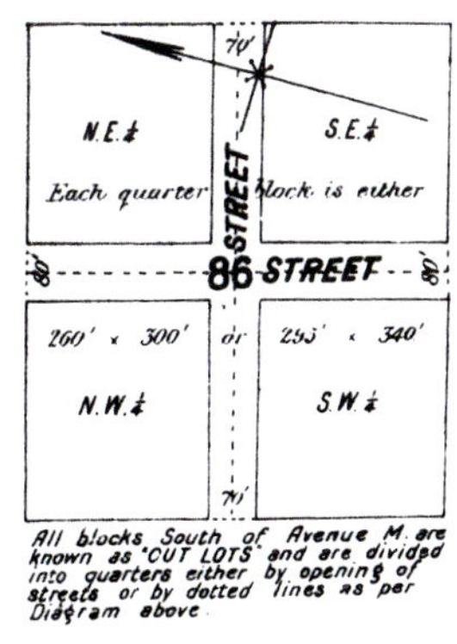

Fig. 53. Sanborn insurance map, 1889. As the city moved south and west, the outlots, which were part of the original plan, were developed. Alleys were usually cut through the outlot quadrants.

Nor did the Johnsons remain for very long at their 1881–82 alley address at "rear 426 Church cor 16th." By 1890, they had lived at four different addresses, including a front-street address on the Tin Can Alley block and two alley locations. Richard Johnson died in 1890. Nettie Johnson moved back to Ward Five, to the alley bordered by Twenty-seventh and Twenty-eighth Streets and Avenues H and I. Her alley neighbors of ten years earlier, Emma Davis and her husband, were living on the alley in the servants quarters on the property where Mrs. Davis worked as a domestic servant. Mrs. Johnson took in a boarder to help pay her rent but soon moved to another alley address five blocks away, where she was listed in the 1893–94 directory, and where she died on July 26, 1893. Like her husband Richard and so many of her fellow alley dwellers, Nettie Johnson was buried in Potter's Field.[26]

Fig. 54. A view from the alley in the neighborhood of Thirty-sixth Street and Avenue M. Photographed circa 1940.

Plants and Play along the Alleys

The alleys then were just dirt. Later on, some of them were covered with oyster shell. And you could have the best time. . . . There was never any threatening feeling about it. There was never any idea that you couldn't play in the alley or that anything bad would happen to you. . . . Alleys were always such cool places. The trees would grow over and they had flowers and dogs and cats. It was a nice place to play. I always liked it in the alley. . . . There was a lot of integrated play in the alleys. You played with whoever was there, including black children. **Irene Ayers**

Children played in the alleys. It really was a safer place to play in. And we used to call it—we used to say that about the beach—that we would promenade. You never went nowhere. You just walk up and down, like you see kids walking in the park, lovers walking in a park. But they did that in alleys. You know, we did a lot of things that were done everywheres else, but we never would think of it like that. The children could just go so far. The teenagers, they'd walk up—"You don't get out of Mama's sight, now"—you know, so they promenade. They have to go up and down. Those little girls walking and talking to one another, fifteen and sixteen. **The Rev. James B. Thomas**

Alleys were a very important part of how we'd go to people's houses. We'd walk through the alley maybe. The Mountain Speedway, the old roller coaster, was right next to my house so we'd go through the alley to go there. The front sometimes.

The alleys were sandy. They weren't paved—at least the alley that I remember. We played in the alley. We also used to play in the streets. . . . In my neighborhood, we used to call it the League of Nations. It was such a diverse group: Scandinavian, English, German, Greeks, Italians, everything you could think of. There were Jewish people, too. It was all one play group. Very few blacks were involved in the play group, but there was also a lot of the blacks that were friendly, and we played with them in the neighborhood as young people.

The blue bloods lived on the other side of Twenty-fifth Street. They didn't associate with us. . . . I noticed a lot of the alleys where blue bloods lived. We used to go down there and rob their pomegranate trees and their pecan trees. Go through the alleys to get to them. **George P. Mitchell**

I thought the alleys were beautiful because of the flowers, especially the poinsettias. They were trees that hung over the fences. I'd never seen anything bigger than something in a pot. **E. Burke Evans**

There were a lot of trees, a lot of fruit trees in the alleys. A lot of vacant lots where there were wild plum trees where we spent many a day eating plums. The alley that I was raised in didn't have as many trees in it but it did have plantings. **Bill Millican**

There were lots of fruit trees. . . . I was talking to my brother in Houston and he says, "What I remember about the alleys is that's where the fruit trees were. Close to the alley fence. That's where we used to steal the fruit. You could reach right over the fence and get your fruit." **Robert M. Tucker**

Some of the alleys were beautiful because they had fruit trees. They had plenty of plum trees, fig trees, what they call a date tree and not a palm tree, pear trees, and peach trees. . . . A shade tree was very important to your house and to your neighborhood. Just think about no air-conditioning and only a few people even could afford fans, so you know what a shade tree meant. It meant the difference between just a barren street or stretch of land and like an oasis. This is a beautiful place if you got a shade tree. **Gerald Z. Clouser**

5 Owning Alley Property

I'm operating thirty-five houses that I own. I have three in the alley. I can't hardly rent them. That stigma attached to them—"I'm not going to live in no alley." Good houses. Well kept. Better than some on the front street but hard to rent.

Gerald Z. Clouser

Most alley dwellers in Galveston either rented the house in which they lived, or resided in housing provided in exchange for domestic services. There were exceptions—people like Peter Brantigan, who owned their property and chose, for reasons of convenience, necessity, or preference, to live in an alley or back house. There were also those who purchased and developed alley housing for income purposes only and lived along a front street.[1]

Brantigan's cabinetmaking shop and residence were located at "rear 1818 Avenue I," on property bought by his wife Francisca and her first husband, carpenter Ferdinand Hendel, in 1859. Hendel died in the 1860s. The Brantigans, both Prussians, were married in 1870. Like their neighbors, they suffered severe losses in the 1885 fire—in their case, property valued at $1,000. Three weeks after the fire, the Brantigans obtained a building permit for a $300 "cottage" that, as shown on the 1889 Sanborn map (fig. 56, top), stood in sharp contrast to the other residences rebuilt on the half-block, including that of their new next-door neighbor, Jacob Sonnentheil. On the front of the Brantigans' lot was a one-story, box-shaped house. To the rear were four small outbuildings, the largest of which was probably the shop, and a long, narrow, one-story dwelling that hugged the west side of the lot and opened into the yard—no doubt, the Brantigans' "rear" residence. The other four front houses on the half-block were imposing two-story, irregularly shaped structures, each with a sizeable carriage house and servants quarters defining the alley line and a backyard free of scattered outbuildings. In 1894, the Brantigans sold their property, whereupon the buildings on the lot were replaced by a residence in keeping with the new scale and style of the neighborhood (fig. 56, bottom).[2]

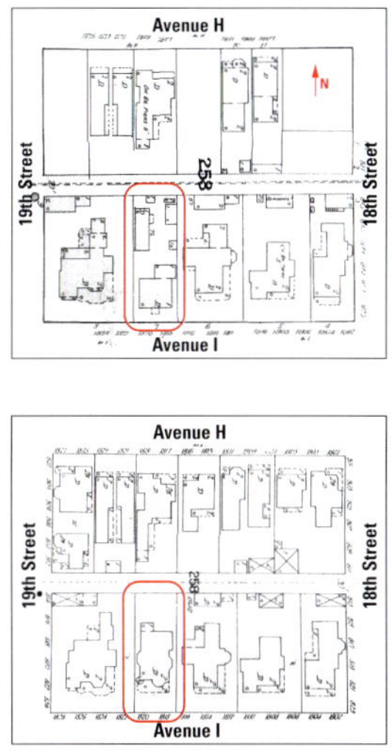

Fig. 56. Sanborn insurance maps, 1889 (top) and 1899 (bottom), showing changes on the Brantigan property. The Sonnentheil house is on the corner, to the west of the Brantigans'. See also fig. 36.

For others, operating their business and residing on the alley side of their property was a frugal interim arrangement. In 1870, Friedrich Eggert, a thirty-one-year-old Prussian immigrant and bachelor, bought a lot on the north side of Avenue K between Twenty-first and Twenty-second Streets. He was still there in 1880, as were his wife and five children. Throughout this period, Eggert maintained a tailoring business in downtown Galveston, but between 1885 and 1889 he replaced the front cottage and a rear dwelling with larger structures and moved both his shop and his residence to the alley building. By the time the 1895–96 directory was published, Eggert had moved them to another property he had bought on Avenue N. He kept the Avenue K property, presumably renting both buildings,

---

There were several people that built houses that lived in the back. I would think that they did it for commercial, for shop purposes. I know of one that's still standing. Walter Cunningham was a painter, carpenter, cabinetmaker. He built his house on the alley, high-raised, double doors in the back, downstairs combination shop, storage, garage. You enter through the front gate and you walk to the back of the lot—the house was back there so that he could get in and out from the alley. I think he had plans to ultimately build a house in front, but he didn't live that long. **Ernest Z. Clouser**

Fig. 55. 2818 Avenue L rear. The three-room commissary or shotgun house was moved to this location after 1912. The two houses in the background face Avenue L, the one on the right being the front house to 2818 Avenue L rear. Photographed 1995.

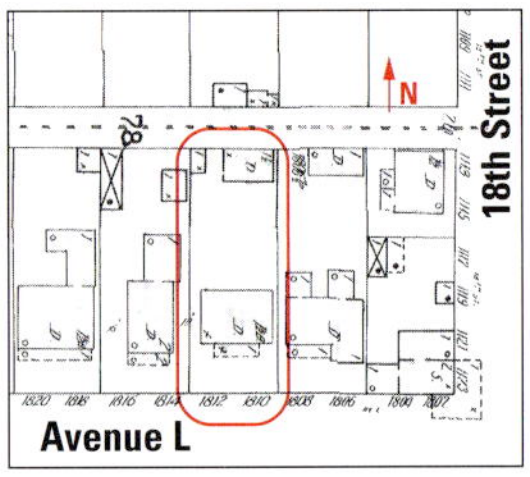

Fig. 57

at least until 1901–2, when four Eggert relatives were living at "rear 2120 K," probably as a temporary housing arrangement following the 1900 hurricane.[3]

Like the Brantigans, Johanna and Conrad Toebleman chose to live in a back building, rather than a front house, on the lot that Mrs. Toebleman owned at 1812 Avenue L. (See figs. 57–60.) But the exchanges of ownership between Mrs. Toebleman and her brother, house-painter Fritz Wedemeyer, are considerably more convoluted than those for the Brantigan property and are reflective of a period when the purchasing of property was often depen-

Fig. 58

Fig. 59

dent upon the financial resources of family, friends, or other personal associations. In 1873, Johanna Wedemeyer Lohmann financed the purchase of the lot for her brother when she was married to Teodor Lohmann and living on an alley two blocks away. In 1878, Wedemeyer paid off the note to his then-divorced sister, who was now living at 1812 Avenue L in "a frame dwelling house on the alley" and paying her brother a monthly rent of $2 against his note. In April 1879, Johanna Lohmann married laborer Conrad Toebleman; in May she rescued the property in a tax sale for $24.75.

In August 1880, the Wedemeyers sold the property to Johanna Toebleman and canceled "the rental of a certain frame dwelling house on the Alley." The Toeblemans sold back to the Wedemeyers all structures and improvements on the lot except the alley house. After the 1885 fire destroyed the block, the two couples signed a fifteen-year lease agreement whereby the Wedemeyers rented the front ninety feet of the lot at a monthly ground rent of $2 and on which they built a dormered cottage (fig. 58). The Toeblemans built another alley residence on the back thirty feet of the lot. Four years later, the Wedemeyers sold the front house, "together with cistern fencing and Outhouses," to the Toeblemans and moved to another location. The Toeblemans now owned both the lot and all the buildings at 1812 Avenue L, but continued living in the two-room alley house and renting the front house to a new tenant, harnessmaker Frederick Lott and his family. The arrangement was maintained until both Toeblemans died and the Lotts purchased the property, at which time they rented the back house, then eventually moved it to form an ell on the front house (figs. 59, 60).[4]

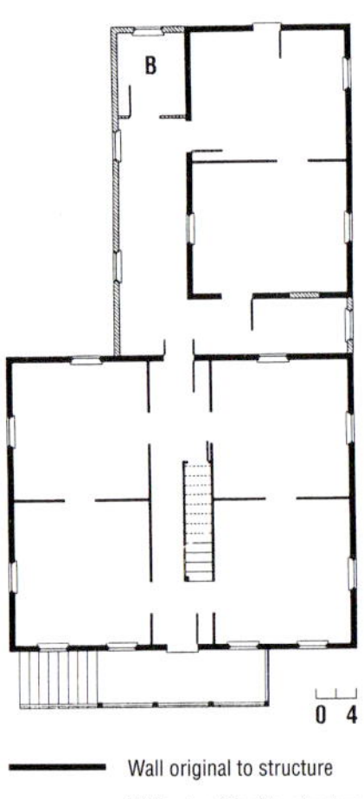

Fig. 60

Toebleman property, 1812 Avenue L, built 1886.
Fig. 57. 1899 Sanborn insurance map shows back house situated on alley line.
Fig. 58. Front house. Photograph early 1890s.
Fig. 59. The back building was moved and connected to the front house to create the wing. Photograph 1983.
Fig. 60. Floor plan showing the two structures connected. Documented 1990.

Other property owners and their families moved between their front and back houses, often when a widow or mother-in-law vacated a larger front house in order to rent it for the income or to relinquish it to the growing family of a younger generation. Mary Allen was among the widows who were property owners listed with an alley or rear address in the 1891–92 directory.

Irish immigrants Mary and Robert Allen lived at several rental properties before being listed on Avenue H between Thirty-third and Thirty-fourth Streets in the 1882–83 city directory. In 1883, Allen, a boilermaker by trade, purchased the property. He died in July 1886. Mary Allen was living on Avenue P 1/2 in 1888–89, but within a year she had returned to the rear address of the Avenue H property and was working at the bagging and cordage factory

Fig. 62. 3205 Avenue M rear. Example of two-room cottage with inset porch, the type of building owned by Kate Wooden. Photographed in 1995.

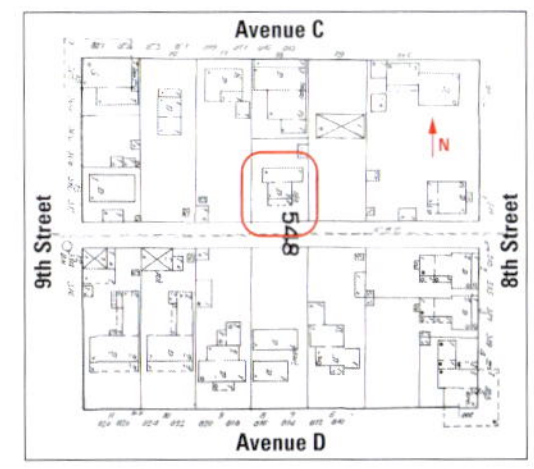

Fig. 61. Kate Wooden's house on 1889 Sanborn insurance map. The section fronting the alley is a two-room cottage with inset porch. The back section may have been a shotgun house.

five blocks away. By 1893–94, she was employed at the cotton mills, and a son, who was also listed at the alley address, was a spinner at the bagging factory.

At the time of the 1900 census, Mrs. Allen was no longer working. She was living alone at "rear 3310 H," which, as shown on the Sanborn maps, was a one-story, fifteen-foot-by-fifteen-foot structure tucked into the northwest corner of the lot. By 1913, she had moved to the slightly larger front house, where she was living with a daughter when she died in 1914.[5]

Most property owners who maintained an alley address owned the lot from front street to alley, but there were exceptions. In February 1867, two women, Kate Wooden and Anna Wells, paid $300 each for the east and west halves, respectively, of lot 4 in the block bordered by Eighth and Ninth Streets and Avenues C and D. In June 1867, the women redivided the lot. Wells became owner of the north (front) half, and Wooden of the south (back) half, in each case "with all the Houses and other improvements on the same."

Koch's 1885 bird's-eye view clearly depicts Wells's front house and a backyard full of smaller buildings and appendages, although distinguishing Wooden's house is difficult (fig. 66). The first clear documentation of both houses is the 1889 Sanborn map (fig. 61), which shows Wooden's house set back several feet from the alley and surrounded by yard, not a typical placement for an alley dwelling in Galveston and one suggesting that the building may have been re-sited. The house was a one-story cottage with an inset porch, a building type that predated the Civil War (fig. 62); originally, it could have been a front house, a detached service building, or the wing of a larger house. Wells's house, which was marked "OLD" and was a larger version of the same house type, almost filled the front of the lot.

On August 17, 1866, Catharine Kansberry (Kate Wooden) had married Daniel Wooden, who died of pneumonia exactly one week later. City mortuary records disclose that he was black, forty years old, born in Delaware, and buried in Potter's Field. Kate Woods, one of the numerous variations of Kate Wooden's name, was listed in the 1870 census as thirty years old and sharing her house with her nineteen-year-old niece, a mulatto woman, Rachel Hawkins, who could neither read nor write. The occupation of both women was "Washing," and both were born in Louisiana.

On February 29, 1896, "Katie Wooden sometimes called Katie Canterbury" wrote her will. She left her niece "all my property real and personal . . . consisting mainly of my homestead and household effects, situated in Galveston County in said State, fronting on the alley between Market and Mechanic Streets [Avenues D and C], and between Eighth and Ninth Street." Wooden died less than three weeks later and was buried in Potter's Field. When her will was probated in February 1898, her "homestead" was valued at $700 and her "Household effects, furniture, etc." at $100.[6]

Rachel Hawkins continued living on the property until fall 1906, when she was committed to the State Asylum for the Insane. The estate inventory taken shortly afterwards valued the property at $450 and her personal effects at $50. Hawkins was still living in the asylum in 1931 when the property was sold.[7]

Some of the houses along the alleys that were owned by their occupants were situated on rented land. Ground rent and house-moving were practices that began very early in Galveston, probably for various reasons: the scarcity and therefore the cost of solid ground; frequent flooding; the impermanence of real estate, both land and buildings, because of the climate and topography; the chronic scarcity of materials; and the limited financing available to laborers—especially black laborers—to purchase both land and housing. But for those who could afford to purchase lots in speculative locations, ground rent produced an interim income with no attendant expense.

I have never been in any other city where houses were moved like they are here. All sizes and kinds. I'm talking about the period from 1946 to 1970. The last massive migration was from the last time the medical school purchased property and moved out a lot of housing down in that area. But you could look up almost any day and see a house going down the street. It was incredible. . . . One of those houses behind the medical school was stolen. It was all jacked up and ready to go, and someone moved in with a flatbed truck one night and just whisked it away. It probably went across the Causeway. It was not found. **Inez R. Lasell**

Moving houses—that was a business. They had four or five house movers. . . . You really wouldn't think much about it. Somebody sitting on top to raise the wires up with a stick. You see houses going down the street. They put them in alleys, too. **The Rev. James B. Thomas**

Fig. 63. Alley between Avenues C and D, looking west across Sixteenth Street. The alley is interrupted at Nineteenth Street by the Anico Tower. Photographed 1995.

The Intimacy of Alley Life

The houses were right on the alleys—and the smells. The windows were open ten months out of the year, and the kitchens were usually on the alleys so you smelled everything everybody was cooking. Awfully quiet. There was no traffic and the people who lived on the alley were awful careful what they said because it was heard. If anybody was having marital trouble or arguments, everybody in the neighborhood knew it—on the alley, that is.

There was a back house next door. It was a b-i-g house for an alley house. It was high-raised with a garage and storeroom underneath. It had only one big room and a small room on the side. The bathroom was outside. In fact, when we first moved there—we moved there in the summer—and the first year I was walking down the alley going to school—everybody short-cut through the alley—the old lady that lived in the house threw her slop jar on me. I'll never forget that. . . . We called her Miss Chicken Brain because we thought she was crazy. She was white. Real old lady, skinny. I'm sure it was a mistake. She was just throwing out her morning slop jar in the alley. That was common.

Fig. 64. Two-year-old Robert Tucker with his older brothers, Walter (left) and O. H., and their aunt Alma Hegar in the backyard of the Tucker house at 912 Avenue F. Behind them is a fence separating the front and the back houses, both of which were rental property. Photograph circa 1920–21.

Fig. 65. In 1928, the Tucker family moved to 1918 Avenue M 1/2; sometime in the 1930s, Robert Tucker photographed the alley behind the residence—which is the same alley he describes in his interview.

The young boy our age that lived next door in the front house married and they fixed that house up for him. He lived there. They put three rooms in that big room, and put a bathroom and a kitchen in that small room, and it was a pretty nice place after that. Still storage and garage underneath. . . . That was the only back house in the block on our side.

Now, across the alley there were two back houses. Right across from us was the Flake house. A black couple lived there and he worked on the wharf and she worked for Mrs. Flake, and it was only a little two-room house. It was raised—they were all raised. They were real nice people. I had a paper route and he would help me work on my bicycle.

Robert M. Tucker

The moving and shifting of houses were never difficult in Galveston because there were no foundations. Houses on both the front streets and the alleys were perched on blocks or built on wooden underpinnings, neither of which encumbered "the faculty of locomotion," as Matilda Houstoun called it in 1844. Picking up a house and moving it to a new location was done with some frequency and with considerably greater ease than in most places. In fact, it was so easy that one black woman, Mary Allen—"a Mrs. Atlas"—was charged in 1869 with taking "one frame house valued at $100." A black man, Aaron Browning, was charged in 1875 with "stealing and carrying off a building."[8]

There were those who viewed such maneuverability as a menace. In November 1885, the City Engineer complained that the streets were being damaged "by the moving of empty buildings," but moving houses was a habit that Galvestonians found difficult to break. Thirty years later, the Galveston Commercial Association denounced the "practice of removing old shacks from different localities to streets on which there were nothing but first-class residences."[9] The narrow alleys obviously placed some limitations on the movement of buildings, but many alley and back houses, as well as smaller sheds and stables, could fit within the twenty-foot alley width.

Owners of houses situated on leased land along an alley or on the backside of a property rented only a portion of the lot. For instance, Joseph Trave, who, according to the 1881–82 directory, was proprietor of the Public Square Saloon at the corner of Twentieth Street and Avenue G, lived at "rear 467 e Winnie," a block bordered by Avenues G and H and Fifteenth and Sixteenth Streets. Trave owned his house, valued in 1881 at $250; the land on which it was located was owned by florist Philip Junker, whose family lived on the front of the lot. In September 1883, the two parties signed a five-year lease agreement whereby the Traves would continue renting, for a total of $300, the same southwest quarter (alley side) of the interior lot. The document noted that "the improvements on said One fourth Lot" were "the property of Lessee and are not Owned or claimed by [Junker]."[10]

Some owners and their houses found their way to more than one location. Scottish immigrant and laborer William Adam moved his house, as well as his wife and four children, three times, the first location being the alley bordered by Tenth and Eleventh Streets and Avenues B and C. From 1880 until 1882, Adam and a Mrs. C. Davis were assessed for improvements valued at $200 and $300, respectively, on lot 4, a lot owned by J. W. Hibert, who lived two blocks away. Adam's house, according to Galveston Insurance Board records, was built in 1880.

By 1884–85, Adam had moved his house to the southeast corner of Eighth Street and Avenue E, where he was assessed, once again, for improvements only. In 1891, he not only moved his house to a third location, 621 Avenue D, a lot that he had bought, but also added a porch and two small appendages. Apparently, the house was destroyed in the 1900 hurricane because the insurance inspector scratched out the references to Adam's 1880 house and noted that his house was built in 1901. Adam's new house was no more stationary than the old one. In 1904, it was one of many small houses that were moved from the right-of-way of the grade-raising canal and placed on a temporary site, where it was still located when Adam died a widower in March 1909.[11]

Adam eventually emerged the owner of both a lot and a house. Other house owners, not so fortunate, ultimately lost their houses and became renters or boarders. For example, two black women, Matilda Day and Winnie Compton, and a black man, James Jackson, were listed in the 1881–82 city directory as alley residents and in the Assessor's Abstracts as owning improvements on the blocks where they lived. In all three instances (as was also true in Adam's case), their taxes were unrendered in 1881.

Matilda Day, who was fifty years old in 1880, was from Kentucky and could neither read nor write. Winnie Compton was sixty and from Virginia. Both their houses were situated on lots south of Avenue J. Day's house, valued at $50, was in the block bordered by Twenty-fourth and Twenty-fifth Streets and Avenues L and M; Compton's house, valued at $100, was in the block bordered by Twenty-first and Twenty-second Streets and Avenues K and L. By the time the 1884–85 directory was published, both women had evidently lost their houses and were residing elsewhere. Neither was listed as owning any improvements on her new block. After 1884–85, Compton disappears from the directories, but Day is listed at three addresses before appearing in the 1898 directory at a front-street address on the same block where she had lived in her alley house.[12]

In 1880, carpenter James Jackson and his wife Jane were living in a house that was valued at $100 and located on lot 3 in the block bordered by Eighth and Ninth Streets and Avenues E and F. (See fig. 66.) It was a neighborhood in which the Jacksons had lived at least since 1870, when they were listed in the census in a household of fifteen people ranging in age from one to seventy years—James Jackson being the only person who could both read and write. According to the census, both Jacksons and four other men owned personal property ranging in value from $100 to $400, but none of them were listed as owning any real estate. This suggests that their personal property, which would have been movable property, probably included several small houses and that the "household" was, in fact, a grouping of owner-occupied houses situated on a leased lot. James Jackson was obviously a respected member of the black community. Following the 1875 storm, he was one of five men appointed to determine the "best means for providing for those of their color who had been sufferers."

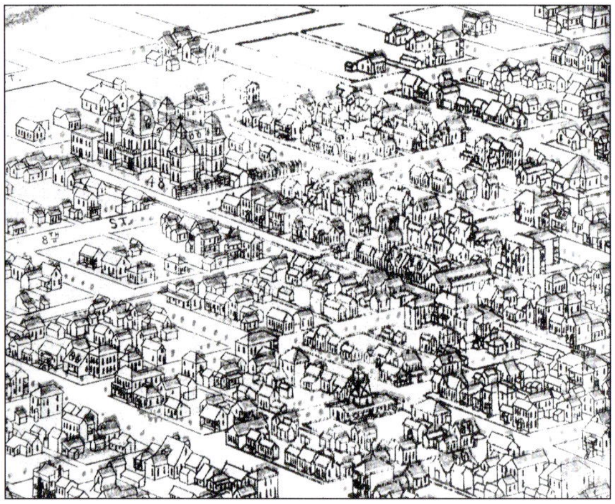

Fig. 66

Fig. 66. 1885 bird's-eye view showing the blocks in which Kate Wooden (left) and Jane and James Jackson (right) owned their houses.

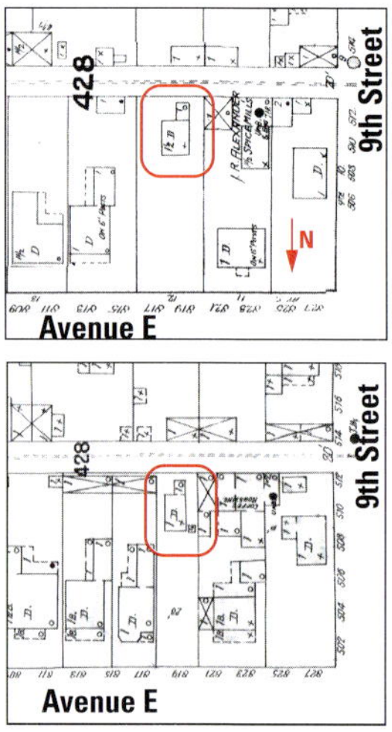

Fig. 67

Fig. 67. Sanborn insurance maps, 1889 (top) and 1899 (bottom) showing the Jacksons' house.

By 1880, Jackson's taxes were unrendered and his name disappears from the Assessor's Abstracts after 1884. The Jacksons, however, continued living at the same location and presumably in the same house, which, according to the 1889 Sanborn map, was a twenty-foot-by-eighteen-foot, one-and-a-half-story house oriented to the main street but placed on the rear of the lot with an open front yard (fig. 67, top). Quite possibly, other houses on the lot had been moved or demolished between 1870 and 1889. Certainly, the Jacksons witnessed major changes on adjoining lots. By 1888–89, Julius Alexander was operating his coffee-roasting and spice-mill business on the alley side of lot 2. Lots 3 and 4 sold in 1894, and a front house was built to the east of the Jackson house (fig. 67, bottom). The last directory listing for the Jacksons at that address was in 1895–96. After that, James Jackson appears at different locations in two directories, once at a rear address at 911 Avenue G. Just where the Jacksons were living when he died at age seventy-seven in September 1898 is difficult to determine, but within a year, a Jane Jackson was boarding at 2621 Avenue C in Ward Five.[13]

The practice of ground rent was always more common in Galveston than official records indicate. At the same time, as the 1880s progressed, the number of tax assessments for improvements that were separate from land ownership began to dwindle, suggesting that the practice was gradually being abandoned. Natural attrition is just one of several possible explanations. A proliferation of finance companies made it somewhat easier, at least for white laborers like William Adam, to acquire both a lot and a house. At the same time, members of the older black population, people like James Jackson, found it difficult to maintain ownership of the houses that they had acquired after the Civil War. Their minimal, fluctuating incomes made it impossible for many to pay their property taxes, even a few dollars each year, and financial assistance was not easily obtained. The amount of land that was available for temporary rent also was decreasing, but even though low-lying and outlying lots were being filled and made more marketable for permanent development, ground rent remained an accepted real estate practice in Galveston well into the twentieth century.

While alley property was home for some owners, it was simply an investment for others. Some alley landlords owned a single plot of land and lived in the front house while renting out a back building. As time passed, the number of single-property landlords grew, as more and more people converted what originally had been servants quarters and other service structures into rental units. Other landlords had multiple property holdings that accommodated an occasional back building. For example, when Mary Hutz died in 1869, she owned four buildings on two lots in Ward Five, including "one Shanty in Alley."[14]

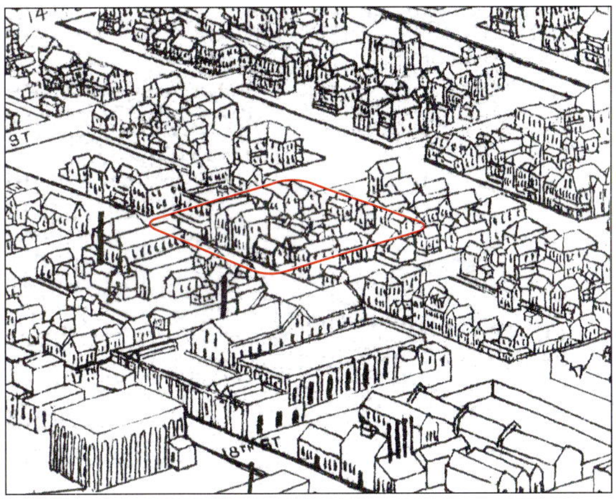

Fig. 68

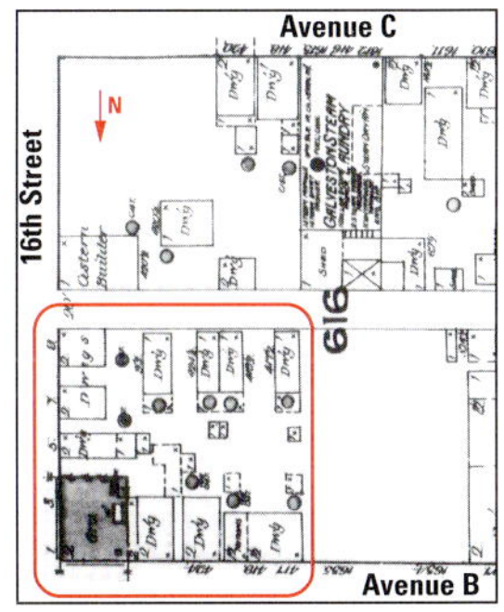

Fig. 69

Figs. 68 and 69. 1885 bird's-eye view and 1885 Sanborn insurance map showing James Cross's property at the corner of Sixteenth Street and Avenue B.

Then there were property owners like Irishman James Cross, Sr., whose real estate holdings were limited in number but lucrative in return from both the front and back sides of their properties. Cross migrated to Galveston in 1866, when he was thirty-seven years old. By 1872, he had exchanged his carpenter's trade for that of grocer and bought three lots in Ward Two at the corner of Avenue B and Sixteenth Street, where he built a two-story corner store and residence, three houses on both street sides, and four dwelling units fronting the alley. It was largely because of Cross's development that the block had six alley listings in the 1881–82 directory, the most of any alley east of Seventeenth Street. Cross also owned improvements (but no land) across the alley, which in 1885 included a dwelling and a cistern shop. The latter explains the unusually high number of eleven cisterns on his properties, including individual cisterns for his alley houses. (See figs. 68, 69.)

After the block was destroyed in the 1885 fire, Cross redeveloped his property but reduced the store building to a single story and the alley buildings to two dwellings and a stable. The block remained, however, one of the more densely populated alleys in the area.[15]

The owners of properties on blocks with a high alley density frequently included both those who lived on their property and absentee landlords. This was true of Blocks 507 and 508, where Tin Can and Fat Alleys were located (figs. 4, 5). On Block 507, the Tin Can Alley block, the fourteen lots were owned in 1880 by twelve individuals, of whom three lived on the block and two had businesses on the block but lived elsewhere. For example, DeWitt and Mary Cunningham bought lot 2 in 1879 but operated a "groceries, provisions & ship supplies, store and warehouse" on lot 7, a lot they did not own, and actually lived eleven blocks away. By 1884–85, the Cunninghams had moved their residence to lot 2, which by then was one of the most densely packed lots on Block 507, accommodating a one-story Chinese laundry and a two-story dwelling on the front side, two detached dwellings in the backyard, and another dwelling and a small shed situated directly on the alley.

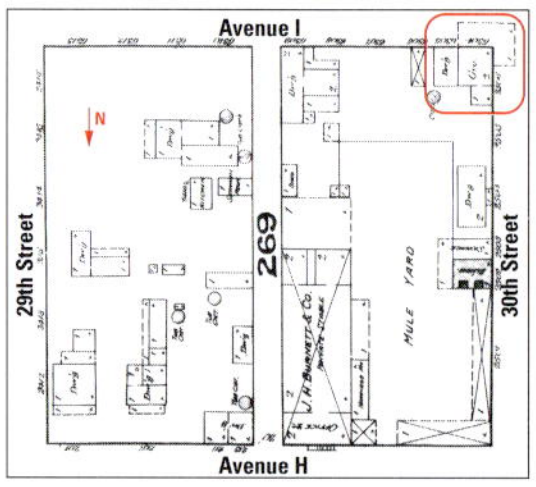

Fig. 70

In 1890–91, the couple for the first time listed "furnished rooms" at their lot 2 address, although Cunningham had dropped his other business listing several years before. The couple proceeded to convert both front buildings to commercial use and the shed on the alley into another dwelling. At the time of the 1900 census, two back buildings were each inhabited by a single white man, the third by two white men, and the fourth by a black laundress, her two children, and four black boarders.[16]

In 1880, the twenty lots on the Fat Alley block belonged to twelve individual owners, only three of whom lived on the block. The latter included William Yowinckle, whose residence and highly flammable wood-sawing business were on the corner of Twenty-eighth Street and Avenue E. In 1901–2, when the directory listed thirty-two alley dwellers on Block 508, the highest number in the city, Yowinckle was one of two property owners still living on the block. Although Yowinckle had retired, his property was anything but idle. He had adapted his buildings that lined the alley into dwellings and tenements, for which there were seven addressees, all blacks, in the directory.

Fig. 71

Figs. 70–72. Burnett's Alley on Block 269. With the corner store as a reference point, the alley dwellings and other buildings on the block on the 1885 Sanborn insurance map (fig. 70) can be matched with the portion of Burnett's Alley that appears in the lower left corner of an 1894 photograph (fig. 71). The two large buildings in the upper right of the photograph are the Ursuline Convent and the Beach Hotel. The 1899 Sanborn insurance map with pasteovers (fig. 72) shows Burnett's Alley after the block was redeveloped and the muleyard replaced with dwellings. Photograph published in *Art Work of Galveston* (Chicago: W. H. Parish Publishing Co., 1894), p. 48.

J. H. Burnett and his family partnership represent another type and scale of Galveston investor, the "capitalist," by his own description. Even though Burnett was always credited in newspaper accounts as being the sole owner of the family's sizeable real estate holdings, including those with alley properties, they were jointly owned by Burnett, his wife, and two children.

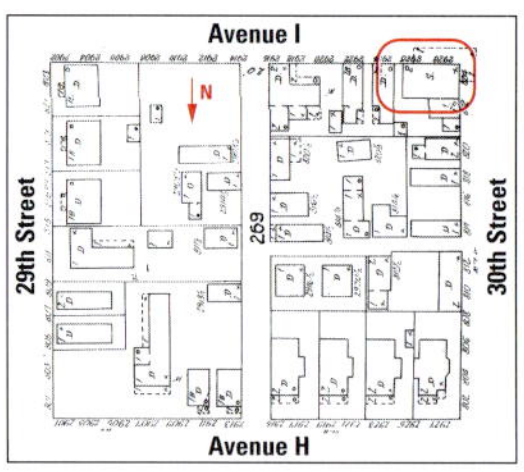

Fig. 72

Burnett first appears as a commission merchant in the 1872 Galveston city directory. His residence remained in Crockett, Texas, where he was living at the time of the 1870 census and where the combined value of his real estate and personal property holdings was $65,000. By 1875–76, the family had moved to Galveston, where Burnett was listed as both commission merchant and partner in a contracting business, and where the family quickly established itself as real estate investors. The annual building report published by the *Galveston Daily*

News in October 1875 stated that "Col. J. H. Burnett" had constructed twenty-two houses at an "aggregate cost of over $40,000," seventeen of which were located in Burnett's own neighborhood of Twenty-fifth Street and Avenue Q. When Burnett's wife died in 1886, the family's Galveston properties were valued at $89,250 and included some lots on blocks with high alley densities.

In fact, one of the Burnett properties became known as Burnett's Alley. Bought by the family in 1884, it was the western half of Block 269 in Ward Five—a block oriented east-west, split by an alley that ran north-south, and bordered by Avenues H and I and Twenty-ninth and Thirtieth Streets. By the time the 1885 Sanborn map was drawn, the half-block was dominated by the Burnetts' mule yard and stable, but the meaning of that cannot be fully understood until we read the inventory taken at the time of Mrs. Burnett's death: The property stabled six horses and ninety-two mules, the latter used for Burnett's general contracting business and freight transfer line. (See figs. 70, 71.)

During the 1890s, Burnett sold the half-block, but not before subdividing and splitting it with a ten-foot alley that ran east-west. Fifteen houses were built on the property, including eight on the alley sides, which increased the alley population substantially (fig. 72). There were just two alley listings on the block in the 1891–92 city directory, in contrast to nineteen alley listings, all blacks and including Isaac and Linda Robinson, in 1901–2. (See page 49.)

The name "Burnett's Alley" lingered long after Burnett's business had been replaced. On December 5, 1908, local newspapers reported that "Lucinda Washington, an aged negress, residing in what is known as Burnett's alley, was found dead in her solitary house."[17]

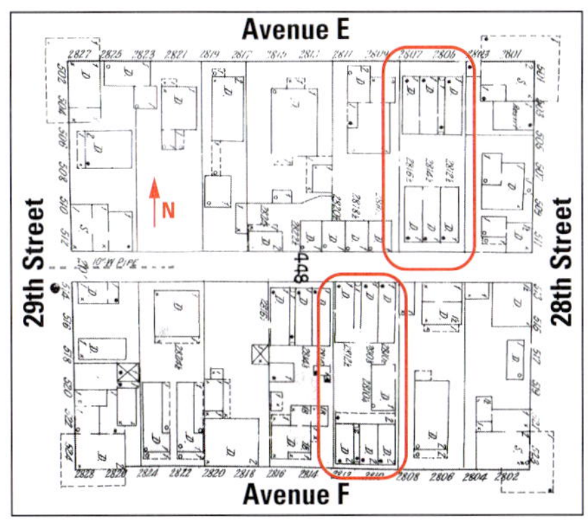

Fig. 73. 1912 Sanborn insurance map showing Robert Palliser's rental properties on lots 6 and 10 in Block 448. Palliser probably also built the units on lot 11.

Robert Palliser established residence in Galveston at about the same time as the Burnetts. Palliser was an English bachelor in his mid-twenties when he migrated to the port city and began pursuing numerous business ventures while residing in a boardinghouse, a thrifty living arrangement that he maintained for almost twenty years. By 1886–87, R. Palliser & Co. was manufacturing Cedar Bayou bricks, and Barnes & Palliser was listed in the directory as "bricklayers, contractors, and builders."

Palliser began buying Galveston real estate in 1884. Over the years, some of his investments would be located on blocks with a history of densely populated alleys. One of these was Block 448 in Ward Five, which was bordered by Avenues E and F and Twenty-eighth and Twenty-ninth Streets. Block 448 already had a history of illustrious investors, including the Bishop of the Diocese of the Galveston Catholic Church and Charles H. Leonard, a mayor of Galveston.

In 1905, Palliser bought lot 10 on Block 448, one of the lots owned by the Catholic bishop, and in 1911, he acquired lot 6. In both instances, Palliser built two sets of triplex housing units—one facing the front street, the other fronting the alley (fig. 73). Long and narrow, the

---

The alley houses were built to rent by the land barons and people who owned mega-houses. Robert Palliser was one of them. He once owned a hundred rent houses. He carried his own insurance and he never bought a whole block in case of fire. His son managed his properties. There were also a lot of Jewish owners.

A lot of these houses were built in the 1930s. The ones with plumbing were built then because it was required by then. They were built by hired carpenters and they were highly profitable because they gave no services.

Robert M. Tucker

---

one- and two-story shotgun units filled the width of the lots; all but one set of the four had a passage giving access to the lot interior. On Sanborn maps, these distinctive units can be identified as Palliser buildings even when they appear on property he did not own, such as lot 11 in the same block.[18] Palliser may have built the units for other landlords, or he may have built them for himself on leased land.

Neither Burnett nor Palliser lived on their rental properties, much less in alley housing that they owned. Such was not the case with Johann Ort, "real estate owner," who, between 1890–91 and 1898, lived in the alley dwelling on his property in the block bordered by Avenues L and M and Twenty-eighth and Twenty-ninth Streets. One of many parcels owned by Ort and scattered throughout the city, the property consisted of two adjoining lots on which there were three separate houses with front-street addresses and one alley dwelling.[19] The alley had always been one of the more densely populated alleys south of Avenue J.

Fig. 74. Alley houses in the 1300 block between Avenues K and L, looking west. Photographed 1981.

Both Burnett and Ort described their occupation in the 1900 census as "capitalist" and in the Galveston city directories during the 1890s as "real estate owner" and "real estate dealer."[20] In contrast, Palliser never adopted any titles that suggested his real estate interests, always identifying himself as a bricklayer and contractor. Galvestonians would have been well aware of his real estate investments, however, because he purchased and developed properties throughout the city. No doubt, there were also those who noted the change in his lifestyle when he moved to a house on Avenue M that he had bought in the early 1890s, then boarded in the house of a recently widowed woman in 1897, and married her the following year.[21]

At some point, Burnett, Ort, and Palliser all owned properties on blocks that had the highest alley populations in the city. Ort tended to concentrate his investments in older, established sections of the city, whereas Palliser and Burnett, probably because of their contracting businesses, also extended their real estate interests to outlying, less developed areas. All three men maintained the status quo along the alleys of their older properties and, in some locations, pushed for higher densities, as Palliser did on Block 448.

Obviously, there were many reasons why people owned alley property in Galveston. For some, like Johanna and Conrad Toebleman and Kate Wooden, residing on their alley property, as well as owning it, can be explained by a combination of convenience, economics, and preference. But for others, like James Cross, J. H. Burnett, and Robert Palliser, owning alley property was solely an investment—a very lucrative one.

6 Devastation and Reconstruction: The 1900 Hurricane

De people cry an' holler an' take on somethin' awful. But de depot station stood de storm good . . . Den after de storm was over an' gone we wen' out dere an' wen' on home. Dead people an' horses an' dogs was everywhere you step. Put your foot down an' you put it on a dead man. I never seen nothing like it. De house where I live was gone an' dere wasn't nothing lef' dere.

Henry Johnson, Texas Narratives

In mid-summer 1900, Federal census takers once again canvassed the neighborhoods of Galveston, this time enumerating 37,789 inhabitants. The most current city directory, for 1899-1900, had listed 21,210 individuals, 1,065 of whom were living at an alley or rear address.[1]

Just where all the alley dwellers were on September 8, 1900, when Galveston was devastated by a hurricane that remains the most deadly natural disaster on the North American continent, is unknown. The hundreds of terrifying tales of survivors do not include a description written by anyone who survived the storm in an alley structure, even though there were those who tried or had to do so, as evidenced by the names of alley dwellers on the lists of dead and missing.[2] There are accounts of people who sought refuge in structures that they believed to be sturdier and safer than their own. For many of those who lived in back houses or servants quarters, that probably meant going to the bigger, higher, and presumably stronger front house. For those who lived in rented alley housing, it may have meant going to a larger neighborhood residence or to a public building.

Black laborer Henry Johnson moved to Galveston "jes' in time to be in the big storm," and was living in a boardinghouse at Twenty-eighth Street and Avenue I in Ward Five. He and his neighbors, many of whom would have been alley residents, fled to the Union Passenger Depot, a brick building on the west side of Twenty-fifth Street between Avenues A and B that "stood de storm good," but his boardinghouse "was gone an' dere wasn't nothing lef' dere."[3]

Fig. 75. Photograph looking southwest from Avenue L and Twenty-first Street after the storm. The small buildings on the right were probably back buildings that defined the alley line in the block. Ursuline Convent is in the background. Photograph copied from *The Great Galveston Disaster,* by Paul Lester [Galveston, 1900], following p. 32.

Fig. 76. "Rear View of Yard of Residence in East End," documented and titled by Galveston photographer Victor J. Biron.

In addition to the six thousand to eight thousand people killed or missing, an estimated four thousand were rendered homeless and eight thousand destitute.[4] The blocks along the Gulf and on the eastern side of the city were totally destroyed. Few buildings, if any, escaped damage. But contrary to the commonly held belief that Galveston was virtually obliterated, portions of the city survived relatively intact.

On September 9, the Central Relief Committee was formed, first for the purpose of "burying the dead and feeding and clothing the living," after which "the most difficult task was to provide shelter for the homeless." Temporary shelters included several hundred tents lent by the government "to those absolutely shelterless" and "living in roofless houses amidst debris that covered decomposed bodies, and over which they were obliged to climb in order to reach the remnants of their homes." Many people had no choice but to live in shelters "built of storm lumber."[5] (See fig. 77.)

Fig. 77. Shelter "built of storm lumber." The structure is not unlike many makeshift shelters that served as housing along the alleys throughout the nineteenth and into the twentieth centuries. Stereoscopic view.

The building subcommittee, which had $450,000 to disburse, adopted a program of both repairing and constructing houses. Four "intelligent" inspectors allocated $118,139.65 for 1,114 repairs, with allowances varying from $16 to $359. The bulk of the funds, $294,478.01, was used to build housing as described in the May 1902 report of the Central Relief Committee:

> *Contracts were made for building three-room cottages (as fast as men and material were available) on lots belonging to families whose residences had been entirely destroyed. No distinction was made between the races. The cost of the first ten cottages was $359.00 each, and when the supply of mechanics and building material became more plentiful this was gradually reduced to about $300.00. Four hundred and eighty-three houses were built on this latter plan, and at this date, over eighteen months after the disaster, are occupied by industrious people.*
>
> *To those who were able to contribute money or labor towards the construction, the committee made cash allowances averaging $265.00 each, and in this wise 1100 houses were built. The houses, being substantially erected, can be made part of more convenient residences whenever the owner becomes able to build.*[6]

What this meant for alley residents is hard to document because there is no known list of people who received assistance in rebuilding or repairing their houses. Preference was given to those who owned both their house and lot, a policy that excluded most alley housing.

However, at least some of those who owned and occupied houses situated on leased land qualified for assistance. Real estate agent H. M. Trueheart wrote a New York client that there was "not [a] stick left" on the client's block near the Gulf, and that some tenants "may decide to rebuild on the property with what help they can get from the Relief Committee."[7]

The architectural landscape of Galveston was altered on both the front streets and the alleys by the erection of the 1,583 houses, at least a third of which were long, narrow, three-room cottages. These were essentially shotgun houses in plan, but were known locally as "commissary" houses, a term that suggests they were disbursed, like other emergency supplies, through the commissaries established in the city's wards immediately after the storm (fig. 78). Over the years, many of the houses were converted to rental units, ofttimes being moved to the rear of a property, while others were incorporated as wings or additions into "more convenient residences," as recommended by the Central Relief Committee.

Fig. 78. Commissary or shotgun houses on alley in 1500 block between Avenues B and C, north side, looking west. Photographed 1990.

The rebuilding program relied as much on private individuals as on public assistance. Agents like Trueheart were pressed by their clients to repair their properties, at least to a habitable level, because there was "a very good demand for rents, and as soon as the houses are put in condition we can no doubt get tenants at a fair price." On September 26, Trueheart wrote to another of his clients, A. O. Slaughter, who lived in Chicago and owned a corner lot on the Tin Can Alley block:

> *Our Mr. Adriance has been out and examined your houses on Post Office [Avenue E] and 27th Sts. The corner house is off the blocks, awning gone, and most of the window sash out. The floor is all torn up. The house adjoining is a complete wreck. The third house is almost a total wreck; the roof and ceiling are good, but all four sides are out but still on the ground.*
>
> *The two small houses in alley are in very good condition, but off the blocks, and one partly in the alley.*
>
> *It will be sometime before we can get an estimate as to what it will cost to repair them, as it is almost impossible to get mechanics. It is estimated that 97 1/2 per cent of all the houses in the city have been more or less damaged by the storm.*[8]

Interspersed with business matters, Trueheart noted that his cousin and business associate, "our Mr. Minor, was lost."[9]

The storm drastically altered Galveston's population. In addition to the thousands who were killed or left homeless and destitute (fig. 79), an estimated 2,000 people chose to leave the island rather than rebuild.[10] Yet despite the reduced population and the efforts of the Central Relief Committee, a severe housing shortage was unavoidable. For those whose housing options were limited before the storm, they became even more restricted after the storm.

The 1,065 individuals with an alley or rear address in the 1899–1900 directory consisted of 827 blacks, 237 whites, and 1 Chinese. In contrast, the 1901–2 directory lists a smaller number of total entries—17,695 as compared to 21,210—but a larger number—1,284—of alley residents. The racial breakdown of alley residents—1,066 blacks and 218 whites—suggests that even under the desperate circumstances created by the storm, alley housing was becoming more and more a black phenomenon.[11] (See table 6.1, p. 78.)

Fig. 79. Family displaced by the storm. The woman and three children (one child is barely visible on the right) were photographed with their salvaged possessions at an alley corner. They may have been residents of a back building. Stereoscopic view.

The cleanup and initial rebuilding efforts were just the beginning of Galveston's response to the hurricane. For the next ten years, the city's energies and attention would be consumed by two monumental engineering projects—the building of a seventeen-foot-high seawall along the Gulf and the raising of the populated area of the island by an average of eight feet—designed to protect the city from a similar disaster and to reassure not only Galvestonians but also the outside world that the city had a future.

The first sections of the Seawall extended from Sixth to Fifty-third Streets and took three years, from October 1902 to October 1905, to build. But what really tested the "pluck and patriotism" of all Galvestonians, whether they lived on a front street or an alley, was the grade-raising project, which "was not," declared one engineer, "a lawn party or pink tea affair." Surely, no one disputed that, once the highly anticipated first loads of fill were pumped into the far east end of the island in July 1904. As Galvestonians watched, their fascination with the technological complexities of the project must have been mixed with some dread when they realized that, for the next few years, sections of the city would be in various stages of the messy process. When the original contract was completed in summer 1910, 10,601,400 cubic yards of sand fill had been used to raise the island as far as Forty-fifth Street, and over $2 million had been spent to give an even and protected slope from the Seawall to the bay (fig. 80).[12]

Funded by indebtedness bonds and remittance taxes, the grade-raising was the first major project supervised by the commission form of government that Galveston adopted in 1901. An appointed three-man Grade Raising Board was responsible for the day-to-day management of the project. The contractor was Goedhart & Bates, a New York-based firm.[13]

Raising a populated area by a hydraulic method was an unprecedented, massive undertaking that depended on the cooperation of every property owner and householder in town. Progressing from east to west, the fill areas were raised at first in sixteen-block sections, an area found to be too large and subsequently reduced to twelve-block sections to facilitate pumping and drainage. When a section was to be raised, a levee was built around it and everything below the prescribed grade level—all structures, appurtenances, sewer and water mains, gas lines, and streetcar tracks—was elevated (fig. 81).

Every property owner was responsible, both physically and financially, for raising the house, fence, sidewalk, privy, and all other structures on his or her property at least eighteen inches above the level to which the block would be filled. For guidance, grade marks were placed in all the alleys and streets. According to the engineers' survey, there were 2,191 houses that had to be raised, including "413 one-story [houses], 62 cottages with basements, 1,226 cottages, 321 commissary houses, and 169 stables, barns, etc.," numbers which presumably included alley dwellings. Citizens were assured there was no cause for "worriment" regarding the cost of raising their houses, because "even the humblest commissary house owner will be able to meet the expense and thus participate in the enhanced valuation of real estate in Galveston." The estimated cost of raising a large two-story house was $20 to $25, an expense that could be reduced, it was suggested, by neighbors hiring one firm to raise several houses in the same neighborhood or by "clubbing together . . . in the manner customary in raising the frames of houses and barns in country districts."[14]

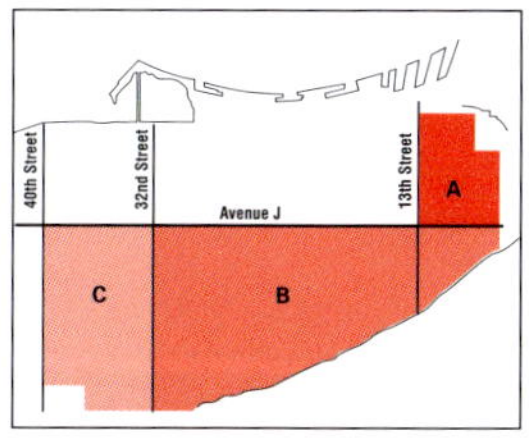

Fig. 80. Map showing the order in which the areas were filled. The average fill was as follows: section A, 2.8 feet: section B, 5.5 feet; section C, 6.6 feet. Source: Map of Galveston compiled by C. G. Wells, 1904.

Most residents dutifully, if not "willingly and cheerfully," raised their houses and back buildings. They had little choice. Many structures clung precariously to frame supports that were anywhere from a few feet to fifteen feet high, depending on the amount of fill that was needed on each block and on whether the owner intended to enclose a lower level. Elevated boardwalks connected structures on the same lot—most crucially, the privy with the house—and intersected streets, but documentary photographs do not reveal a network of catwalks along the alleys (figs. 82, 83).[15]

Fig. 81. Before and after grade-raising. The area to the right has been filled while the buildings on the left are being prepared for the process. The bracing in the side yard of the two-story house is supporting a fence. The pipes will be used to pump fill into the area.

Once preparations were complete, the actual filling of the streets and alleys was accomplished by European-imported dredge boats that excavated water-soaked sand primarily from the bay, and then maneuvered through a distributing canal to connecting stations (fig. 84). At these points, the fill was discharged through long pipes that were moved from street to street and from alley to alley in each designated area.[16] Out-of-town excursionists flocked to see the "city on stilts," as did the locals, especially on Sunday evenings when "hundreds of people" would "go out and view the work from the Seawall." Ella Belle Ramsey was one of those who "use to walk down dere at night an' watch 'em work," taking a special interest because she worked as a domestic for Mrs. James Alvey, whose husband was chairman of the Grade Raising Board. When interviewed in 1937 at age ninety-five, Ramsey was still living at 1228 Avenue I rear on what had been the Alvey property, which was in one of the first sections of the city to be raised.[17]

Fig. 82. Panoramic view of grade-raising. The lower rail of the long white fence indicates the height to which the area will be filled. On the left is a grouping of small residences that are typical of alley buildings. Various outbuildings and sheds are also visible, most notably on the right in the background.

Although the pumping of sand and water into the streets and alleys may have been the messiest—and most picturesque—part of the process, it was by no means an end to the ordeal. Once a section drained enough to be safe for horses and wagons, additional fill was delivered to each lot at no cost. The property owner was responsible, once again both financially and physically, for leveling, grading, and resurfacing the property, and for installing sidewalks and curbing. The contractors leveled and graded the streets and alleys, which the city then resurfaced. It was a slow process—one that could take more than a year.

The lives of alley dwellers, like those of all Galvestonians, were altered by the grade-raising project. Because most alley residents were renters or domestic workers who lived on their employer's property, many of them may have been spared the direct costs associated with the project. At the same time, there were, no doubt, some landlords and employers who gave their tenants and servants a choice: either raise, at their own expense, the back building in which they lived or move.

Local newspapers and project records seldom refer to service buildings, suggesting that domestic servants living on their employer's property were the alley dwellers least inconvenienced by the project. Property owners with servants were most likely to be able to afford the cost of raising all their buildings or to pursue what was considered the ideal solution: fill their lot with dry material, protect it with a bulkhead, and avoid the "disagreeable conditions" when wet fill was pumped into their block.[18]

Edmund R. Cheesborough, secretary of the Grade Raising Board, kept voluminous records and files as he almost single-handedly kept track of contractors and subcontractors, city officials and staff, and literally hundreds of property owners and renters throughout the course of the project. His correspondence and listings of buildings that were raised or

moved from one location to another and back again are full of references to alley properties and residents.

The cost of raising a house, however small, was prohibitive for some who owned their alley house. As the date approached for the filling to begin in the first section, Cheesborough prodded owners like "Mrs. Mosely (Col'd), Alley Part N.E. Cor. 12th & 'B,'" who had not yet raised her house. Reminding Mrs. Mosely that she had promised to raise her "cabin," Cheesborough pleaded, "We now beg to notify you that the filling will begin in your section within ten days . . . and, therefore, beg to kindly ask that you give the matter of raising your house, prompt attention."[19]

Two other parties in the same section flatly refused to raise their improvements. The Board's response was to "throw up" an earthen bulkhead against the buildings. One of those who refused was Rachel Hawkins, who had inherited the south half of lot 4 and the alley house at 813 Avenue C from her aunt, Kate Wooden (figs. 61, 66). Cheesborough asked the contractors to send someone to the site to explain that the bulkhead would "prevent the salt water from covering the lower floor," adding that "you will observe . . . [these people] are practically destitute of means and are not inclined to do anything one way or the other."[20]

Obviously, some property owners who lived along the alleys, like Rachel Hawkins and probably Mrs. Mosely, had neither the money to have their houses raised nor the resources to do it themselves. Cheesborough defended the policy of placing bulkheads around their buildings because to "raise one house everybody in the area to be filled would demand and expect the same right." But the policy created another problem: When the bulkheads were removed, the lots were left "down in a hole." There is no way of knowing how many alley residents were among the people who simply had no choice but to leave their house and have it "half way buried," like the commissary house that "stands as a warning . . . of what

Fig. 83. Backside view of area being raised. The alley line of the block is clearly defined by privies and a long shed.

may be expected by those owning houses and who fail or refuse to raise same."[21]

The most complicated logistics of the project involved the building of the distributing canal, which, when completed, measured 200 feet wide and 20 feet deep (fig. 84). The canal followed the eastern outline of the island from the channel to Twenty-first Street, where it turned west and ran to Thirty-third Street. Fifty-eight blocks were altered, the changes ranging from cutting off the tip of a corner lot to eliminating an entire block. An undetermined but substantial number of buildings—almost all small houses—had to be moved from the canal right-of-way, either to a different location on the same lot or, more frequently, to a vacant lot leased by the city. There was a trade-off for property owners whose houses were moved. The city assumed all moving costs, paid all taxes on the properties while the canal was used, rented the lots on which the buildings were temporarily placed, and, finally, filled the canal and returned the houses.[22]

Most residents accepted their assigned location without complaint, but there were exceptions. The Leonard and Lewis families each owned lots and improvements on the same block of Avenue M 1/2 between Twelfth and Thirteenth Streets. The Leonards were white. According to the 1903–4 city directory, Thomas Leonard was a nurse, but it was his wife Isabella who was spokesperson for the family. The Lewises were black and counted at least six family members who had to sign the lease agreement, but only one Lewis, Theresa, was listed at the address in the 1903–4 directory.

Fig. 84. The dredgeboat *Holm* maneuvering in the northeast end of the grade-raising canal. The Seawall is on the left.

The two families did not live on adjoining lots on Avenue M 1/2 but were scheduled to be next-door neighbors in their temporary location during the grade-raising project. Cheesborough informed the contractors that Mrs. Leonard objected "vigorously to being located alongside of the Lewis family" who, in turn, "also object vigorously to being located alongside 'poor white trash,' therefore it becomes necessary for us to separate the pair." The altercation was complicated further because the Lewis family felt they "will be somewhat crowded on one lot, although, that is the amount of their present holdings," and "there seems to be a contention about who is to live on the alley." Cheesborough found another lot in another block for the Leonards and gave the Lewises the two adjoining lots, but he did not record if any member of the Lewis family lived along the alley in their temporary location.[23]

Many of the properties that had to be moved for the canal were owner-occupied but situated on leased land. Several ground renters, like longshoreman A. E. Wentzel, chose to secure a permanent location that would require moving their house only once. Prior to the building of the canal, the Wentzel household of seven lived in "a 2-room house on the alley" of Mrs. Julia Schmiedeberg's property at 618 Avenue G. The Schmiedeberg "dwelling house" was moved to one location and the Wentzel "shack" to another lot, not on an alley, where it would remain, "Wentzel having rented the new sight for his own account."[24] Wentzel, as well as other individuals identified in Cheesborough's records as ground renters, is not listed in the Tax Assessor's Abstracts as owning improvements, just one more indication that the practice of ground rent was far more prevalent than is suggested by standard documentary sources.

During the grade-raising, alley residents endured the same discomforts and inconveniences as other Galvestonians. Once their houses or quarters were raised, they, like everyone else, waited for the fill, which, when started, gushed every one or two hours, frequently day

Fig. 85

Fig. 86

Fig. 87

Fig. 88

Photographic series showing the filling of one block.
Fig. 85. Two men—one black, one white, and both in bowlers—survey the process from the back fence.
Fig. 86. Filling on the front side. For orientation, the hipped roof of the corner store is visible in the background of the other photographs.
Fig. 87. The house on the left in this photograph is the house on the right in fig. 86.
Fig. 88. Catwalks connect houses and privies.

and night, and for what could be several weeks, depending upon the grade level to which their block and section were to be raised (figs. 85–88). After the water drained, the odor lingered, and householders were left with "pure sand," which, if not quickly surfaced, could shift with heavy rains or become so dry that it "drifts like snow" and so fine that "it penetrates everything." It was also hard to ignore the resurfacing material most widely used—the sweepings of livery stables.[25]

Indirect losses and hardships caused by the project took a heavy but inestimable and silent toll on many people. Such alley dwellers as washerwomen and seamstresses, whose income depended on services that they offered from their houses, suffered when their neighborhood was being raised, as did woodsawyers, draymen, junk collectors, and others whose livelihood relied upon their freedom to move about the city. Although widow Mrs. L. A. McCashin did not live on an alley, she and many alley residents had much in common. Prior to the grade-raising, Mrs. McCashin made her living "by taking in sewing and renting out a part of her little home." Once the project was underway, a sympathetic Cheesborough wrote the city attorney that "no one will rent her rooms, and she finds it very difficult to get work as people object to going over the sandy area in order to reach her." In May 1905, Cheesborough begged the city not to sue Mrs. McCashin for back taxes, as it was threatening to do, noting that "this party had saved up about $40 with which she intended paying off her back taxes, but was compelled to use same in raising her house."[26] Cheesborough's letter refutes

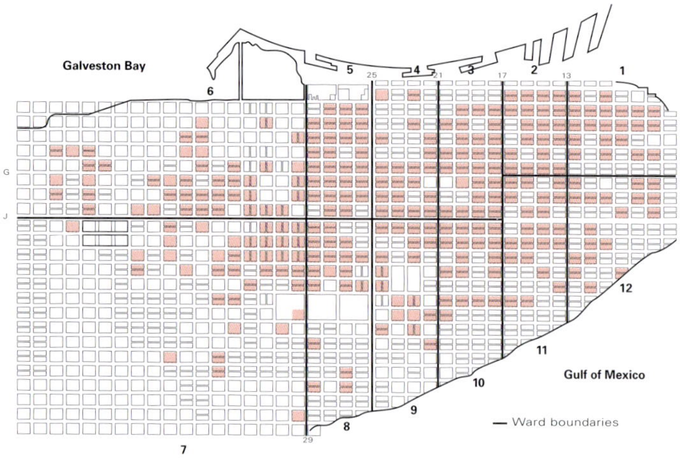

Fig. 89. Distribution of 290 inhabited alleys before the grade-raising project, based on 1,284 alley addressees listed in 1901–2 city directory.

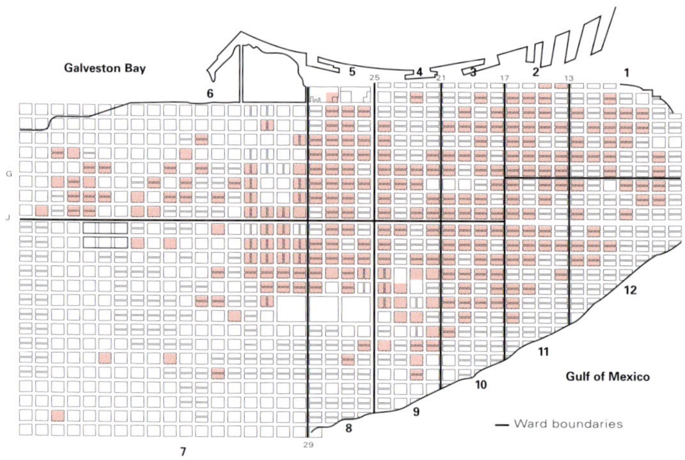

Fig. 90. Distribution of 271 inhabited alleys after the grade-raising, based on 1,221 alley addressees listed in 1911–12 city directory. Two alleys are outside the map area.

the earlier claim published in the newspaper that the cost of raising a large two-story house was $20 to $25.

The grade-raising project may have ensured steadier employment for some men living on the alleys, particularly draymen who worked for specific dredging companies and livery stables. Transporting dry fill and resurfacing materials was "furnishing employment for many teams" in January 1905, but many jobs created by the project were not filled by Galvestonians, as had been promised at the outset. House-movers and house-raisers obviously were in demand at certain times, but newspapers periodically reported a "lack of work" for laborers, because construction, as well as many other businesses and industries, experienced a general slowdown.[27]

Arranging temporary quarters for animals that were needed to produce income or food was especially difficult for alley residents and others living in small, already cramped houses. There were several possible solutions. Animals might be confined to a raised platform in the yard or to a porch or stoop (if the house had one) or even brought into the house. They might be sheltered elsewhere, but that was an option more likely for people with greater resources than many living on the alleys. Some people were forced to sell their animals and equipment, such as the families who advertised "HORSE and wagon for sale; cheap; no

Table 6.1
Alley listings in Galveston city directories before and after 1900 storm, by race

		Alley Listings			
Directory Year	**Total Listings**	**Black**	**White**	**Chinese**	**Total**
1899–1900	21,210	827 (77.7%)	237 (22.3%)	1	1,065
1901–1902	17,695	1,066 (83.0%)	218 (17.0%)	0	1,284
1911–1912	22,194	1,035 (84.8%)	183 (15.0%)	3 (.02%)	1,221

Source: Data from *Morrison & Fourmy's General Directory of the City of Galveston, 1891–1892; Morrison & Fourmy's General Directory of the City of Galveston, 1901–2;* and *Directory of the City of Galveston, 1911–12.*

room on account of grade raising," and "One good family cow and calf." People living in the first sections of the city to be filled discovered that temporary arrangements might have to be tolerated much longer than predicted. Eight months after the filling was completed, owners had not been given street and alley lines, which meant that there were still no fences enclosing many properties, and "those who are ambitious to raise chickens are prevented from doing so because they can not confine them."[28]

Alley residents who had a garden, small as it would have been, probably lost at least one year's crop and perhaps more, depending on how long it took a property owner to resurface a lot. Projected dates for filling an area changed frequently, and there were those who lost "the benefit of [their] truck garden." Nor was it always possible to gauge how long an area would take to drain—or, in the worst cases, if it would drain at all—and allow the planting of a garden. Ornamental painter Henry L. Eimer complained that, as a result of the filling, the back part of his property at 3627 Avenue M "is a quivering mass of silt and of such a character that a horse cannot stand on same," a condition neither conducive to animals and gardens nor exclusive to Mr. Eimer's block.[29]

When the original contract for the grade-raising project was extended from February 18, 1907, to February 18, 1910, Galvestonians must have wondered if the project and the mess would ever end. However, in mid-October 1908, they saw a hopeful sign: A house that had been moved for the canal was returned to its original location.[30] Over the next two years, as the filling continued on the west side of town, the canal right-of-way was filled. Eventually, most of the houses and accompanying structures were returned to their old addresses. Modifications to some original agreements were necessitated by houses or lots being sold, landlord and tenant disputes, divorce settlements, and an occasional cantankerous owner.

Some property owners used the grade-raising project to replace the temporary housing that had been built by the Central Relief Committee after the hurricane. Several commissary houses that were moved from the front of a lot to the alley side for the canal right-of-way were kept at the alley location "so that the front part would be available for another building." Other commissary houses were sold. One was bought by attorney Miles Crowley and moved by the city "to the rear end" of Crowley's lot rather than returned to its original location. Crowley requested that the house be moved again and a fence installed, but Cheesborough refused. On other occasions he acquiesced. Cheesborough asked the house-movers to raise the chicken-house belonging to butcher Oswald Killi, but grumbled that "any ordinary individual would raise his own chicken-house and say nothing about it." The project already had paid to raise the "negro cottage on the alley, stable and back fence" on Killi's lot at 1019 Avenue L.[31]

The grade-raising project did not substantially alter the number or the racial percentages of alley residents. A comparison of the 1901–2 and 1911–12 city directories shows only a slight reduction in the number of alley and rear addressees as well as in the number and distribution of inhabited alleys.[32] (See figs. 89, 90; also table 6.1.) What changed dramatically, however, was the number of individual alleys with a much larger population, most of them, not surprisingly, in Ward Five. There were now eight alleys in the ward with twenty or more addressees, whereas in 1901–2, the number was two. (See appendices D and E.)

In many respects, the visual changes along the alleys were only temporary, as was true throughout the city (fig. 91). Gradually, vegetation resprouted and fences were rebuilt. Some alley buildings were left at a noticeably higher level because the owners wanted to enclose a

Fig. 91. Photograph taken looking east along Avenue J (Broadway) after the grade-raising. The Texas Heroes Monument is located at the intersection of Avenue J and Twenty-fifth Street. The brick house in the background is Open Gates, the Sealy house. (See fig. 120.)

usable, lower floor. The two-story back buildings that originally consisted of a stable or carriage house on the lower level and living quarters on the upper level changed very little with regard to their height and relationship to the ground. Actually, other factors in the very near future would have a greater long-term impact on the alleys than did the grade-raising.

Whether or not Galvestonians could *feel* that they were on higher ground is unknown. Certainly, they believed that they were on safer ground and, for property owners, on real estate that was more valuable, a major rationale for both the Seawall and the grade-raising project. But the increase in property values was, of course, a benefit from which most alley dwellers were excluded.

Galvestonians took pride—and justifiably so—in the grade-raising project. It was an unequaled technological feat and one of extraordinary community cooperation. Nevertheless, between the hurricane and the grade-raising project, those first ten years of the twentieth century must have been almost unimaginably harsh and disruptive for many Galvestonians, but most especially for the city's poorest citizens—like many of those who lived along the alleys.

7 Change along the Alley: Technology and Housing Reform

The alley is both a blessing and a curse.

Lawrence Veiller, 1911

For James Hanna, the most vivid recollection of the Galveston grade-raising project was being terrorized both on and off the schoolyard by "the offspring of the dredge boat and pipeline workers . . . the dregs of humanity."[1] Aside from these encounters, Hanna writes of an almost idyllic childhood, much of it revolving around the backyard of his family's two-and-a-half-story house at 1417 Avenue D (figs. 92–95). He also writes about a period when major technological changes began to alter the everyday backyard activities and appearances that had existed since the mid-nineteenth century.

To Hanna and his five siblings, their backyard playground on a spacious lot-and-a-half seemed "as large as a circus lot." There were the servants' house in one corner and the chicken house and run on the opposite side. The elevated cistern adjacent to the house was "almost as high as the roof," and was used for laundering, watering the lawn, and emergencies such as the 1900 storm. Instead of outbuildings, the Hannas' house had a raised, floored basement where the family stored wood and coal for heating and cooking and their washerwoman's "gunnysacks of charcoal." There was also a toilet for the servants, a darkroom for Mr. Hanna's photography hobby, and a play area. The front yard "was given over to lawns and flowers and, other than an occasional excursion in the lawn swing," the children did not play there.[2]

Fig. 92

Fig. 93

Fig. 94

Fig. 95

Hanna family photographs taken by John Hanna.
Fig. 92. Hanna residence, 1417 Avenue D, taken after 1900 hurricane.
Fig. 93. East side of house looking toward the servants quarters.
Fig. 94. Hanna children in the backyard in their Mardi Gras costumes, February 22, 1898.
Fig. 95. Margaret Hanna and Nancy (last name not given on photograph), on June 18, 1899.

According to Hanna, the children and their friends, who were "from prominent families and of the same social strata as our own," had the run of the backyard every day but Monday. That was washday, when the Hannas' laundress Becky and "her helper" began the two- or three-day ritual of washing and ironing the family's clothes and linens, and for which there were hundreds of variations in backyards and alleys all over Galveston. The hand-laundering process required at least three tubs and followed "long-established standards," with the pieces "hung on ropes strung all over the yard, for drying in the sun." The ironing was done the following day and, if necessary, another day in Becky's quarters.[3]

At the time of the 1900 census, John Newberry, a black longshoreman, and his wife Stella were renting the one-story back house in which Becky later lived.[4] No one was living there in 1910, a signal that the Hannas' gradual acquisition of their first automobile had begun.

When Becky decided to share a house with some members of her family, Father had the old servant's house torn down and constructed a new building in order that we could keep our horse and buggy at home. For many years they had been kept at the livery stable downtown where the horse was well cared for, the harness kept oiled and its brass buckles polished and the buggy washed and polished as often as necessary. Each morning, promptly at eight o-clock, a Negro boy would drive the horse and buggy to our house and secure it to a hitching post at the curb. Then going around to the back of the buggy he would unfasten a bicycle with specially made iron towing arms and return to the livery stable to make another delivery. At whatever time of the day or night that Father had no further use for the vehicle he would telephone the livery stable and in a few minutes the boy would appear, fasten his bicycle to the rear of the buggy and drive off.

After the construction of our new carriage house and stable, it became my job to get up early and hitch up old Maud and drive around to the front of the house and tie her to the hitching post. I didn't object to this as it added substantially to my allowance. . . . Whenever Father would not need the buggy in the afternoon I would unhitch it, put a riding bridle on Maud and ride her bareback all over the neighborhood, sometimes with one or two of my friends seated behind me.

As might be expected, however, this was just too good to be true to last. Father had decided to buy a car, and old Maud was sold to Grandma. Her stall and manger were ripped out and the stable converted to a garage. The change for me was not too hard to take, for at that age and era, an automobile was far more thrilling than anything else.[5]

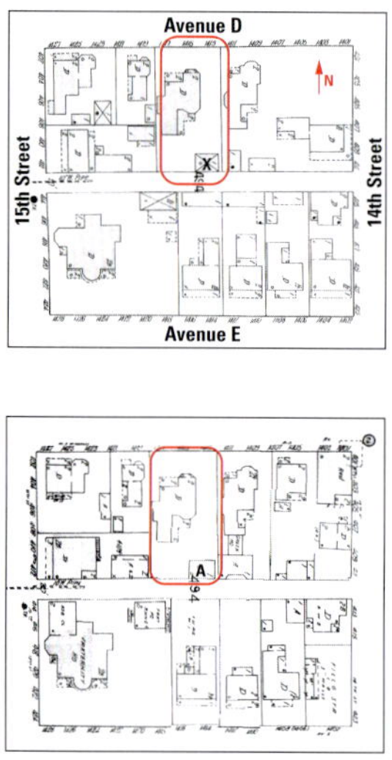

Fig. 96. Original 1912 Sanborn insurance map (top) shows a stable on the Hanna property at 1417 (marked "X") Avenue D. The same map with an early pasteover (bottom) indicates that the Hannas had adapted the building for use as a garage (marked "A").

Many households converted carriage houses, stables, and sheds into garages, a process that took place on the Hanna property sometime after 1912, when the Sanborn map still shows a stable where the servants quarters had been located (fig. 96). In 1912, there were only four properties with "AUTO" garages on the twenty-eight blocks in Ward Two, the ward in which the Hannas lived. Adrian Levy remembered that his widowed mother bought the family's first automobile in 1912, his freshman year in college, and kept it in "a garage, just a one-story thing" behind their house. By 1915, the *Galveston Daily News* regularly listed building permits for garages ranging from a $50 "portable garage" to a $1,000 "concrete and hollow tile garage and servants' house." The local newspapers also reported the names of proud new automobile owners along with their car make and dealership.[6]

There was a two-and-a-half-story house that belonged to the other side of the family, the Niemann side of the family, at 1219 M. We had a stable out in the back. . . . It had bunks on the wall for people to sleep in, had places for the wagons, places for the buggies, and stalls for eight horses back there. My great-granddaddy was a mounted officer, his son was a mounted officer, and then, back in those days, they'd lease drays to the city, and one of his sons-in-law drove a dray for the city, and his other son was a carpenter and a contractor and he'd use it to haul lumber and everything to build houses. Everybody in the family kept their horses there.

In fact, the neighborhood was full of animals. Mrs. Greve kept six cows on her property at 1218 L and you bought your milk from her. The Wegners owned the house at 1328 K and kept five horses and four cows in their backyard. He sold milk, loved horses, and had pens for them. On the corner of Twelfth Street and Avenue L, that used to be Mr. Fritz's meat market where he regularly killed and processed his own weenies and other meats, blood and liver puddings, and hogshead cheese—right there on that corner. You could get all the fresh meat you wanted. **Oscar T. Ekelund Jr.**

Other families and individuals were slower in replacing their horse and stable with an automobile and garage. In June 1915, plumber P. C. Stewart obtained a permit to build a stable and bathroom valued at $100 at 3624 Avenue R. Real estate advertisements continued to list a "good stable" or "large stable" among the assets for residential properties. When the 1910 census was taken, there were 1,802 horses and 519 mules stabled in a city of 36,981 people. Ten years later, there were 847 horses, 642 mules, and 44,255 residents. The automobile was replacing the horse for personal use, but a machine was not, as yet, replacing the work animal.[7] (See fig. 49.)

In the late nineteenth and early twentieth centuries, technology introduced the most obvious and drastic changes along the alleys in Galveston, at least in those blocks where residents like the Hanna and Levy families could afford indoor plumbing, gas heating, and automobiles. Concurrently, a perceptible shift in attitude towards the alleys and alley dwellers had taken place.

By the late 1880s, local newspapers were reporting fewer incidents involving alley residents. With the black population firmly secured in the lowest economic positions, white Galvestonians were no longer as threatened by economic and social uncertainties as they had been after the Civil War. Consequently, they were less interested in reading stories that confirmed their prejudices. Only occasionally did the newspapers report what was considered a noteworthy alley-related story, as in 1904, when Heywood Scott received a verdict of justifiable homicide for shooting W. H. Singleton, a twenty-eight-year-old widower and "embryo Baptist preacher." Singleton was killed when he broke into the house of Scott's sister on the alley between Twenty-ninth and Thirtieth Streets and Avenues G and H, one block north of Burnett's Alley.[8]

Most Galvestonians were content with a well-established housing pattern that included alley housing consisting primarily of servants quarters or rental units and which, in both cases, usually meant housing for blacks. To supplement their minimal income, many domestic servants lived in housing provided by their employer, an arrangement that ensured white Galvestonians of a servant class. Galveston was also a city of renters and rental housing, a status confined neither to blacks nor to alleys, but home ownership definitely was much less a possibility for blacks than for whites. According to the 1910 census, 87 percent of "Negro homes" in Galveston were rented and 8 percent were owned. In contrast, 60 percent of white-occupied houses were rented and 36 percent were owned. On both the national and state levels, Galveston ranked very low in the number of houses owned by blacks.[9]

Events in the early 1900s compelled some Galvestonians to address the alleys that were in the most deplorable condition, most notably those in Ward Five. The hurricane and the grade-raising project had only worsened conditions by damaging or destroying already deteriorating buildings throughout the city and forcing more people into those blocks where housing on both the front streets and the alleys always seemed available, however crowded.

Outside factors as well as local conditions motivated the civic clubs in Galveston to begin pressing for sanitation and housing reforms. The most militant groups were the Women's Health Protective Association (WHPA), founded by sixty-six professional and nonprofessional women in 1901, and the Galveston Commercial Association (GCA), which consolidated three existing businessmen's organizations in 1910.[10] Both groups saw themselves as part of a national urban reform movement. It was a movement that had produced a literature, including an alley literature that identified and illustrated alleys and alley

Fig. 97. Illustration of backyard view and alley house entitled "Where the Other Half Lives in Columbus [Ohio]," published in *Survey*, July 1, 1911. The caption explains that the backyard was within view of the state house and that the two-room dwelling rented for $8 a month.

housing as a national, not just a local, problem (figs. 97, 98). Undoubtedly, reform-minded Galvestonians were familiar with journalist and photographer Jacob A. Riis's book, *How the Other Half Lives: Studies Among the Tenements of New York,* first published in 1890, then republished in 1900 and 1903 with more graphic photographs, including alley scenes.

In November and December of 1911, *The Galveston-Dallas News* featured a twenty-nine-part series on housing conditions in Galveston, Dallas, Fort Worth, Houston, and San Antonio. Written by reporter George Waverly Briggs, the series was reprinted in a pamphlet entitled *The Housing Problem in Texas: A Study of Physical Conditions under which the Other Half Lives*, an unabashed borrowing of Riis's title. With Briggs declaring alley housing to be "the worst example of house congestion that Galveston affords," the city's alleys and alley houses—those that opened into the alleys—entered a new phase in their history.[11] It was a selective crusade: back houses and servants quarters—those that provided a service to a front house and were more likely to be oriented to a yard—were exempt from the campaign.

Fig. 98. "Throw It in the Alley," a Detroit alleyscape published in *Survey*, August 5, 1911. The alleys are lined with tenements in what were identified as "the most crowded districts" in the city, which "has probably the most complete alley system in the country."

Briggs attributed Galveston's housing problems to the city plan, although he acknowledged that the regular blocks and intersecting alleys expedited traffic movement, facilitated fire protection, and allowed adequate air passage. The original town planners, however, had not anticipated the overcrowding that developed as space became more restricted and land values increased beyond the commercial core. To match income to value, property owners, according to Briggs, were forced to build on "every inch of available space," whether dwellings were large or small. As a result, houses in Galveston were so close that they neglected "that greatest attribute of home life, so indispensible [sic] to proper conditions of living and the rearing of children—privacy."[12]

Overcrowding, wrote Briggs, was at its worst on those alleys that had "more persons living in houses facing the alley than there are living in the dwellings behind them, facing the street." Sanitation, trash, and animals compounded the problems, which were visible all over town. Many of the smaller houses were without sewerage connections, either because they were too remote from sewer mains or because property owners refused to make the connection as required by law. The small, cut-up backyards and "the jamming together of rear ends of dwellings, separated only by narrow strips of ground divided by makeshift fences," were "congregating points of filth." In addition, "the small premises fronting the alleys usually have as an important part of their complement a cow or two, a horse, a donkey or a pack of dogs."[13]

Briggs claimed that conditions along Galveston's alleys were far worse than those in the other four cities, and only in passing cited problems with alley housing in Dallas and Fort Worth. At the same time, he declared that shotgun houses were the "bane of housing experts throughout the world," but reserved his most heated criticism for shotgun houses in San Antonio and Dallas.[14] Briggs may have made a distinction between a shotgun house and a commissary house, but it would have been a distinction based primarily on terminology; the two were virtually the same house type.

Examples of "civic attractiveness" and "civic unattractiveness" were illustrated but not identified in the articles. Scenes that were unmistakably taken in Galveston, including two backyard views and one view of an alleyway, were all examples of "civic unattractiveness" (figs. 39, 99). The alley that was illustrated was in Block 448, bordered by Avenues E and F and Twenty-eighth and Twenty-ninth Streets. It was consistently one of the most densely populated alleys in town and the one on which contractor Robert Palliser had built his multiple shotgun houses.

Fig. 99. Galveston alley in Block 448, looking west. Illustration used as an example of "civic unattraciveness" in newspaper series, *The Housing Problem in Texas: A Study of Physical Conditions under which the Other Half Lives* by George Waverly Briggs (*The Galveston-Dallas News*: 1911), p. 63. It is also the alley on which Robert Palliser owned and built rental property. (See fig. 73.)

Galveston was "fortunate" because there was "a comparative lack of poverty" and the majority of laborers were homeowners, which Briggs attributed to the healthy though somewhat erratic wages of dockworkers and their frugal wives. Most working-class houses were occupied by a single family, with "the lodger evil" a temporary problem only when shipping was at its peak. In such times, five- to ten-member families who normally lived in houses with three to five rooms rented space to additional boarders and lodgers. Briggs specified that this was true of the white laboring class, but not "the negroes . . . [who] crowd into their houses without regard for sanitation, ventilation or decency."[15]

Briggs advocated the passage of a state housing law and local ordinances that would apply to alterations to existing dwellings and to new construction. He recommended that rear tenements be forbidden altogether, but if that was determined to be unconstitutional, he proposed that they be discouraged through strict sanitation codes. Briggs also called for stricter enforcement of existing municipal ordinances, crediting Lawrence Veiller, director of the National Housing Association and a housing-reform activist, as the inspiration for many of his recommendations.[16]

The series did not elicit an immediate response to improve housing conditions in Galveston, but Briggs believed that it would alert an ignorant public, the first step in correcting the problem. As in the past, city commissioners continued to act upon individual petitions regarding dilapidated buildings, including some that were located on the alleys.[17]

Figs. 100 and 101. 1912 Sanborn insurance map and detail of circa 1912 aerial view taken from "Little Frank's Balloon" showing "model arrangement" of rental housing on outlot bordered by Avenues M and M 1/2, and Twenty-sixth and Twenty-seventh Streets. The aerial view shows only a portion of the outlot: Central High School, the black high school, is the large structure. (For later changes to the block, see fig. 11.)

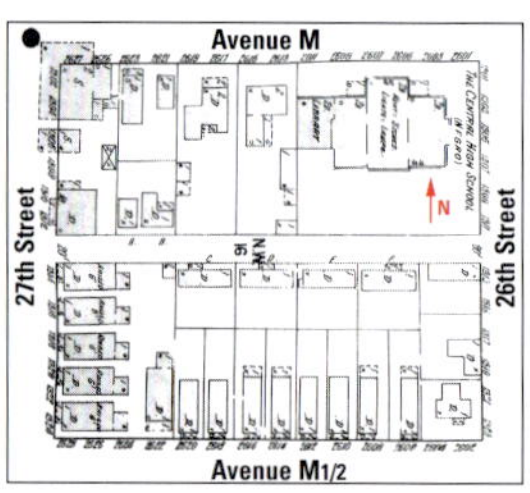

Fig. 100

On February 20, 1913, the Women's Health Protective Association and the Galveston Commercial Association submitted to the city commissioners a joint petition with two requests: the appointment of a city building inspector; and the adoption of a policy whereby the alleys in the city would be used for "residence purposes only (as an adjunct to the buildings situated in front) for servant quarters, or otherwise, with access to these buildings through the front of the lot." The WHPA submitted a separate petition "to bring about clean alleys," to which the commissioners responded that it was the citizens, not the city, who were at fault. The health inspector lamented that even though arrests were made "by wholesale," convictions were impossible.[18]

Soon thereafter, the GCA, wanting the city to be "a model of cleanliness and healthfulness," commissioned Dr. James Persons Simonds, chief of the laboratory of preventive medicine at the University of Texas Medical College in Galveston, to conduct a sanitary survey. Whereas Briggs's newspaper series presented a comparative survey of housing conditions in cities throughout the state, Simonds's report, which was published in pamphlet form, addressed a wider range of health issues specific to Galveston, many relating to the alleys.[19]

Housing conditions were one of Galveston's "crying shames" and were due, wrote Simonds, to two forms of overcrowding: too many houses built on a single lot, and the alley house. He cited the blocks between Avenues D and G and Twenty-fifth and Twenty-eighth Streets, the center of Ward Five, where conditions were "disgusting beyond expression," and where the streets and alleys, but not the lots, had been filled to grade. Sewer mains had been laid in the district, but alley houses were not connected, even though "most of the property on these particular blocks brings abnormally high rent, because it is rented for purposes that are socially and legally outlawed." As a result, standing water and the overflow from privy vaults filled the yards almost year-round. It was no coincidence that the city's highest death rate from tuberculosis was in the same area where "the miserable type of dwelling and the crowding together of the buildings" facilitated, if not actually caused, the spread of disease.[20]

Fig. 101

As an alternative, Simonds pointed to a specific "model arrangement" of rent houses on the south half of the block bordered by Avenues M and M 1/2 and Twenty-sixth and Twenty-seventh Streets. Most of the houses were shotgun or modified shotgun houses. Four of them opened into the alley (figs. 100, 101). "These are," wrote Simonds, "occupied by negroes; they are neat; the alley is clean; and the tenants are able to retain and even develop their self respect." Among the property owners on the half-block was the Ort family, longtime owners and developers of rental property.[21] (See chapter 5.)

Simonds believed that the only new housing law that Galveston needed was "a vigorous law regulating the building of houses, especially in alleys." Like Briggs, Simonds felt that there should be provisions for adequate inspection and fair, even enforcement. Both men obviously feigned ignorance when they claimed not to understand why some property owners were not required to make sewer connections in accordance with existing ordinances. Enforcement was particularly important to Simonds because the people most affected by poor housing conditions were those "without influence or 'pull.'"[22] It was the kind of sentiment never expressed by Briggs.

Simonds's report initiated action, most of it focusing on the "restricted district" in Ward Five. In February 1914, two county commissioners submitted their own list of dilapidated buildings to the city commissioners.[23] In April, a grand jury reported that the consumption of cocaine was so great in Galveston that it "was peddled indiscriminately upon the streets and alleys of the 'restricted district' at all hours of the day and night," having "assumed alarming and tremendous proportions." Prostitution and the illegal sale of liquor were cited in the same report as "serious matters."[24]

In late May, the streets and alleys committee of the GCA—chaired by none other than George Waverly Briggs, now a Galveston resident and editor of the *Galveston Daily News*—inspected "some of the poorer quarters of the city," where it found "housing conditions so frightful as to challenge adequate description." A newspaper report described the inhabitants of the area:

> *Races are indiscriminately mixed in this district. Mexicans pursue their "happiness" as they desire; negroes, of course, predominate; but white women and white men, driven to the last stages of life, also live here. . . . There are washerwomen and dairymen, idlers and hangers-on, criminals and drug-fiends, the careless, the ignorant, the sick, the brutal, all living in a more or less common state of destitution.*[25]

Briggs's committee submitted a list of recommendations: demolish some structures, fill premises to grade, require tenants and property owners to clean their premises and keep them clean, require sewer connections where service was provided, and clean the gutters in the area.[26]

Under pressure for the city to take action, on June 4 the Mayor requested that the Dilapidated Buildings Committee, composed of the City Health Officer, the City Engineer, and the Fire Chief, investigate a list of buildings "situated on the alley portions of said lots" in Ward Five. A week later, the committee recommended that seventeen structures be demolished after proper citation and hearing procedures had been followed. On July 23, the Health Officer reported that most owners had ignored the citations, with the exception of two widows: Mary Cunningham and Minnie Yowinckle, longtime residents of Blocks 507 and 508, respectively, who demolished their "shacks" and cleaned up their properties.

The housing projects—all of that was alleys, okay? Look what's happened to it. It may not be the best you've got but when it was originally built for what it was built for, it was beautiful. It got a lot of people out of alleys but now it's gotten to something else. I feel like it was, it had to be done. It was a must, you know. . . . As I remember, they had five government housing complexes. Some were built before World War II—built for military personnel and converted into residential. There was one called Bayview where, when I got married, we moved to because of being in the military, I had access to it. Of course, during that time everything was segregated. **Bill Millican**

Fig. 102. Alley cleanup during 1920 outbreak of bubonic plague. See also fig. 49.

(See chapter 5.) The commissioners voted for the city to demolish the remaining buildings if the owners failed to do so.[27]

On October 29, 1914, the city adopted its first building code. It must have been something of a disappointment to Briggs and Simonds because it did not disallow alley housing, as both had recommended. In an effort to curb alley dwellings, particularly those that qualified as "shacks," the code stated that sheds could be no larger than 150 square feet and 8 feet high. Exterior privies and wood or coal houses could be built of wood with incombustible roofing and walls to the same measurements, but there were limitations: they could not be built on the front of a lot; only one shed could be built on each lot; and none could be used as a dwelling, as an addition to a dwelling, or for business purposes.[28]

The 1913–14 demolition campaign focused on a defined section of the city, one that was viewed very differently, both "socially and legally," from other parts of town. However, when two Galvestonians died of bubonic plague in June 1920, the alleys became a primary target for a cleanup campaign on a massive, citywide basis. The United States Public Health Service dispatched a representative to Galveston to supervise the "plague control program" of trash removal, trapping and dissecting rats, and ratproofing buildings. By December, when the plague was considered under control, 12 people had died, 90,000 rats had been killed, and untold quantities of rubbish collected and buildings demolished along the alleyways (fig. 102).[29]

Although the city had adopted a rat-control ordinance in 1912, a stricter ordinance followed the 1920 outbreak.[30] Property owners were required to ratproof "every building, outhouse and other superstructure, stable, lot, open area and other premises, sidewalk, street and alley now constructed or hereafter to be constructed." Buildings were classified, with some requiring cement floors and others requiring underpinnings or pillars of specified heights. Property owners also were required to meet certain maintenance standards regarding the removal of trash from under their houses.[31] Although the requirements may have become more stringent, the ordinance was but the latest—and certainly not the final—plea for cleaner alleys. It is a plea that Galvestonians have heard since 1839.

Back House Observations

Back houses had their own kitchens. Lots of families had servants and they stayed in the back houses. Chimneys and wood stoves determined the location of the kitchen. Kitchens were downstairs in some of the bigger houses. Wood stoves were outlawed in the 1940s—that's when gas really came in.

Outhouses were on the alley line. In some cases, there was a separate outhouse for the property owners and their servants or tenants. In others, they used the same outhouse. It was up to the whims and wishes of the landlords. The problem was keeping them clean. People who cleaned outhouses were called "scavengers." They were independent and worked citywide. Both blacks and whites did them. The indoor plumbing trend started in 1927–28. Then it became mandatory.

People kept horses in back, in the alley, and on empty lots next to the house. I remember a few backyard stables, one at Fifteenth and N 1/2. People in the back houses couldn't afford to keep or feed their families, so they sure couldn't keep a horse. After the 1920s, people had to get rid of animals, but until the late 1920s, they had those.

The alleys themselves were not well maintained in the 1920s and later. Some were well kept by the desires of the people who lived there. For some, the alley was their home and they kept it clean. There were mostly blacks and a few Mexicans living in the alleys. Those that stayed was because of their economic situation, not because they were happy. They made themselves happy with the situation. People didn't move around a lot. When rents got high, that's when people got more mobile.

It was uncommon for servants to live in the main house. Some servants quarters were very nice. . . . Most entrances to the back houses were on the alley, but some went through the main yard. The average one was three to four rooms, but some were larger. Lots of them were shotgun houses, and some were one room, but most were more.

Living in a back house was something of a status barrier. People living in the front thought that they were superior economically, but that wasn't always true. Often, people in back were saving money to get a better house. Lots of people did that. Rents of $10 to $25—that's what induced people to rent a back house and that was true up until the early 1970s. The rents were upped then because of a lack of housing and the influx of medical students looking for a place to live.

There was a stigma about alley houses but not today. Back houses are as good as front houses. The stigma was before the 1960s and 1970s, and was true for blacks and whites. The students made it feasible to live in them. Leon M. Banks Sr.

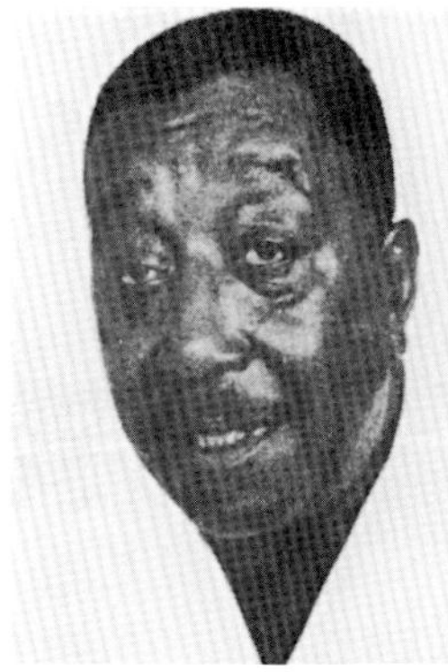

Fig. 103. Leon M. Banks Sr.

8 Alleyscapes

It's like looking over a back fence. It's the same idea. It's just that your neighbors are at these funny angles to you. . . . There was a couple who used to live there and they didn't take care of their garbage. I never did think about such things in my whole life, but then when it's your front yard, you do.

Pam Diamond

Since the founding of the city, Galveston's alleys and back buildings, like its alley residents, have been evolving, adapting, and changing. The placement of buildings along the alleys and the evolution of two distinct alleyscapes in the residential neighborhoods have responded to necessity, economics, technology, and social and racial attitudes.

Service buildings, especially the larger ones, were placed to the back of the long, narrow lots for very practical reasons. It allowed more yard space and helped define an alley wall—important considerations, since the daily routine of a household revolved around the backyard. Animals were kept to the rear of properties in stables and sheds. Smells associated with the animals, the privies, and the daily slop were confined, at least in theory, to the backside of the properties. And most Galveston properties, certainly those on single lots, simply were not wide enough to accommodate both a front house and the entrance to a carriage house or stable (and eventually, an automobile).

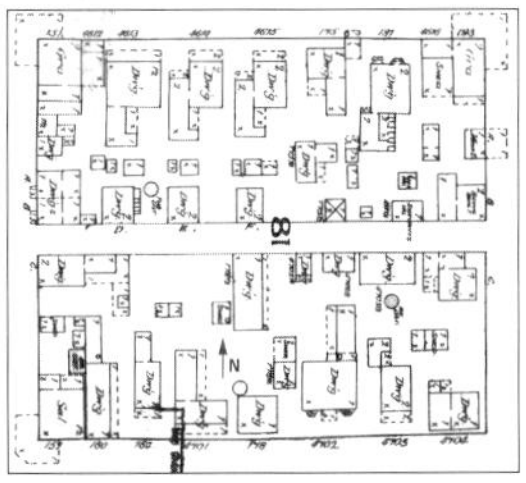

Fig. 105. 1885 Sanborn insurance map showing block with small- to medium-size houses and numerous detached back buildings, including utility buildings and dwellings.

The racial and social attitudes that pushed slaves and servants into back buildings determined the placement and availability of housing, particularly for blacks, following the Civil War. Rental housing built along the alleys gave maximum use and economic return to the long narrow lots and answered a desperate housing need. By placing the houses and their primary entrance directly on the alley line, the front and back buildings—and their inhabitants—were separated as much as Galveston's city plan permitted.

In addition to the buildings situated along the alley line, backyards were full of other structures that often seem randomly arranged on Sanborn maps. There were freestanding dwellings and tiny "servants rm[s]" located on lot interiors as well as second dwelling units in the wings of primary structures. Small front houses could have a surprising number of back buildings, because they could not absorb heating, cooking, and plumbing functions as easily as could larger structures (fig. 105). Cisterns appeared on the early maps but began to disappear in the late nineteenth century. By the time the first Sanborn map was made in 1876, detached kitchens had become more the exception than the rule. The maps were too small to label the use of every little back building on every lot, but the smaller buildings that were sometimes labeled include sheds, woodhouses, washhouses, henhouses, greenhouses, and dwellings. Like most buildings on the front streets, back buildings were usually frame, the masonry exceptions being either service structures that matched a primary residence or an early detached kitchen or commercial oven.

The evolution of almost any alley in town can be documented by using a Civil War map, the 1871 and 1885 bird's-eye views, the succession of Sanborn maps, and the buildings and alleys themselves. Two blocks in Ward Two illustrate the different residential alleyscapes and back buildings seen throughout the city. Block 496, bounded by Avenues D and E and Sixteenth and Seventeenth Streets, represents the alleyscape that is dominated by service

Fig. 104. 1628 Avenue E, back building, on Block 496. Kruger house, Nicholas J Clayton, architect, built 1888. Looking west toward Seventeenth Street. Photographed 1990.

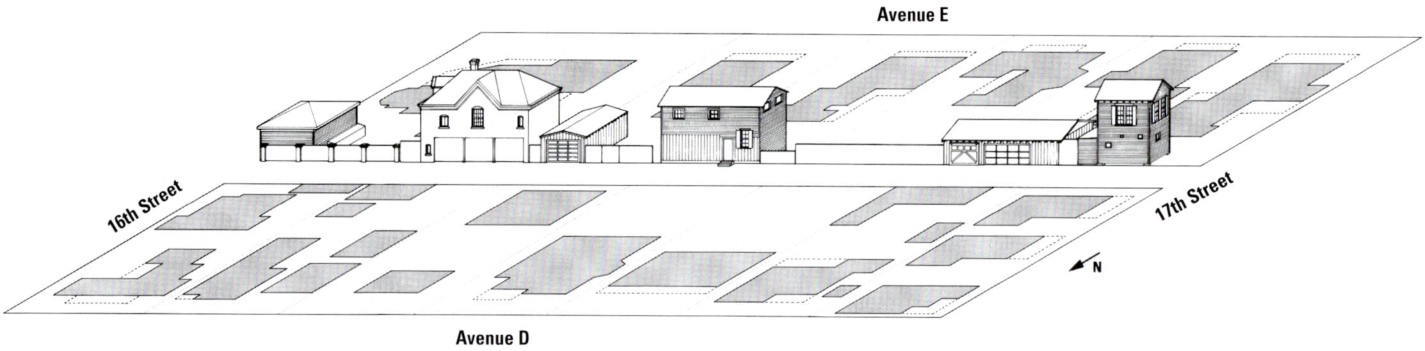

Fig. 106. Alleyscape, Block 496, Avenue E side. Documented 1991. The Landes property is on the Sixteenth Street side of the block; the Kruger property with its two-story servants quarters is on the Seventeenth Street side.

buildings oriented to the yard and front structure, whereas Block 375, bounded by Avenues F and G and Fifteenth and Sixteenth Streets, is typical of the alleyscape in which the buildings are oriented to the alley. (See figs. 106, 109.)

Although it is difficult to tell a great deal about either block from the Civil War map, it is at least clear that Block 375 contained six primary properties and a considerable amount of open space, whereas on Block 496 there were ten properties that combined a greater mix of large and small primary structures. Both blocks had a healthy number of back buildings, most of them placed directly on the alley line.[1]

More precise characteristics begin to emerge for both blocks in the 1871 bird's-eye view (fig. 107). The buildings on Block 375 were modest in size and height and scattered in their arrangement. Block 496 was far more dense, due to the number, placement, and size of its buildings and to several residences with large attached wings. The strongest definition of an alley line was on the south side of both blocks.

By the time the 1885 bird's-eye view was drawn, Block 375 had experienced the greater change (fig. 108). The gaps in the earlier view had been filled with the gabled and hipped roofs of small to modest-sized buildings, although the jumbling of buildings, as well as their size, makes it difficult to determine the alley line. In contrast, on Block 496 there were, if anything, more back buildings, especially small ones, marching down the alley line, but little change is evident in the primary structures.

Block 496 burned in the 1885 fire. Consequently, there were drastic changes to the block by the time the 1889 Sanborn map was drawn, the first Sanborn map to include Blocks 496 and 375. By 1889, the Avenue E half of Block 496, as well as two lots on the Avenue D half, had been rebuilt (fig. 110, left). In terms of back buildings, the Avenue E half of the block followed the earlier pattern: A definite alley line was created by a series of two-story service buildings. Three of the buildings were stables, probably with living quarters on the second floor, as was a fourth structure labeled as such on a later Sanborn map. A fifth one-over-one structure served as servants quarters.

Fig. 107. Detail of 1871 bird's-eye view showing Blocks 375 (top) and 496 (bottom).

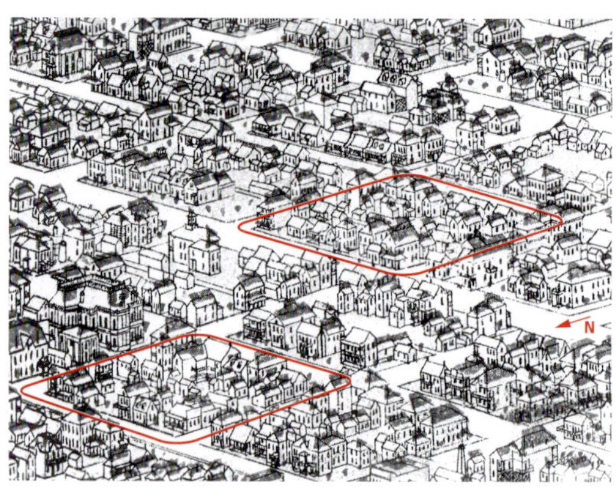

Fig. 108. Detail of 1885 bird's-eye view showing Blocks 375 (top) and 496 (bottom).

Fig. 109. Alleyscape, Block 375, Avenue F side. Documented 1991. Reading from the Fifteenth Street side, the house numbers of the first two alley dwellings are 1505 and 1511 Avenue F rear.

The primary structures on Block 375 changed very little between 1885 and 1889. The 1889 Sanborn map makes it possible, however, to decipher the uses of the various back buildings on the block (fig. 111, left). On the Avenue F half of the block, three small buildings directly on the alley line and a fourth on the interior of a divided lot were marked "D," the symbol for a dwelling and, in this instance, probably rental housing. Across the alley were two stables, a shed, and one "D" structure. Other miscellaneous one-story buildings also hugged the alley line.

By the early twentieth century, most primary structures on both blocks had assumed their present appearance except for minor modifications (fig. 110, right; fig. 111, right). The most noticeable changes that would take place in the blocks over the years would be along the alleys. Block 375 acquired more dwellings on both sides of the alley, with the Avenue F side gradually developing the almost continuous facade of alley houses that is there today. On Block 496, the alleyscape was altered not so much in appearance as in use, through the conversion of stables and servants quarters to garages and rental property, and the construction of additional one-story garages and, eventually, a one-story duplex.

The distinction between the two types of alleyscapes can still be seen today. Alleys that are dominated by service buildings, such as the alley in Block 496, have a greater sense of space and height for several reasons: the distance between buildings is greater; the buildings are taller because they are a full two stories or have a lower level that is raised, usually four feet or more; proportions, including roof pitch, are more generous; and many buildings are placed parallel to the alley line, a siting that contributes to their alley presence. (See figs. 104, 106, 113.)

Frequently, the raised lower level on the alley side of these structures has few if any openings, or the openings are covered with solid doors or panels. In either case, the effect is much the same—a solid wall. In fact, some buildings are still aligned with a substantial masonry wall or wood fence, as many were in the nineteenth and early twentieth centuries. The primary facades of back houses or service buildings are clearly oriented to the yard, although there may be an entrance with a stoop or small canopy on the alley side.

In contrast, on alleys dominated by alley houses, such as the alley in Block 375, the alley wall is defined by the primary entrance facades of tightly arranged, sometimes cramped,

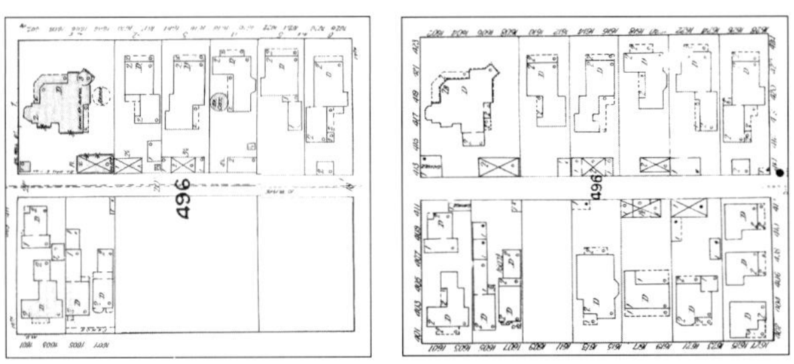

Fig. 110. Block 496, 1889 (left) and 1912 (right) Sanborn insurance maps. The maps are oriented to match the alleyscape drawing in fig. 106.

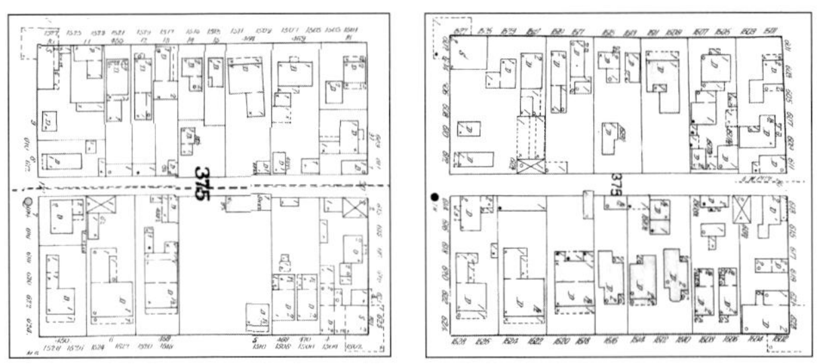

Fig. 111. Block 375, 1889 (left) and 1912 (right) Sanborn insurance maps. The maps are oriented to match the alleyscape drawing in fig. 109.

structures. These buildings tend to be smaller, with the entrance level placed closer to the ground. Orientation is clearly to the alley, with openings, stoops, small canopies, and porches frequently interrupting the alley wall. There is little space for trees or shrubbery. (See figs. 109, 115; see also frontispiece.)

Alley houses have more appendages than do back houses and service buildings. These appendages take various forms, such as a rear addition or multiple additions, the juncture of two adjoining alley houses to make a larger house, a vertical boxed attachment that usually denotes a hot-water heater, or a small enclosure on the porch that often contains a toilet. Two-story alley houses do exist, but many of these began as one-story dwellings that were raised to accommodate a second, separate living unit.

There are many alleys in Galveston in which all the back buildings were originally service structures for the front houses, an arrangement most likely to occur on blocks like 496, where residences were larger and predominantly owner-occupied (figs. 112, 113). Many of these alleys and buildings retain their original appearance, even though uses have changed—servants quarters are now rental units and carriage houses are garages. On other

Fig. 112

Fig. 114

Fig. 113

Fig. 115

Figs. 112–113. Block 496, 1600 block Avenue E. Photographed 1995.
Fig. 112. Front-street view, north side of street, looking west. The brick house on the right is the Landes house.
Fig. 113. Alley side, looking west. The Landes carriage house is in the foreground.

Figs. 114–115. Block 375, 1500 block Avenue F.
Fig. 114. Front-street view, south side of street, looking east. Photographed 1995.
Fig. 115. Alley side, looking east. Photographed 1990. (For alley view looking west, see frontispiece.)

alleys, both types of back buildings are visible. In such blocks, the two building types may be intermixed on the same side of the alley, or they may be on opposite sides, as on Block 375 (figs. 114, 115). Finally, there are still vestiges of alleys in which most, if not all, of the back buildings on both sides were built as high-density rental housing. These were the alley buildings and blocks most vulnerable to total demolition.

Unfortunately, Sanborn maps and early views cannot disclose the social practices surrounding back buildings, such as the gates that residents used, how spaces within property lines were allocated, and how those elements changed with time. Presumably, most housing that was oriented to an alley was entered through the alley. This becomes less certain in the case of living quarters that were located in secondary structures with entrances on both the alley and the yard side, such as carriage houses, and for dwellings and servants rooms that were located on lot interiors. Whether residents of these structures could use the front gate or always entered through the alley side probably depended on their relationship with others living on the property, racial and social attitudes, and perhaps, to some degree, convenience.

Fig. 116. Detail of 1930 aerial photograph showing Blocks 375 (bottom) and 496 (top).

On properties where the main house was owner-occupied, family members who had "taken a permanent abode in the back building" and some renters of back buildings might have used the front gate.[2] Most servants, especially black servants, probably did not.

The greatest possibility for conflict regarding access to a property or the use of a privy and cistern existed on properties where all the occupants were renters. Some lease agreements anticipated such problems. In October 1866, James Codling leased a lot with "free use of the Cistern on the adjoining Lot for all the water for the use of his family." A year later, Calcedorcia Muscat leased a house and kitchen on the corner of Nineteenth Street and Avenue D, "including the front Yard about 30 feet square." In addition to keeping "a clean House & yard quiet & respectable," Muscat agreed that "the adjoining tenants on the Westside has to have the privilege to enter through the gate into their house & also have the use of the Privy and also the use of the Cistern for drinking."[3]

Property owners were required to build a fence enclosing their property, but fences also defined spaces within lot lines. In 1867, Rebecca McLeod wanted to lease the front portion of one of her Galveston properties while also accommodating a former slave's shop and house to the rear. She wrote to her real estate agent that the house "only occupied a small fraction of the lots, the fence separating his shop," suggesting that "the balance of the lots could . . . be rented to any one wishing a small dwelling." She clarified the division by sketching the property footprint, including the fence. Fifty years later, when Dr. James Persons Simonds conducted the sanitation survey of the city, he noted that "a fence or low wall" separated the front houses from rows of "the most dilapidated often very unsanitary hovels."[4] Fences also separated front houses from servants quarters and back houses, as documentary photographs show (figs. 36, 64).

Obviously, fences served several purposes. They defined spaces and separated renters from owners, renters from renters, servants from employers, and animals from people. They kept animals in—and out. They provided a minimal degree, or at least the suggestion, of privacy and helped to buffer front house occupants from the backyard and alley noises, smells, and sights of everyday chores and activities.

9 Stepping into the Yard: Service Buildings and Back Houses

It was convenient living here, and I would not have to go back and forth over there to do things during the day. I would have my regular time. I would go in the morning—I guess around nine and around twelve or one, I was through. I wasn't on call and I didn't work Saturdays and Sundays.

Willie Mae Clay

Service buildings were first and foremost utilitarian structures, and viewed as such by Galvestonians. Even the most elaborate carriage houses were ignored in nineteenth century newspaper accounts that described, sometimes at length, new residences considered architectural achievements in the city. Still, there was a hierarchy to service buildings in Galveston, beginning with those structures that were associated with the larger residences and borrowed architectural details from the front house. It was a distinction acknowledged by the laborer who protested that an ordinance adopted after the 1885 fire and requiring homeowners to use treated roofing material was "all right for the wealthy citizen, erecting a handsome residence and outhouses to correspond but how will it work with the poor man, whose little 10x10 board kitchen attached to his residence is supposed to only cost from $10 to $20? The roof will cost more than the entire building formerly did."[1]

It was the larger, more elaborate and architecturally detailed back buildings that were most likely to have the services of at least an experienced contractor, if not an architect. On February 28, 1860, William H. Williams, property owner, and W. S. Deats & Bros., builders, agreed upon the specifications for a building complex that consisted of four structures: a two-story primary residence; a "rear building" that would be a "two Story house connected with the mane [sic] house" and include the kitchen; a forty-four-foot-by-fourteen-foot stable and carriage house; and a privy. Many details of the "rear building," including the roof, brick piers, and weatherboarding, were to be "like the mane house," while other details, such as the cornice, were to be "like that on the mane house but of lighter proportions."[2]

When building his brick Italianate residence in 1859, Henry Rosenberg followed the customary arrangement for larger properties by building separate support structures that were placed along the alley line and that quietly echoed the shape and detailing, as well as the material, of the front house (figs. 118, 119; see also fig. 18). Two of Rosenberg's outbuildings flanked the rear of the main house: The carriage house was situated on the alley corner; and what was probably the slave quarters, as suggested by the labeling on the 1889 Sanborn map, was placed on the lot interior. A third brick outbuilding, the stable—and the one with the most unpleasant odors—was built at the opposite end of Rosenberg's six-lot property.[3]

One of the most elaborate service buildings to be built in Galveston was the stable, carriage house, and servants quarters at Open Gates, the residence of banker and entrepreneur George Sealy, located on the northeast corner of Avenue J and Twenty-fifth Street, the most prominent intersection in the city (fig. 120). The design of the Romanesque residence is credited to the New York firm of McKim, Mead, and White, an attribution based on a set of specifications for the house interior that was prepared by the firm in October 1888. The supervising architect for the residence was Nicholas J. Clayton, the most influential and prolific architect to practice in Galveston during the late nineteenth and early twentieth centuries. In September 1889, Clayton produced a set of plans for the stable, as he referred to the building, and for which he submitted a statement of expenditures in March 1892. Sealy

Fig. 117. Looking toward the front house from the service building. Photographed 1995.

Fig. 118

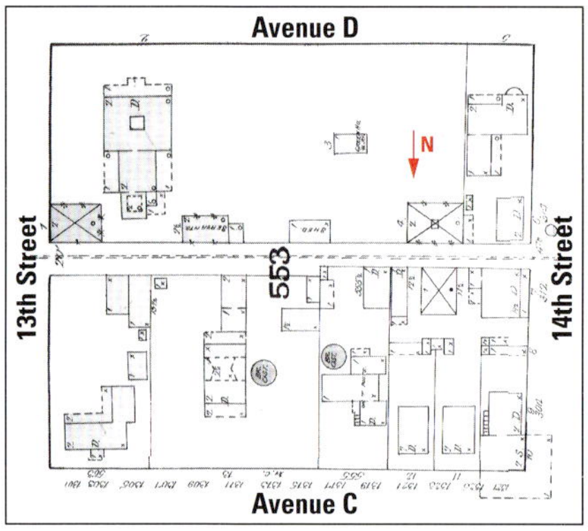

Fig. 119

Figs. 118 and 119. 1871 bird's-eye view and 1889 Sanborn insurance map showing the Rosenberg property. The 1871 view is relatively accurate for larger properties like the Rosenberg house. Changes to the property between 1871 and 1889 include construction of the larger stable on the west side. See also fig. 18.

paid $15,842.90, for the building plus another $8,500.48 for enclosures and approaches, including walls, fences, gates, lighting, and sidewalk and driveway surfacing.[4]

Although the primary residence commands the corner of the property, Clayton's stable building, also constructed of brick with a tile roof and terra-cotta trim, is not intimidated. Its placement and interior arrangement gave efficient carriage access to the house. Carriages were kept on the west side of the building; on the east side, the side farthest from the house, were stalls for two horses, two cows, and a pony for the seven Sealy children. The harness room was on the first floor of the tower. According to Clayton's plan, the second floor had a feed room in the northeast corner, five bedrooms, and a bathroom, but no common social space for servants. Some rooms may have shifted in use and function by 1900, when the census lists only three white servants, two women and a man, living and working in the Sealy household.[5]

Two features distinguished the secondary buildings on properties like the Rosenberg house and Open Gates: their architectural detailing and their visibility. Carriage houses

Fig. 120. Open Gates, the George Sealy house, northeast corner Avenue J and Twenty-fifth Street, attributed to McKim, Mead, and White, architects, built 1888–89; carriage house, Nicholas J. Clayton, architect, completed 1892. Photographed 1992.

connected with the wealthier residences were placed to the rear of the properties but were frequently approached, and therefore publicly visible, from more than one side, an arrangement that was possible for Galveston residences that were situated on multiple or corner lots. Consequently, there was reason to pay greater attention to the architectural detailing on these structures (and the money to do so) than to their simpler counterparts that were hidden behind a front house on a single lot and accessible only through an alley.

When Jacob Sonnentheil built his flamboyant frame house on the northeast corner of Nineteenth Street and Avenue I in 1886–87, he and his architect were well aware that the two-story carriage house with servants quarters was a major element in the design. The building was placed on the alley corner of the property, with the carriage door opening into Nineteenth Street (figs. 36, 37). Although the facades of the carriage house were unadorned, it had a carved cornice that repeated the cornice of the main house and a patterned multicolored slate roof. A circa 1895 photograph shows an aproned servant and another woman, probably Mrs. Sonnentheil, standing in front of a solid wood fence that separated the main house from the back building.

Fig. 121

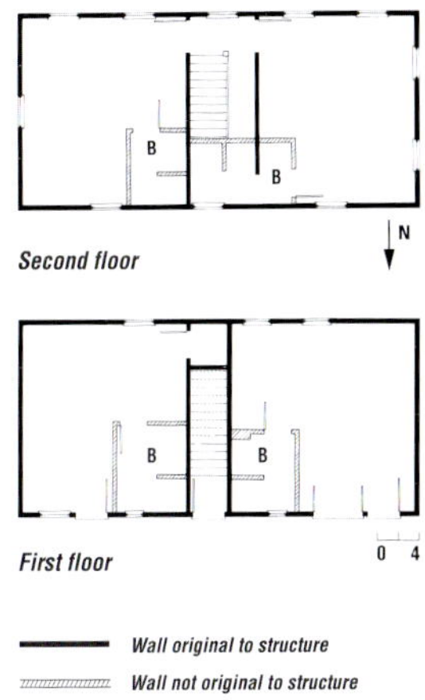

Fig. 122

The floor plan of the Sonnentheil outbuilding (fig. 38) was a standard plan in Galveston. The entrance, which was centrally located on the yard side of the building, opened into a tiny foyer. Rooms on either side of the foyer were devoted to stable and carriage-house functions, and a staircase led to the two-room servants quarters on the second floor.[6]

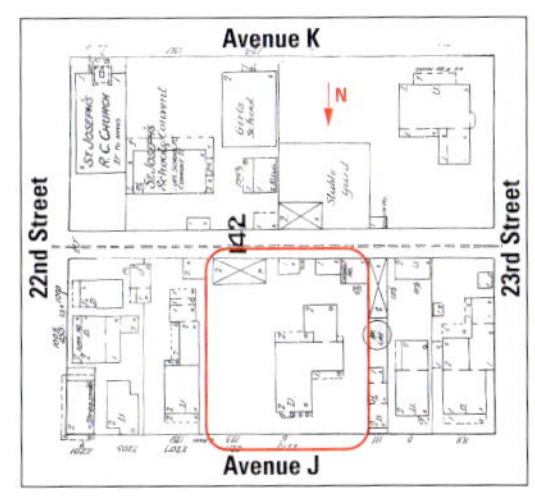

Fig. 124

In 1884, J. F. Smith, hardware merchant and building supplier, used essentially the same floor plan but slightly larger proportions when building the stable and servants quarters for his Italianate house on the south side of Avenue J between Twenty-second and Twenty-third Streets (figs. 121–124). Smith's property, however, was located on the interior of the block rather than the corner. Several other outbuildings were placed along the alley, including a separate carriage house that terminated a carriageway running the length of the property on the west side. In 1900, there were two black servants, a man and a woman, living and working in the household, which consisted of widower Smith, his four sons, and a daughter-in-law.[7]

Fig. 123

J. F. Smith house, 2217 Avenue J, Nathaniel W. Tobey Jr., architect, built 1884.

Fig. 121. Yard-side view of stable and servants quarters. The building has been adapted for use as an office and a bed-and-breakfast. Photographed 1990.

Fig. 122. Floor plans of stable and servants quarters. Documented 1990.

Fig. 123. Stereoscopic view circa 1885. Smith family members are posed at the front entrance; servants are to the side and back, two standing in front of the carriage house.

Fig. 124. 1889 Sanborn insurance map showing a string of buildings along the alley on the Smith property.

While Jacob Sonnentheil was building his house, the towered and slightly eccentric brick residence of merchant Henry Landes was under construction on a double lot on the

Fig. 125

Fig. 126

Henry Landes house, 1602 Avenue E, George E. Dickey and D. A. Helmich, architects, 1887.
Fig. 125. Looking north across the backyard. The flush dormer is on the east facade of the carriage house. Photographed 1991.
Fig. 126. Photograph copied from *Picturesque Galveston* by W. W. Dexter (Galveston: Clarke & Courts, [1900 ?]), p. 82.
Fig. 127. Floor plans of carriage house. Documented 1990.

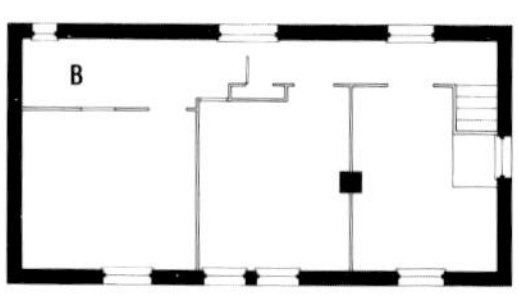

Second floor

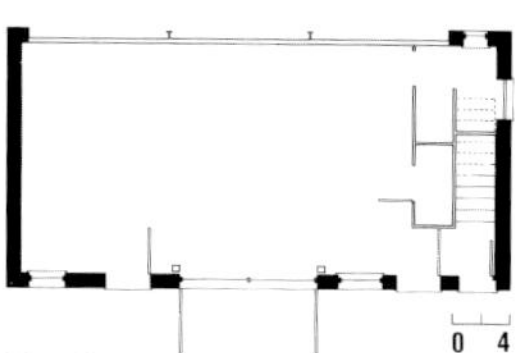

First floor

Fig. 127

northwest corner of Sixteenth Street and Avenue E, on Block 496. (Both Sonnentheil's and Landes's blocks had burned in the 1885 fire.) Brick residences were rare in Galveston, but even more unusual were brick back buildings such as Landes's two-story stable and carriage house, which was placed on the alley line of the inside corner of his property. The primary approach to the Landes carriage house, like Smith's, was a carriageway running the length of the property on the interior side, in this instance, passing under an arbor and servicing a side entry to the house (figs. 125, 126; see also figs. 24, 106, 112, 113).

The floor plan of the Landes carriage house was typical of the period (fig. 127). The first floor was a large space with divisions for horse stalls, as well as a place for a carriage. An enclosed stairwell on the east side of the building led to the second floor, which, according to a Galveston Insurance Board report, originally consisted of two servants' rooms and a hall. Sharing the servants quarters in 1900 were three black servants: fifty-year-old Elsie Mitchell and her two children, twenty-one-year-old George Mitchell and twenty-four-year-old Maude Stanley, whose duties for the seven-member Landes family were those of cook, carriage driver, and laundress, respectively.[8]

In 1899, dredging contractor Charles Clarke began construction of his stuccoed residence on a three-lot parcel on the corner of Eighteenth Street and Avenue I, a short distance from the Sonnentheil and Landes houses. There was, however, an enormous stylistic distance between the two earlier residences and the house that Clarke built twelve years later (figs. 128–130). Clarke situated his carriage house/servants quarters on the lot interior and deviated from the norm by building it of a different material from that of the main house. Although the frame carriage house is almost chaste in appearance, the quoining, wide eaves, and bracketing connect it with the primary structure and hint of the Colonial Revival style. The floor plan shows some similarity to that of the Landes building, but Clarke's structure is much more generous in its proportions and, as noted in the Insurance Board Records, had two closets on the second floor.

Fig. 128

Charles Clarke house, 1728 Avenue I, George B. Stowe, architect, 1899–1900.
Fig. 128. Front-street view. The carriage house is the large opening on the right. Photographed 1990.
Fig. 129. Elevations of carriage house and servants quarters.
Fig. 130. Floor plans of carriage house and servants quarters. Documented 1990.

Fig. 129. South (yard) side.

North (alley) side

0 4

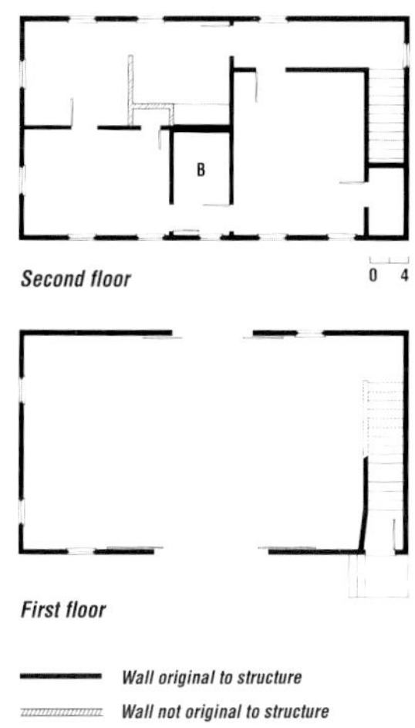

Fig. 130

According to insurance records, Clarke's house was "not complete" in March 1900, but by June 6 it was listed in the *Galveston Daily News* as among "Galveston's New Buildings" and during the summer was photographed for inclusion in *Picturesque Galveston*, a promotional publication. Assuming that Clarke's service building was completed at the same time, it can also be assumed that the four black servants listed in June by the census takers as working in the Clarke household of nine—a typically extended family of children, grandchildren, and a boarder—were living in the back building.[9]

Just who designed these larger carriage houses, servants quarters, and back buildings is not always certain. As the Sealy residence and stable demonstrate, there is no guarantee that the same architect designed the primary structure and the secondary building(s). We

Fig. 131

Fig. 132

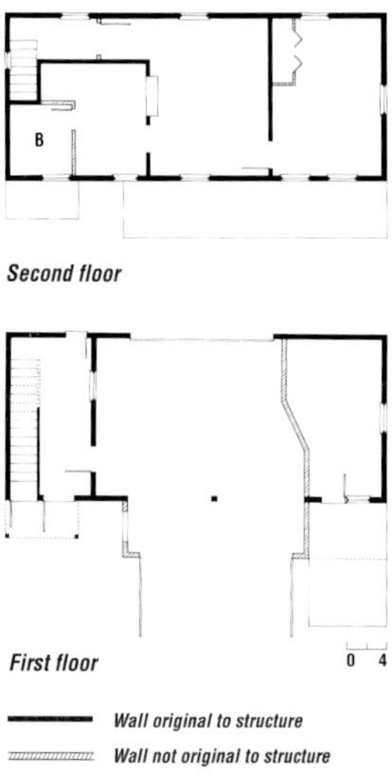

Fig. 133

August J. Henck house, 1412 Avenue I, built 1897.
Fig. 131. Alley view of stable building, looking east. Photographed 1990.
Fig. 132. Detail of 1930 aerial photograph. The Henck property is in the block above the intersection and is the second house to the left of the vacant lot. The Henck back building is very prominent—the stripe on the roof matches the roof of the front house. Sacred Heart Cathedral is in the foreground.
Fig. 133. Floor plans of the stable building. Documented 1990. The first floor was extended on the yard side in 1928 to accommodate a new Cadillac.

know that the architects of the Landes, Smith, and Clarke houses were George E. Dickey and D. A. Helmich, Nathaniel W. Tobey Jr., and George B. Stowe respectively, all of whom had active practices in the Houston and Galveston area.[10] The architect of the Sonnentheil house is unknown. Whether the same architect designed the support buildings in each instance is not documented, but the placement and function of the service buildings are so integral to the properties that it is difficult to imagine their having been designed at a different time.

Most back buildings in Galveston followed a standard form and plan that would have been familiar to contractors and carpenters in the city and were probably built without the services of an architect. In 1897, August J. Henck, real estate and rental agent, built his one-and-a-half-story cottage on an interior lot on the north side of the 1400 block of Avenue I. With its fanciful porch, bay window, and fish-scale detailing, the house was almost as wide as the lot, which was also true of the accompanying two-story stable built on the alley line.

Although Henck's stable was not visible from Avenue I and was strictly a utilitarian structure void of any detailing, its length and height established a formidable presence on the alley, a characteristic of many back buildings in Galveston (figs. 131–133). An enclosed side entrance opened into both the alley and the yard as well as to the stairwell. According to a 1903 Insurance Board report, a stable, harness room, and woodhouse occupied the first floor, while the second floor consisted of three rooms that were "c & pntd," indicating that the rooms were finished with a ceiling and painted. Back buildings such as Henck's were not always inhabited, at least not by servants. When the 1900 census was taken, the only people living at the address were bachelor Henck, his father, and two other older Henck males, probably his uncles.[11]

Many service buildings combined living quarters with carriage-house and stable functions, at least on those properties where owners or residents could afford it. There were, however, other back buildings that were solely residential but had some relation to the front house—as slave or servants quarters, as the residence of a nonrenting family member, or perhaps as the residence of the property owners themselves. These are called *back houses,* and although the distinction between back houses and alley houses can become murky, the distinction is not just one of orientation. It is also one of association: Originally back houses were not intended to be rental property.

Fig. 134. 2020 Avenue J, front house, built 1905. Photographed 1992.

Fig. 135. 2020 Avenue J, back house, alley side. Photographed 1990. Demolished 1996.

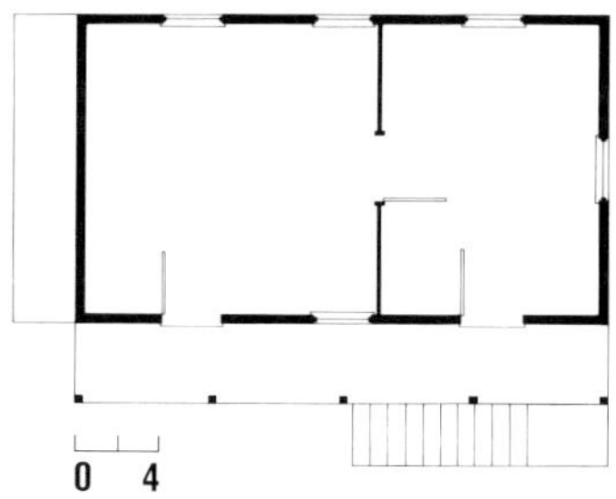

Fig. 136. 2020 Avenue J, back house floor plan. Documented 1990.

Fig. 137. 2020 Avenue J, back house, yard side. Photographed 1990.

One of the earliest building types to be used for back houses was the one-story rectangular cottage with two rooms, often with separate doors opening directly onto an inset or attached gallery. These structures were built before and after the Civil War, and, as Sanborn maps show, the backyards as well as the front yards of Galveston were full of them. It was the house type described by Lucy Shaw in 1839 and bought by Kate Wooden in 1867 (figs. 61, 62). These were also one of the building types most often moved from property to property or shifted on the same property and altered as necessary. Consequently, they can be difficult to date.

The cottage to the rear of 2020 Avenue J is considerably older than the front house, which was built in 1905 (figs. 134–137; see also fig. 2).[12] The 1885 Sanborn map shows a one-story dwelling without a gallery on the back of the property and other galleried cottages and building wings on the block, any number of which could have been moved to this location. The outside stairs on the yard side of the building lead to the dwelling level, consisting of two rooms, each with an entrance opening onto the attached gallery. The interior walls are unfinished single-thickness plank boards. The raised lower level is an undivided space and, on the alley side, a flat wall with large hinged doors.

The two-room back house was built in various forms and proportions over the years. (See fig. 48.) Following the 1885 fire, when Johanna and Conrad Toebleman rebuilt their residence, which was a back house at 1812 Avenue L, they constructed a simple rectangular building with a gabled roof and windows in the gables, a form that could date anywhere from the 1860s into the twentieth century. Originally, the roof pitch ran parallel to the alley, but after the Toeblemans died and the property was sold, the back house was eventually turned and attached to the main house (figs. 57–60). This was not unusual. Back buildings were joined to front houses usually to create an ell, as in this instance, but sometimes they were placed parallel to the front house.

There were two-story back houses in which both floors had always been used for

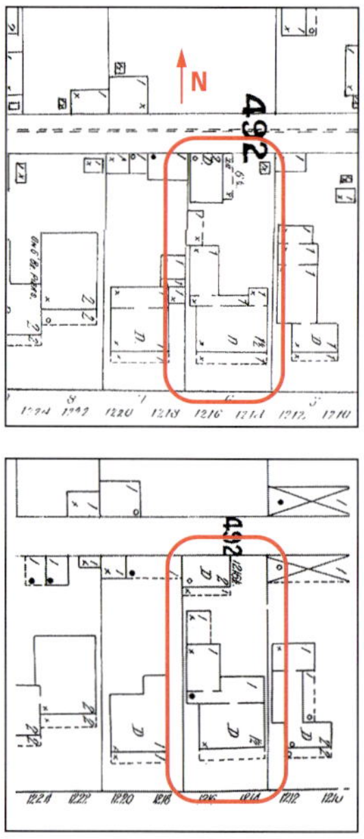

Fig. 138

Figs. 138–140. 1216 Avenue E, back house. On the 1889 Sanborn insurance map (fig. 138, top), the back building is perpendicular to the alley; on the 1912 map (fig. 138, bottom), the building has been turned.

Fig. 139. Back house viewed from across the neighbor's fence. Photographed 1995.

residential purposes, but these were not as common as two-story service buildings where uses such as a stable, carriage house, or kitchen on the first floor were combined with slave or servants quarters on the second. The removal of cooking functions to the main house resulted in the conversion of many two-story service buildings into two-story back houses.

The building at the back of 1216 Avenue E appears to be an example of a two-story structure that was built to accommodate residential use on both floors (figs. 139, 140). The front house is an imposing one-and-a-half-story classical dormer cottage that could have been built shortly after the Civil War. The back house has two rooms on each floor, an interior stairway, and floor-length windows opening onto a suspended balcony on the second story. On the 1889 Sanborn map, the building is perpendicular to the alley, and a double gallery overlooks the side yard, not the back of the house (fig. 138, top). By 1912, it had been turned lengthwise on the alley, which, with the addition of a shed-garage on the east side, made the backyard inaccessible from the alley (fig. 138, bottom).

There are other examples of two-story back houses. In 1888, Nicholas Clayton designed a house for confectioner Rudolph Kruger at 1628 Avenue E on Block 496—the same block on which the Landes family lived. Clayton also designed the only back building on the Kruger property, a compact, two-story, twelve-foot-by-sixteen-foot, one-over-one servants quarters with an enclosed staircase (figs. 141–143; see also figs. 104, 106, 186). In 1900, two black servants, Becky Washington and William Owens, occupied the back house, but not as servants of the Kruger family. The Krugers had moved to a house that they did not own and had rented their property to the Ralstons, a family of seven plus the Ralstons' five boarders.[13] Over the years, the back house at 1628 Avenue E acquired the small, one-story appendage that

Fig. 140. View from across the alley. Photographed 1995.

Mother had help—a Swedish woman who stayed in a spare room in the house. There never was any place in our yard for a dwelling. Not like across the alley. There was just the man there who took care of the property for the Krugers and did different things—carried in the wood, the logs for the stove, stacked those, and did the mopping of the kitchen because it was just bare boards. It was a German family that lived there, named Kruger, and everything was spic and span. The same way this man was, an older man, and he, too, was very neat. As far as any people living there, it was just that particular man. "Servants quarters" they called it. He had the upstairs and the downstairs. **Helen O'Rourke**

Fig. 141

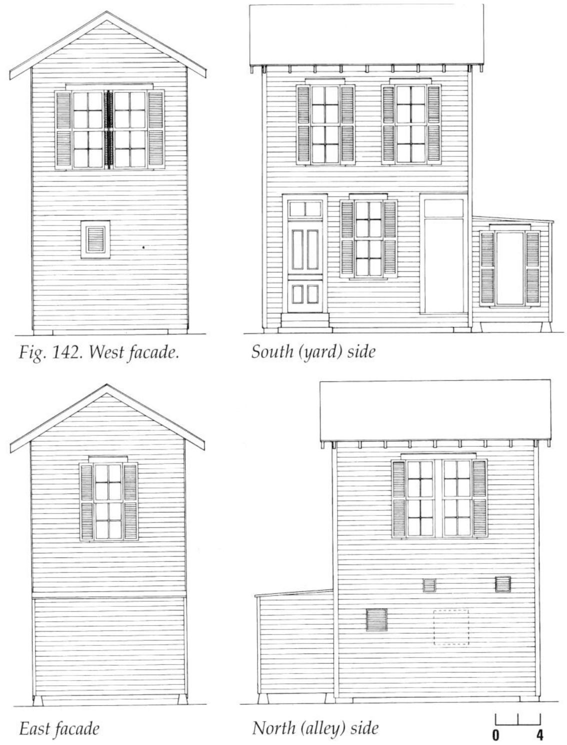

Fig. 142. West facade.

South (yard) side

East facade

North (alley) side

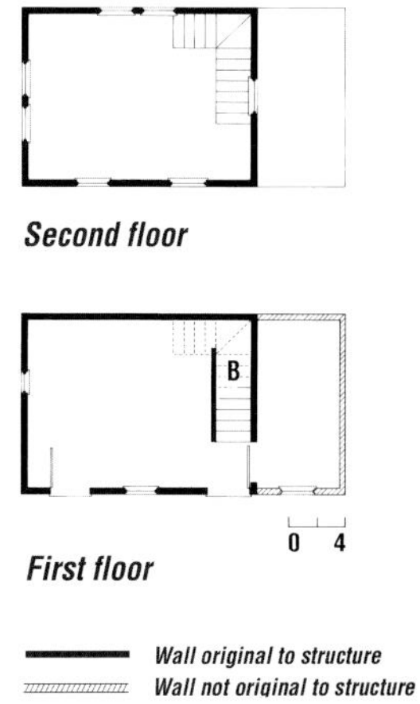

Fig. 143

Rudolph Kruger house, 1628 Avenue E, Nicholas J. Clayton, architect, built 1888.
Fig. 141. Front house. Photographed 1995.
Fig. 142. Elevations of Kruger back house.
Fig. 143. Floor plans of back house. Documented 1990.

is still visible on the east side, and a garage on the west side, which was removed.

One-room, single-story back houses were common in Galveston and probably include many of the smaller unlabeled buildings on the Sanborn maps, as well as many of those labeled "servants rm[s]." The latter ranged anywhere from makeshift structures like the stable in which real estate agent Lucian Minor put a door and window "to make it a servants' room," to finished rectangular or, more likely, square structures with a gabled or hipped roof (fig. 144). The Toeblemans' next-door neighbor, Henry Bautsch, had a "1 Story Servants room" that the insurer valued at $75.[14] As common as these one-room back buildings were, extant examples are most likely to be found when incorporated into or attached to another structure such as an alley house.

Fig. 144. Example of a raised one-room back building. Photographed 1990.

10 Stepping into the Alley: Alley Houses

I had never been in these houses that were built to face the alleys until I married and went with my husband on his calls. . . . I was often struck by the fact that they had nice rugs and furnishings and everything. They just had a regular house. So, one of the things I think I learned is that you really don't judge people by the cover. . . . Some of these were the neatest little homes—very clean, very neat.

Izola Fedford Collins

In contrast to service buildings and back houses that were oriented to a backyard and front house, alley houses were oriented to an alley. Some were owner-occupied, but most were built as rental housing and obviously were profitable or "there wouldn't have been so many," as one Galvestonian observed.[1] There were also service buildings or back houses that were moved to the alley line and adapted for use as alley housing. Because of their size, frequently poor construction, and poor maintenance, alley houses have been susceptible to demolition, relocation, and absorption into other structures.

Fig. 146. Looking across an alley from the porch of an alley house. Photographed 1995.

Although there are many variations to alley houses, they share several basic characteristics: They are oriented to an alley, built of wood, usually one story in their original form, and small. Many were only one or two rooms, such as Eva Lynn's "little 10 x 12 shanty in what is known as the Can alley" as described in 1885 (fig. 26). In December 1899, the city commissioners gave Nicholas Morratti permission to move his "one-room house 8 x 8." Although city minutes do not indicate whether the house was moved from or to an alley, its size matches that of many unlabeled buildings shown situated along the alleys in the Sanborn maps. During a housing inspection campaign in 1914, the *News* described one alley house as a "shack that originally had only one room, but had been cut up into two rooms by a matchboard partition," with the front room measuring about ten feet by twelve feet.[2]

One of the most common types of alley houses had two rooms, the roof pitch running parallel to the alley, and a central entrance flanked by a window on each side. It was the house type described in the 1875 advertisement that hailed: "HOUSEKEEPERS, ATTENTION! For sale at a great sacrifice–ONE SMALL TWO-ROOM HOUSE, New, with fine CISTERN attached, on leased ground, to a cash purchaser."[3] According to records of the Galveston Insurance Board, Sanborn maps, and extant examples, many of these houses measured about twenty-six feet wide, which meant that only one structure could be placed along the alley on a standard lot. It was also the alley house most likely to have multiple additions, the first being a single room that gave an ell shape to the house. The ell might be enclosed and, if space permitted, another room added to the rear.

Fig. 145. Alleyscape with alley houses in block bordered by Twenty-fifth and Twenty-sixth Streets and Avenues L and M. Photographed 1975 by E. Burke Evans.

These two-room houses frequently were placed to the rear of a corner property but turned to face the cross street, not the alley (fig. 147). In this location, the porches were usually larger and more pronounced as facade elements. The houses framed the entrance to the alley and were given a separate cross-street address, even though the property usually was not subdivided. As a result, they assumed an elevated status over their alley-oriented neighbors, which were given the number and street address of the front house along with the label "rear," "alley," or, less commonly, "1/2."

Fig. 147. Houses framing alley corner, west side Fourteenth Street between Avenues K and L. The building on the left, originally a stable with living quarters, has been demolished. Photographed 1981.

The houses on the alley corner at 1112 Twenty-second Street (fig. 148) and on the alley at 1505 Avenue F rear on Block 375 (fig. 109) are variations of the two-room house. The former is typical of many alley houses, but does not qualify as such because of its orientation to the cross street. In April 1893, an inspector of the Galveston Insurance Board noted that the twenty-six-foot-by-fourteen-foot, two-room house at 1112 Twenty-second Street was to be enlarged with a thirteen-foot-by-sixteen-foot addition and "occupied by Tenant." Eventually, another thirteen-foot-by-six-foot section was built in the ell (figs. 149, 150). At the time the additions were made, the house was one of three rental units on the lot, all owned by the estate of grocer Peter Gengler.[4]

The evolution of the house at 1505 Avenue F rear is not as easily determined. The original two-room house, which measured eighteen feet by fifteen feet, was probably built in the late nineteenth century but was moved to its present site either from another location on the same lot or from a different property. The house has multiple additions and now consists of four rooms and a bathroom. The present owner, who has lived on the property since the late

Fig. 148

Fig. 149

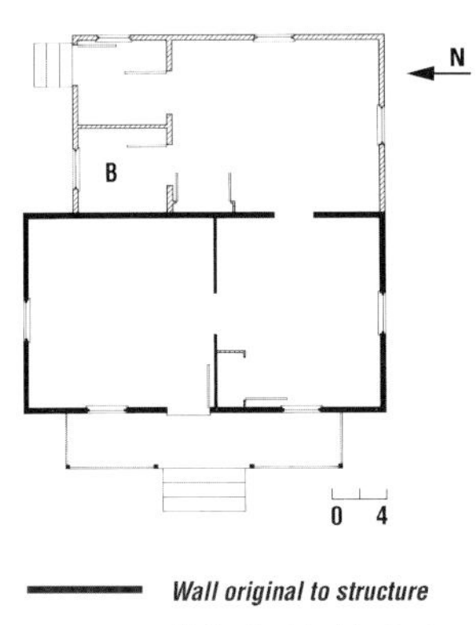

Fig. 150

1112 Twenty-second Street, built 1870s, enlarged 1893. Situated on an alley corner (fig. 148), the house faces the cross street. Photographed 1995. The double gable (fig. 149) is a common profile on small houses in Galveston and usually denotes two sections that were built at different times or were moved and joined. Photographed 1990. The two front rooms (fig. 150) were the original house. Floor plan documented 1990.

1940s—originally as a renter—moved the house away from the alley line to allow space for plantings and a larger porch than is usual for alley houses (fig. 178).[5]

Another familiar alley-house form was the two-room house with the gable turned to the alley and the entrance placed in the gable end (figs. 48, 163). The outside measurements of these houses are essentially the same as those at 1505 Avenue F rear and 1112 Twenty-second Street, but the proportions are very different, including a steeper roof pitch. Basically, this was the same house type built by Johanna and Conrad Toebleman, but once again, their nomenclature is determined by placement and orientation (figs. 59, 60). They may be among the alley houses that are marked "1 1/2," indicating the number of stories, on the Sanborn maps. With windows in the gables, some residents of these houses converted the attic area into a usable and perhaps finished space.

Dormered cottages—in fact, diminutive versions of the front house on the Toebleman property—were also among the "1 1/2"-story houses on the Sanborn maps and were probably among the earliest houses built or placed along the alleys. This may have been the house type that auctioneer A. F. James was selling in December 1847 when he advertised a "STORY AND HALF BUILDING . . . on the alley."[6] The dormered cottage at 1515 Avenue L rear appeared at its present location on the 1889 Sanborn map, the same year in which the Insurance Board records state that the house was rebuilt (figs. 151, 152). It may be an example of a house that originally fronted the main street and was moved to the back of a lot to make room for a larger front house. Then, as now, the house was situated several feet from the alley line and straddled lots four and five. The house consists of four rooms, a narrow enclosed stairwell, one large space on the second floor, and a later bathroom enclosure on the south porch.

Fig. 151. 1515 Avenue L rear. The bathroom and water heater are the enclosures on the right. Photographed 1990.

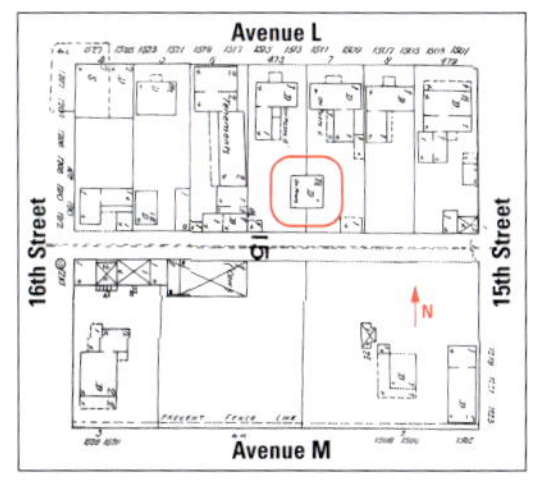

Fig. 152. 1889 Sanborn insurance map showing 1515 Avenue L rear situated on the property line of two lots. Note the "Tenements" next door and the large cow stable and open lot to the south.

If the six listings—five black women and one white man—in the 1901–2 city directory are any indication, 1515 Avenue L rear was full of renters. But it could also be an incorrect address, a not unusual occurrence: 1517 Avenue L rear, the property next door, is labeled "Tenements" on the 1889 Sanborn map. The owner of 1515 Avenue L, widow Helen Schwarzbach, lived in one of her front houses during the 1880s and 1890s but, by 1901–2, had moved to the 1600 block of Avenue L, although she, and then her estate, retained ownership of the 1500 block property through 1909.[7]

The three-room alley house can usually be equated with the shotgun house, or "commissary" house, as it is known in Galveston (figs. 55, 78). This long, narrow house type, with the primary entrance on the gable end and a floor plan of two or three successive rooms and no hall, was ideal for the city's long, narrow lots.[8] The building type clearly appears on the alleys in the 1885 bird's-eye view and on the 1885 Sanborn map, but it was the 1900 hurricane that swelled its numbers and secured its local nomenclature. Most shotgun houses in Galveston were built as single detached units, two of which could fit easily on a standard lot. Some attached multiple units were also built, such as the double unit that grocer James Cross built on the alley of his property on the southwest corner of Sixteenth Street and Avenue B (figs. 68, 69), and the triple units with a covered passageway connecting the alley

Fig. 153. 2808 and 2810 Avenue L, front houses, built 1908. Photographed 1995.

Fig. 154. 2810 Avenue L rear, east facade, built 1908. The alley is on the right. Photographed 1995.

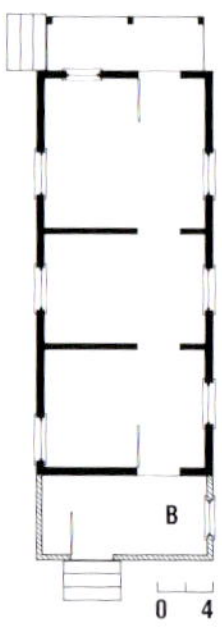

Fig. 155

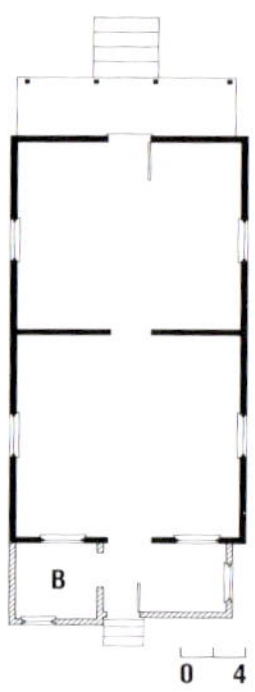

Fig. 156

Fig. 155. 2818 Avenue L rear, floor plan of three-room commissary or shotgun house. Documented 1995. (For photograph see fig. 55.)

Fig. 156. 2810 Avenue L rear, floor plan of two-room commissary or shotgun house. Documented 1995.

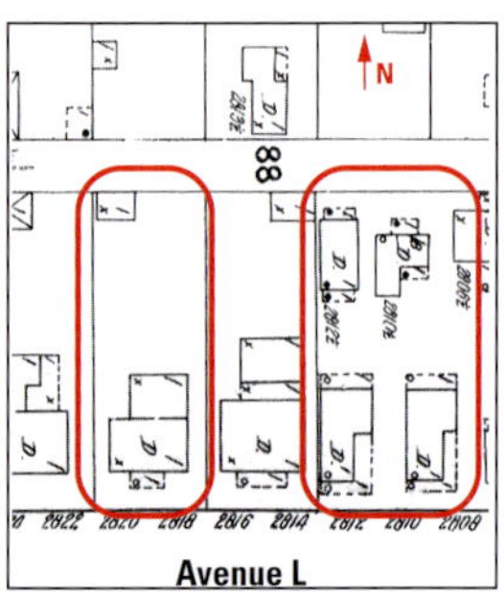

Fig. 157. 1912 Sanborn insurance map. The circled houses on the right are the front and back houses at 2808 and 2810 Avenue L. There was no house as yet at the rear of the property at 2818 Avenue L (left).

and lot interior that contractor Robert Palliser built on his properties in Ward Five (fig. 73).

Galveston alleys are full of houses that, in theory, were built as temporary structures to meet emergency needs but, in reality, contributed to the next generation of alley housing. Following the 1885 fire, the *News* reported that "the houses being hastily thrown up are of a character designed merely to afford temporary shelter, and be subsequently used for outhouses when more permanent structures can be erected." After the 1900 hurricane, the Central Relief Committee provided financial assistance to build 1,583 houses, most of which were probably commissary houses that, "being substantially erected, can be made part of more convenient residences whenever the owner becomes able to build."[9] Instead, as documented in the records of the grade-raising project that followed the 1900 hurricane, some of these cottages, like some of the "temporary" shelters resulting from the 1885 fire, found their way to the alleys to become permanent alley houses.

One such example may be the three-room shotgun house at 2818 Avenue L rear (fig. 155; see also fig. 55). Insurance Board records state that the front house, a worker's cottage, was built in 1871 and owner-occupied, an arrangement that has not changed. The rear dwelling, however, is not accounted for until a later pasteover on the 1912 edition of the Sanborn map, suggesting that its construction predated its placement on this lot in Block 88.

Two lots to the east, at 2810 Avenue L rear, is a two-room shotgun house (figs. 154, 156) that was probably built on site as part of a rental complex owned by David Rossi, an agent for the Houston Ice & Brewery Co. Rossi bought lots nine and ten in 1908; one year later, he was assessed not only for the land but also for improvements valued at $800, which, according to the 1912 Sanborn map, included the two-room shotgun house on the alley and two front houses on lot ten (figs. 153, 157). The front houses were variations of the same house type but larger with hipped roofs and ell-shaped porches. By the time the 1911–12 directory was assembled, Rossi had rented his house at "rear 2810 L" to Amanda White, one of thirteen alley addressees, all black, on Block 88. No one was listed at a 2818 alley address.[10]

A commissary house is just one room after another. Built as commissaries, places for quick shelter for people. Plenty of them around. They were meant, built, so they could be added onto, really. Putting one next to another or putting one halfway down into the side of another one or rooms added onto them.

Robert M. Tucker

Fig. 158. 2621 Avenue K, front house. Photographed 1995.

Fig. 159 (and figs. 160, 161). 2621 Avenue K rear. Photographed 1995.

Many alley houses are an amalgamation of one- to three-room houses or sections of buildings (such as the wing of a house) that were moved and connected to make a larger dwelling. The house at 1511 Avenue F rear on Block 375 is one example (frontispiece, fig. 109). Insurance Board records and Sanborn maps document that two units, a three-room commissary house and a two-room house, were moved to the lot after 1912 and connected in 1968.

The alley house at 2621 Avenue K was originally two separate dwellings (figs. 159–161; see also fig. 3). The main section that fronts the alley was a one-room square house with a hipped roof and a fireplace, that was probably the building on the east side of the lot marked "D" on the 1899 Sanborn map. At some time, the square building was moved, and a two-room house with a gabled roof was attached to the structure on the yard side. The resulting ell was enclosed and extended four feet from the front plane of the building, creating a house with four rooms and a narrow bathroom.

It is unlikely that very many alley houses were originally built as two stories with separate living units on each floor. However, the number of two-story, two-unit alley houses (such as the one in which the Millicans lived—see figs. 9, 10) increased with time as one-story alley houses were raised to create a second unit, and as more and more two-story service buildings, such as those with a carriage house or kitchen on the first floor and living quarters on the second, were converted to residential use on both floors and reoriented to the alley.

The two-story alley house became more practicable in the early twentieth century when the Seawall and the raising of the island provided greater protection against flooding, and city ordinances required that the lower level be floored for sanitary reasons. Most two-story alley houses that began as single-story buildings are easily discernible. The lower or first-floor level usually exhibits fewer details and rougher construction than the upper level, which was the original building (fig. 163).

Tenements were another building type associated with alley housing in Galveston, although they were neither confined to alleys nor always distinguishable from other building forms. For example, on the 1885 Sanborn map, there are three small ell-shaped detached houses marked "Tenements" fronting Fat Alley (fig. 4), while on the block bounded by Avenues J and K and Twenty-seventh and Twenty-eighth Streets, there is a lot with three small, detached dwellings in single file from front street to alley that are marked "Negro Tenements." Obviously, the term "tenement" was applied loosely, because there were other, more distinctive tenement buildings indicated on the Sanborn maps. These had one or two stories and could be several shapes: a single row of connected units that ran parallel to the alley line and sometimes crossed property lines; a bulky, box-shaped building that usually filled the width of a single lot; or a long, narrow structure that abutted a front building and extended to the alley (fig. 162).

On Block 375 is a three-unit building on the alley that is similar in form to the tenement

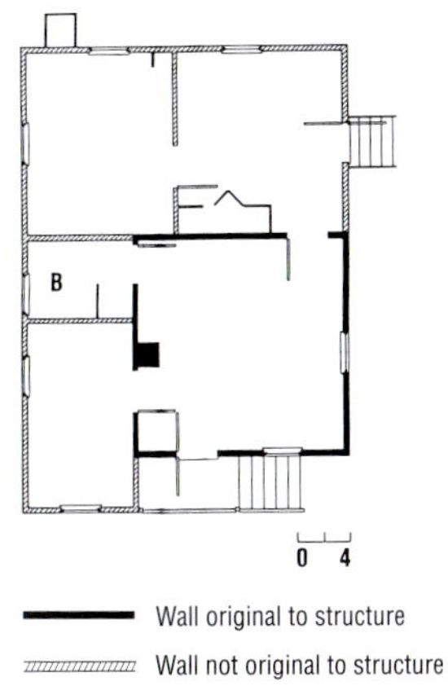

Fig. 160

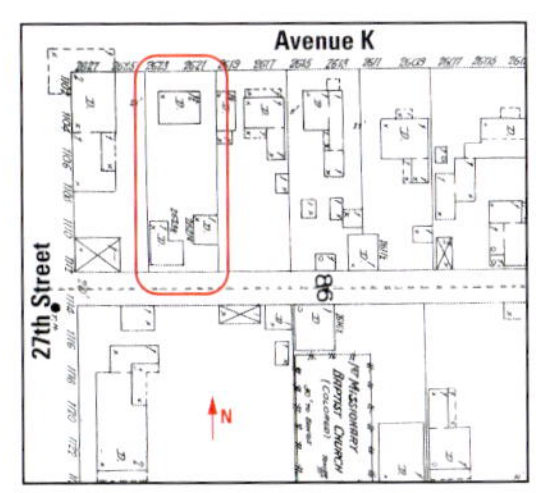

Fig. 161

Fig. 159. Yard side looking west. This part of the house has two rooms. The small enclosure on the right houses the water heater. (See fig. 3 for view of alley side.)
Fig. 160. Floor plan. The house consists of two separate buildings that were joined: a square, hipped-roof structure on the front side and a two-room gabled-roof structure to the back. The ell was enclosed. Documented 1995.
Fig. 161. 1899 Sanborn insurance map showing two separate back houses on the property.

Fig. 162. Example of multi-storied rear tenement. The one-story wing on the front house may originally have been a separate back building. Front and rear structures demolished. Photographed 1991.

rows that appear on the early Sanborn maps (frontispiece, figs. 109, 115). According to the Insurance Board records, these "apartment" units were built in 1944, each with two rooms, a bath, and a door and window on the alley side. The city's first building code, adopted in 1914, differentiated between a "tenement" and an "apartment." In tenements, inhabitants lived independently but shared all or some of "the halls, stairways, yards, water closets or privies." In apartments, three or more households lived independently.[11]

There was a hierarchy in alley housing just as there was for service buildings. On the bottom were the structures that the local newspapers called "shack," "shanty," "cabin," "hovel," and "rookery," terms that were more allusive—and derisive—than descriptive. But Galvestonians knew what was meant. These structures were defined more by condition and size than by building type and constituted the city's poorest housing, whether they were on a front street or an alley.

References to alley houses usually were made in the context of either demanding or applauding their removal, as when the *News* reported new developments at the intersection of Avenue D and Nineteenth Street in April 1880:

> *On the southwest corner of the alley a two-story building of very imposing appearance has been very recently finished and yet unoccupied. It is a frame house, which . . . adds greatly to the appearance of the corner, and hides the ugliness of the frail wooden structures in the rear. On the opposite corner lot . . . a foundation of a good sized brick building is being laid. The small wooden shanties which were on this lot have been removed, and in a short while that corner will bear a very respectable appearance.*[12]

Disasters gave the newspapers—and the citizens—an excuse to attack the poorest housing in the city. Although not directly stated, this included alley housing. The *News* credited, for example, the 1885 fire with clearing away "all the hovels and dilapidated shanties that had so long infested the neighborhood" in which the fire originated, an area that contained a high concentration of alley dwellings, including those built by James Cross.[13] (See figs. 68, 69.)

Documenting the builders of alley houses is even more difficult than discovering those who designed the larger, more elaborate carriage houses and back buildings. Some alley houses were built, or existing structures made habitable, by their occupants or the property owners, especially after the Civil War and in times of emergency.

Many alley houses were built by the never-ending flow of transient laborers who stayed in Galveston for short periods of time and worked at whatever jobs they could find. Eugene Marshall is an example. He arrived in Galveston early in December 1859, and during the forty-four days he stayed on the island, worked on construction crews that built a stable, a two-story house, and a kitchen. For one day, he worked, with little success, as a writer at the newspaper. On January 10, 1860, he noted in his diary the arrival of "a new recruit of 20 carpenters offering to work at 1.25 per day Mr Dillard who is rooming with me is almost fighting mad on the subject." Many of these men did not stay long enough in Galveston to be listed in a city directory, much less a census. Marshall decided to "become rich by degrees" and return to his native Minnesota, where he owned property and had "character and standing."[14]

Fig. 163. Two alley house types. On the right is an example of a house with the gable turned toward the alley. Demolished in 1995. The house on the left is typical of many two-story alley houses that were originally one-story, then raised to accommodate a second unit on the lower level. Photographed 1990.

There were a lot of alley houses just one room, and everything happened in that room. On one side was a cookstove and then, a little table and a bed and a wash basin and the other thing they called a "slop jar."

The Rev. James B. Thomas

On October 3, 1875, the *News* published its annual report of building activities in the city. The paper estimated that "250 houses of all kinds" had been built in the preceding year and listed the architects, contractors, and owners for the larger dwellings and cottages with front-street addresses. Alley houses and their builders probably were among those lumped together in the single paragraph summarizing "small cottages" and "mere cabins."

> *The remaining one hundred and twenty-four to make up the number of houses of all kinds that have been erected during the past twelve months are mainly small cottages, some of them mere cabins, yet they are inhabited and form a portion of the taxable property of the city. Owing to the fact that many of these small cottages and tenements were put up by the day or by journeymen carpenters, no clue could be obtained to the owners, and as the cost in the majority of cases could only be approximated, the plan was adopted of making a general summary of their value, which may be safely set down at $60,000.*[15]

The building of alley houses was not confined to transient laborers. Some were built by skilled carpenters who were or who became permanent residents of the city. Before the Civil War, they included slaves like the "No. 1 Bricklayer and Plasterer" who was advertised for hire in 1857 and the slaves who were owned by builders listed in the 1860 census. These are individuals who also remain nameless in the history of Galveston. After the Civil War, the builders of alley houses would have included former slaves like carpenter and cabinetmaker Horace Scull, who "in the early days of freedom carpentered and built many houses for the ex-slaves, nearly all on leased ground." The list of carpenters, brick masons, painters, and plasterers who worked with Scull included both blacks and whites who appeared in the city directories and census records over the years.[16]

Scull was among those blacks who prospered in the midst of blatant efforts to keep "freedmen mechanics from being encouraged to settle in our city and compete with worthy white mechanics."[17] Building alley housing, especially on a single-structure basis, however, may have been viewed by whites as permissible construction work for black carpenters and laborers because it was predominantly housing for blacks and was among the least expensive housing in the city.

Builders and contractors probably built alley houses when constructing the front

---

Living in an Alley House

You didn't worry about a front house in those years, '39 and '40. If you lived in the rear, you didn't care, you know. That was all right. It didn't make any difference if it was a front house or a back house or what we called "in the alley." I didn't worry about that. . . . People didn't worry about living in the alley. It was nice and clean. They kept things nice and clean, so it was no problem.

Fig. 164. Annie Mae Charles, née Fiedler. The photograph was taken in 1936, the year Charles moved to Galveston.

When they say "shotgun," they mean straight through. Some of them had only about three rooms. You didn't worry about a living room and all this kind of stuff. We lived in one. That was between Forty-third and Forty-second, and Avenue I, in the rear. It was up high, raised high. . . . You had to go up steps. I think nine of us lived there, and it was two bedrooms and a kitchen, and out on the side, that's where the commode was attached.

It was my cousin, Elzina Scurry, and her husband, Mitchell Scurry. She was my cousin and we all lived together. She had two children. They had five with her brother-in-law, and me and my two brothers, so that was eight, and then my mother would come and stay, oh, a month at a time, and that would make it nine sometimes. . . . That was the funniest thing. All four of us slept in the bed together. You couldn't do that now. I mean that was just a double bed and we got king-sized beds now. Nobody was worried about it. You slept good, got up the next morning, and went on to work.

I been thinking to myself, where did we put our clothes? I can't remember chest of drawers. I don't know. And we were clean all the time and we had clothes to put on to wear to church. What you did in that corner over there in that bedroom, you took a broomstick and put it across there and then you hung your clothes there. You put it at a diagonal. You'd hang your clothes up and you'd make you something to drape over it,

---

houses on a lot, especially when the front houses were speculative or rental housing. Contractor Robert Palliser built alley housing, at least on property that he owned and developed in Ward Five (figs. 73, 99). Whether he built alley housing for other landlords is uncertain, but the similarity between the alley houses on his property and on adjoining properties suggests that he did, or that some of his buildings were situated on land he leased from other property owners.

Like Palliser's alley houses, many back buildings along the alleys in Galveston were duplicated, but with all the alterations, additions, adaptations, and relocations, few, if any, retained their original form. There was—and is—a tremendous variety to the alley houses, service buildings, and back houses. The same can also be said about the alleys: Although two distinctive alleyscapes developed in the residential areas, no two alleys were ever alike. As Galvestonians often remark, "There was another whole world on the alleys." It was a world created not only by the people but also by the compactness and the density of the buildings and the spaces that they occupied.

---

like a curtain or something. It was no problem. I was thinking of where we put our underwear. Where did we put our undershirts and panties and all that? I can't remember.

When people came to visit, we would sit in the bedroom. I was wondering the other day, how many chairs did we have? When we stayed on Forty-second and between Winnie and Church [Avenues G and F], we had a living room then, and we had this porch, you know, we could sit on this porch. . . . We moved from that little house to that larger house. . . . We had three bedrooms there and a kitchen and a living room, but the toilet was outside, the flush thing was outside. We still had to take the baths in that kitchen in a tub. We didn't have a bathroom.

In the '30s and '40s, a lot of black people lived together. . . . We didn't pay but $9 a month rent, but that was like pulling your eye tooth out to get that. See, me and my cousin were working for about $3 a week. You have to pay your rent out of that and then buy your food, clothes and the what-not. . . . I never have paid no higher than $14 for rent and I lived from '36 to '46 or '47, and the highest I ever paid was $14 . . . on Fortieth and Broadway.

We walked everywhere. Can't walk to the corner now. Our church is right down on the corner of I, and after church, we'd walk from there to the beach, Thirty-ninth and Beach. Didn't think nothing about it. We didn't buy a car until 1960.

You used the alley just like you did the front street. You thought nothing about it. You put on your clothes, you came out through the alley, went to church, wherever you had to go. Everybody had a car to pick you up, they came in the alley and picked you up. You never was ashamed. You just said, "Well, I live at 4210 Church rear." You didn't say nothing about it. I don't know what people think about it now. . . . Some people don't want to say that they living in the back.

Annie Mae Charles

11 Speaking of Alleys and Back Buildings . . .

It takes a special kind of person to enjoy sitting in an alley, don't you think?

Alfreda Houston

The alleys and back buildings of Galveston offer endless possibilities for discovery because their spaces are filled with the lives of those who have lived in them and those who give their history and their use a continuity. From the city's founding well into the 1960s, there were few Galvestonians who "just weren't into alleys" at least sometime during their childhood or adult years.[1] Some, like Bill Millican and Annie Mae Charles, knew the alleys as residents. Others knew the alleys as observers or as daily users.

In many ways, the voices describing the alleys and back buildings in the twentieth century could be the voices of nineteenth-century Galvestonians. But while these voices depict a daily life that in many respects has hardly changed for decades, they also document that the alleys and back buildings are constantly being adapted to changes around them and are as integral to the evolution and history of the city as the larger structures on the front streets.

Whatever their age and color, Galvestonians share the history of their city's alleys and back buildings. The recollections of one person, however, may seemingly contradict those of another. This does not mean that one is correct and the other is not. Rather, people's experiences as well as their vantage point will differ. The alleys and back buildings can also symbolize different things to different people, even different things at different times to the same person.[2]

Just Walking, Wandering Around, Looking

There are several reasons why the Clouser brothers Ernest and Gerald have been familiar with alley life in Galveston from the time they were children in the 1920s. Their childhood home, owned by their parents John and Hazel Clouser, was located at 1415 Thirty-sixth Street, on an alley corner (figs. 166, 167). That location gave them, says Ernest Clouser, "a command—a twenty-four-hour view—of the entrance to the alley." In the 1920s, their father, a school teacher, began his lifelong crusade to improve the health and living conditions of black Galvestonians. The Clouser children, including a third older brother, John, often accompanied their father on his surveys of the city as well as on his calls as a representative of the Atlanta Life Insurance Company.[3]

Fig. 166. Hazel Zachary Clouser, John H. Clouser, and their sons (left to right): Ernest Z., Gerald Z., and John Z. Photograph circa 1932.

An interview with Ernest Clouser, the middle brother, follows.

I was born in 1922, and began roaming the streets and the alleys of Galveston like '27, '28, and '29. It was one of the pastimes, just walking, wandering around, looking. We had the run of the whole city, but we had to be in by the nine o'clock whistle. There was, at the waterworks on Avenue H, a big whistle—whoooo—at nine o'clock. That was a curfew.

Fig. 165. Alley between Avenues D and E, looking east from alley corner at Twelfth Street. This is the alley behind the Lasell house at 1122 Avenue E described in the interviews with Inez Lasell and her son Danny. Photographed 1995.

Galveston had pretty well-kept alleys. The alleys were fairly safe. Not well lighted, of course. Even the streets were not well lighted. People accepted that. Many people went to bed early, but people who were up after nine o'clock, they'd go through dark alleys. Nobody would bother them. But I'm speaking in a limited way. If you were a woman, I guess, you would have seen it differently.

Large animals were quite prevalent all over town. There were a few riders in the evenings, saddle up and ride, but during working hours, from early morning until after five, mules and horses were used as working animals—pulling wagons. They were well cared for. The owners just came on through the alleys, opened the double gates, pulled on in, put some hay on the ground, unbridled them and the horses stood up all night and ate hay. Our next-door neighbor, Uncle Gunner [Walton], had a horse. Jetta was the horse's name. He kept the horse long after he had bought a car, but I remember him with a horse and a wagon. Even after he got the car, he would still go see about Jetta—in the alley. I used to pet Jetta.

Fig. 167. Clouser residence, 1415 Thirty-sixth Street, where the family had "a command—a twenty-four-hour view—of the alley." The entrance to the alley is on the right.

There were the policy shops in the alleys. A fellow, they called him "Strawberry," was down in our alley. They used nicknames and aliases then. I never did know his name. Mr. Strawberry. He had just a little hut. They had a little kerosene heater in there—year-round. They had a drawing Monday through Saturdays. Daily drawings—a twelve o'clock drawing and a five o'clock drawing, and I think he wrote for two wheels. . . . He didn't live in that hut. That was the office. People frequented that. Came in, gave him the numbers, he wrote them down, gave you a copy, those were your numbers, and you paid him off. And you came back after the drawings. After the twelve o'clock drawing, you'd see him walking back with a sack, and you'd go in and ask for the list. He'd have a list of numbers that came out in the drawing. You'd examine the list against your numbers. Any of your numbers came out on the list, you'd win. He'd pay you right out of that sack. But you didn't win much. Nobody won, really. . . . and people just played themselves broke. It kept many people broke and hungry and ragged because they played numbers every day.

I knew several policy houses. There was one up there on Thirtieth in the alley, in the 3300 block of M 1/2. Mr.—I knew his name well—Mr. Ernest. He had one of those little huts. They were six by six, something like that. Six by four, six by ten. Just large enough. One door, one window, one little desk, one seat, one waiting seat, one bulletin where he put the list. . . . Kind of a slant roof. Some had a little stoop, one or two steps up.

There was never any trouble at all, never that I know of, with the policy shops. But now, the whiskey stills . . . There was a whiskey still that was raided in our alley. You could smell whiskey on the ground. It flowed like water in the rain. . . . There was a lot of it made in the alleys. We called it bootleg whiskey. Lot of it in Galveston. . . . The medical students knew how to do it.

I don't know of any stores in the alleys. No beer joints that I know of were in the alleys. Mechanics, auto mechanics. I knew of one or two charcoal shops in the alleys. Charcoal was used as a heating fuel. You could get a bag of charcoal, a ten- or fifteen-pound bag for ten or fifteen cents. They bought it from someone else. They were retailing it.

The vendors used to go in and out of alleys and then, the sounds in the alleys, you know, like a fish man. If he were walking, he'd have a burlap sack with fish in it or crabs and he would have a funny way he would intone. You'd know that's the fish man and you could hear him a block away—[sing-song sound]. The junk man had another call and you'd know that's the junk man.

Several junk men come through and this wasn't just blacks. It was a white business, too. Some very prominent people started out that way. . . . The garbage, the city sanitation people [were in the alleys]. There was the driver, one horse, a single-horse, two-wheel wagon, and he'd get down and pitchfork, throw it up on that wagon, get back up there, and go to the next one.

Jack Johnson, the world heavyweight champ, and his family lived in the alley behind West Point Baptist Church, in the 3000 block of Avenue M. That was before he attained fame.

When I was an insurance agent in the '40s, the condition of the alleys was fairly good. Steps were good, some of them were painted, clean, throw rugs, furniture, fan. You know, they were employed. They had some kind of work. They either rented or they were servants.

Fig. 168

In 1948, Ernest Clouser moved to Houston where he taught school and served as principal of Paul Lawrence Dunbar Elementary School until retiring in 1980.

Here's the Famous Alley Life

The youngest Clouser brother, Gerald, was born in 1927 and has always lived in Galveston, except when he attended college and served in the Merchant Marines. In 1994, Gerald Clouser retired after teaching vocational classes in the public schools for forty years.

Pointing to a photograph taken in the late 1930s by his father, Gerald Clouser says: "Here is how we lived. I mean, it was so far below standard it was pitiful. Here's the famous alley life. Here's the alley right behind the existing Post Office."(See figs. 168, 169.)

Fig. 169

Alley views photographed in late 1930s by John H. Clouser. Fig. 168. Alley between Avenues F and G and probably Twenty-eighth and Twenty-ninth Streets, looking east toward the Federal Post Office and Custom House. Fig. 169. An unidentified alley but in the same area. Much of the area is now vacant land.

The rent was cheaper in the alley house or the garage apartment or the back house. It was always cheaper than on the front street. Now, we could live on the front streets, could rent on the front streets, could buy on the front streets, but it was an economic problem. Many of us didn't have enough money to live on the front streets. Didn't have enough money to buy on the front streets.

During the Depression, and I'm talking about all the way up to 1940 or '41, people who were employed and had a little education and a little clout and any industrial job, could have black servants for $2 a week and, of course, many of them did. And, of course, the black servants used to say, "Well, I got to stay in that house because for $2 a week I can't live anywhere else and ride the trolley or walk to this work." And many of them wanted the black servants to be what you call live-in servants, on call all the time and everything else. So the black servants used to want *to live on the premises and be connected to their utilities. And, of course, some of those back houses had inside toilets, but most of them didn't have a bathtub in them.*

Now, land in Galveston was very valuable until they expanded the island. The city limits used to stop at Fifty-seventh, at Fifty-ninth, and they used to talk about how expensive land was and very few blacks could buy any land. They didn't start buying land on a large scale until about the '40s. . . . We were feeling the effects of the war and the prosperity of the war around '39 and '40. . . . We started shipping a lot out of here. . . . We used to have all kind of factories here. . . . [but] those were jobs that we didn't get, only a little of it was black skill. Blacks couldn't buy houses on the front street with those kind of jobs, but after '41, blacks were able to get good industrial jobs. . . . Listen, 1940, '41, we were able to just get better jobs. They needed us. They flat needed us, and opportunities started unfolding and we were able to buy on the front street and wouldn't buy in the alleys.

Fires were a real problem in the alleys. They used to call them "chimbley fires.". . . People were burning anything they could get. Of course, wood was fuel then. I can remember as a kid, a side hustle for me to make a little money—I sold kindling. Would load it up in a cart and sell it. . . . I'd go through the neighborhoods and alleys selling kindling wood for about fifty cents a bundle.

They peddled fish, wood, charcoal. The peddlers were black and white and some of them were something else. I think we used to think they was gypsies or something. We didn't know what they were. We used to say, "Well, they're not black and they're not white. What are they?" And they also used to say, "They're gypsies." Well, I didn't know what a gypsy was except maybe what we would call an Arab today. . . . They could be just anything but they would always say, "Gypsy."

There was a lot of prostitution, gambling joints, and fish fry houses—just any kind of hustling you could come up with in these alleys. Black and white, and transient rooms. . . . I can remember little home laundries in the alleys. . . . They'd have about five tubs: you wash; then you boil; then you washed and rubbed; then you went to this one, that's first rinse; second rinse, don't forget bluing was used; then, finally, the last one was clean rinse. Well, that's the biggest problem with the home laundry—where to throw the water. So many of those yards kind of looked like an old mud slop place, but some of the people built trenches and channeled it all out to a drain.

Everything had a odor. All those old outhouses had a odor. And the sulphur. And people used to burn rags and sulphur to run the flies and mosquitoes away. And they was always cooking with hog lard. That had a odor. You could smell that old coffee plant which was on Thirty-ninth and Avenue N all the way up to here. And then a pickle plant, sauerkraut plant, all kind of stuff. Bake shops all around here.

My father did that survey trying to prove to the world that Galveston, one of the oldest entry cities of the Texas coast . . . had the worst slum in the world for us. He was trying to disprove this old myth you could hear from time to time, people say, "Galveston was always different from other places. We got along good here. Blacks did fine here. Blah, blah, blah, blah, blah." Well, we didn't have plantations here and, of course, that made some people think we were better off.

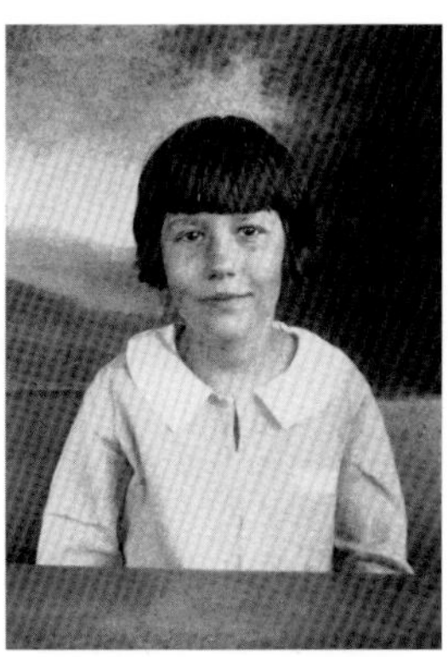

Fig. 170. Inez Rather Lasell, circa 1930.

The Noise Was Terrible

Inez Lasell became acquainted with Galveston alleys and back buildings in the same era the Clouser brothers did. When she was a child, Lasell would travel with her mother, her brother, and a sister from Gonzales, Texas, to Galveston to spend several weeks with her aunt, Tommie Gill, who lived at 1818 Avenue J. Lasell eventually moved to Galveston as a permanent resident. It was the noises of the city that impressed the eight-year-old girl in 1930 (fig. 170).

For a country girl, the noise was terrible. Broadway [Avenue J] was a loud street. A scissors and knife sharpener man came down the alley. You could hear his whistle a block away. . . . He'd blow that loud, piercing whistle to announce his arrival. If you needed something done, the maid went trotting out the back door with whatever it was and stopped him, and if it was a pan or a pot to be mended, he just stopped there in the middle of the alley and worked on it. He had a cart, hand-pulled, full of materials related to his trade. I suppose he had a means of heating solder to repair the aluminum pots and he had a grinder's wheel to sharpen knives and scissors. He went from one end of town to the other, and then started back again. That old man was still here when I came back in the '40s.

One of the most typical things that traveled down the alleys was "the worker" (fig. 171). *He had this cart that was something he had fabricated. I don't know what he started with, but he had put wheels and added more wheels to it, and he did yardwork, and he carried all his tools on that cart, and he picked up objects. Anything that was out there in the alley that someone had thrown away he thought he might utilize, he picked up. And it just got bigger—and bigger—and bigger! The police were always after him about obstructing the view and obstructing traffic because he would park that thing on the sidewalks when he was cutting grass. You couldn't get around it and you couldn't see around it. So, in order to make it visible and not create traffic hazards, he put those little colored pinwheels—he had them stuck on everything. They were on all the bamboo rakes, on the sides. They were red and blue and yellow and green, and there were so many of them that they made a noise. When the wind was blowing, you could actually hear them. . . . He was a white man, a very dirty white man. He was still going strong in '39 and '40, and he had been around for some years before that.*

Fig. 171

Fig. 172

Drawings by Galveston artist Emil Bunjes.
Fig. 171. "The Worker," circa 1935.
Fig. 172. View of alley between Avenues D and E and Fifteenth and Sixteenth Streets, published in the *Galveston Daily News*, October 6, 1935. Bunjes lived on an alley at one time.

Vegetable and fruit vendors also came down the alleys. . . . They would go down the front streets and the alleys, but Broadway [Avenue J] was such a busy street that they always used the alley. They'd come through the yard, particularly if they knew it was someone that frequently bought something. They'd come and knock on the door or call. There was a great deal more freedom. People walked through your yard and you thought nothing about it. They were fenced, but if someone had to get somewhere else and didn't want to go all the way around, they would cut through. That didn't offend anybody.

Hardly any vehicular traffic used the alleys. It was uncommon. The garbage men had trucks, but that was once or twice a week, and people came home in the evening and parked their cars in their garages, but for the most part, no one drove down the alleys. Kids played in the alley all the time. I didn't play in the alley, but there were children back there.

I have been told by old friends and neighbors that there were many white cooks, laundresses, and maids, some of whom lived in the alley houses. A number of those small houses facing the alley, as opposed to facing the backyard, were lived in by the German and Irish domestics.

Sort of a Lover's Nest

Dr. Mavis P. Kelsey Sr. observed the alleys and back buildings in Galveston when he was a medical student at the University of Texas Medical School between 1932 and 1936, and again in 1937, when he returned to teach for a year in the school's Pathology Department (fig. 173).[4] During his student years, Kelsey lived just a short distance from the university at 1426 Avenue E in the Alpha Kappa Kappa fraternity house, which had been the Swedish consulate. (See fig. 96: the 1426 Avenue E property is in the lower left-hand corner of the block.)

Fig. 173. Dr. Mavis P. Kelsey Sr. The photograph was taken in 1936 when Kelsey graduated from medical school.

The house was situated on the corner with an adjoining interior lot that was open. To the back was an old carriage house with an apartment upstairs. . . . The fraternity brothers lived in it some, but many times it wasn't occupied, and so it was a place where they had parties. They had some romantic interludes up there. That was sort of a lover's nest up there. [Mrs. Kelsey: Listen to that. I'll learn a lot of things I never knew.]

On the backside of the alley, the neighbor I remember most of all was Dr. George Herrmann, professor of medicine. He was a famous teacher and all his students loved him. He would make jokes during class about the noise that came across the alley from the AKK fraternity house and also how they used to throw Old Quaker whiskey bottles in the alley. Old Quaker was a brand of whiskey that came out just after Prohibition ended.

Everybody made homebrew all over Galveston. People did it in the attics. You could go downtown to the grocery stores and buy all the ingredients to make homebrew as well as the instructions. We made it in the fraternity house, all of it, and we used to make it back in that old garage, but we usually made it up in the attic.

We nearly always went to school in the alley. It was closer to go out the house and go to the back. You saved a few steps by going through the alley. That was true of all the fraternity houses up and down that row.

There were a lot of servants still living around. Lot of blacks that lived in the back buildings. It was kind of beginning to decline at that time and there were a lot of people had daytime help, but there were a lot of people who had live-in servants. And you know, when they had such segregation, they used to kind of limit the blacks to the alleys. I'm talking about when they went to a white man's house to work, they came through the alley. They didn't come in the front door. They came in the back door. Even in those times, some of the servants had cars. They'd park on the side street, come through the alley, and go in the back. That was anywhere and it was true in Galveston. These things that I'm describing used to be the way of life for everyone. Things were changing. The Depression was on when I was in medical school and it made a lot of difference.

Alley between Avenues D and E and Eighth and Ninth Streets. Photographs taken September 8, 1930, when gas lines were being replaced throughout the city. The photographs are from the period described by Ernest and Gerald Clouser, Inez Lasell, and Mavis Kelsey.
Fig. 174. Looking east from Ninth Street.
Fig. 175. Same alley looking west from Eighth Street. The alley is defined by an almost continuous line of sheds, garages, and dwellings. The block has been redeveloped by the University of Texas Medical Branch and is no longer residential.

Fig. 174

Fig. 175

People lived on an upper level in practically all the back buildings. On the lower level was the garage, storage, and some of them were converted to living areas, because they built the Seawall and there hadn't been any great floods in the town in a long time, so a lot of them were being converted into living quarters. . . . A lot of these places were not down deep in the alley. They were frequently on the corner of the streets and the alleys. And the bigger houses were usually on the corner.

People frequently took care of the alleys pretty well if they lived there. In our neighborhood at least, they weren't trashy. I don't think people littered then like they do now. People had a little more respect. However, as I say, Dr. Herrmann accused us of throwing whiskey bottles out in our alley. You know, after one of these big parties, he'd come into class and all these medical students there and he would say, "Sure were a lot of Old Quaker liquor bottles in our back alley this morning." And everybody would roar with laughter.

The number of students living in buildings along the alleys in the East End grew as the medical school and hospital complex developed and as the number of married students increased. Garage apartments especially appealed to the latter. Housing was tight for everyone, and became even more so after World War II. In 1953, when Inez and Al Lasell purchased their house at 1122 Avenue E, the medical students, according to Inez Lasell, "took what they could get. Primarily, students wanted to be close to the hospital, particularly those in the upper levels who were on call. . . . I remember them running down the alley with their stethoscopes flapping to answer their calls."

Every Kid . . . Played in the Alley

Danny Lasell, who was almost seven years old when his family moved to 1122 Avenue E, grew up observing the alleys and back buildings in his neighborhood (figs. 165, 176). There are similarities between his impressions of the 1950s and 1960s and those of his mother when she was visiting Galveston as a child during the 1930s. But, as Inez Lasell notes, "Danny was always the wanderer and he knows a lot of things I don't know." Danny Lasell is now living in Houston.

In going down the alleys, you would see outbuildings that were washhouses. I don't recall any really being used that much as laundry facilities, but they were installed when the laundry was still done by hand. (See fig. 40.) *They had sinks and washboards and clotheslines. Frequently, they were ten by sixteen feet—long and narrow. I remember three specifically. They even had screen doors so that the washwoman could iron without the flies or whatever. The screen doors went into the yard usually. Some did open onto the alleys.*

Many people lived on the alleys. Most of the people I recall living on the alley were either blacks who worked as domestics or medical students, and the servants quarters had been converted into apartments for medical students. I do remember women who worked as maids living in some of the alley apartments. I remember one caught on fire one time, probably in the 1000 block of Market [Avenue D], and all the kids in the neighborhood rushed over to see. When it was all over, we went up the stairs. The stairs were so rickety, I don't know how it held anyone over 200 pounds. And the sink was probably no bigger than a foot by a foot, and it was a cold water flat. She was using a wood stove to heat the apartment with, and this was in the early '60s and I think kerosene had ignited too quickly when she tried to start the fire. It was just amazing to see how stark this little structure was and what little it had in it.

One of my strongest memories is black women dragging wood through the alleys. Many of them had wood stoves and they would pick up two by fours, planks that were discarded from carpentry work. It really didn't occur to me that this is what they were doing until I saw one splitting it with an ax and taking it inside and she told me that that was for her stove—to fuel the stove with.

Many did catch on fire. That happened every now and then, and especially on the other side of Twenty-fifth Street where the real tenements were. I have a vague recollection that there was constantly something catching fire there.

Fig. 176. Birthday party in 1954 in backyard of Lasell residence, 1122 Avenue E. Left to right: Danny, Cindy, and Sally Lasell, Barbara Jarvis, Carroll Ladt and Pam Jarvis. The building in the background is across the alley from the Lasell residence and was originally a servants quarters. (See fig. 165 for another view.)

Many of them did not have indoor bathrooms. They still bathed in washtubs or the big galvanized bathtubs that were sold in hardware stores. Frequently you would see the tub hung on the outside of the house. The outhouse was a flush toilet and all the blacks who lived in these houses allowed other blacks to use their outhouse because that was during the days of segregation and they had nowhere else to go. You would see them walking down the alley. There was a corner grocery store near our house, and occasionally one would drift over and I remember specifically following one old man because I was going home and that's, I'm sure, what he had to do. It was just understood by the people who lived in these places that that was open to them.

In our neighborhood, going towards Thirteenth and Twelfth Streets, I remember the garage apartment that Pauline Hertz lived in, which was a new building.[5] *Her mother had apparently bequeathed the house to her sister, and they provided for her by having this garage apartment built in the back. She had become a religious fanatic, and we took everyone to see Pauline's garage apartment because it had a light that hung over the garage door that had inscribed in black crayola, "God Strike Every Dishonest Thief with a Nervous Breakdown, Especially the Devil." Pauline rode a bicycle. She was an interesting person to talk to because she was very literate and spoke very intelligently and was rather captivating. She'd been a teacher and she knew how to talk to children and anyone, really, and was just a very nice teacher-type friend. But she got on these religious tangents and when she was really on a tear, these cursing tirades would issue forth. I never was the recipient of one, but I walked by the apartment and heard this, and all the kids would cluster underneath to listen.*

I would say that she was one of the few whites that lived on the alleys. I remember having a friend named Arthur Collins who was black and he lived on the alley in the 1200 block of Market [Avenue D]. It was a cottage that had a kitchen, a combination living room–bedroom, a small bedroom, and a little entrance hall, and no bathroom. The sink was a cold-water sink. They had a hoosier cabinet—I remember that distinctly—and a hall tree was in this little entrance hall, and that was about all that was there. You could sit on the floor and shoot marbles but not much more. Then the kitchen and then it went into this combination all-purpose room that was a living room, bedroom. The couch folded out into a bed and then there was a little tiny bedroom that must have been no more than nine by ten. Three people lived there, and I think at one time, four. The older brother had already left. But that also had one of the outdoor toilets, and the tub was either on top of that outhouse or hanging on the side of the house, and various people would come by to use the commode.

There was so little yard at Arthur's. I think all they could do was hang clothes in it. A little shed, maybe for bicycles and whatever they might have, but there was very little yard space. . . . I don't recall any of them going through the yards of the main houses at all. I don't remember Arthur even walking into the front part.

We played in the alleys all the time. All of us did, constantly. We were always running up and down the alleys. They were a safe place to play at that time, certainly. We played hide-and-go-seek, chase. Frequently, it was foot races, and we'd throw a football and baseball. We weren't supposed to because of the windows that might be broken, but it always happened. I don't know what they are today, but every kid in Galveston played in the alley at some point, and frequently, black and white together. I don't recall Galveston being especially segregated because of that and because many blacks did live throughout the city.

Most of the blacks that lived in alley houses did not live behind the houses where they worked. There may have been a few, but not many. Most of them caught the bus and went elsewhere. You would see them standing on the corner.

Another vivid memory, though, is to see the maids or hear them—you would hear them before you'd see them in the morning—get off the bus on Market [Avenue D] and turn down Twelfth Street and come through the alley from Twelfth towards Eleventh on Postoffice [Avenue E], and then one by one they would file into the various houses that they were employed by. They always entered by the alley side at that time. I don't remember any mention whatsoever by my mother or my father telling anyone to come to the back door but, in those days, they did. It was just an understood means of entrance.

The black men primarily were doing yardwork that I recall. Certainly, they had other jobs. I would have to say the ones I knew were probably out and away more than anything else. They occasionally would come through as junk collectors, picking through the trash for cans and scrap iron.

I remember one woman who pushed a huge perambulator all through the alleys, and she rooted through garbage cans looking for silverware and valuables that she could resell to a pawn shop and it would be interesting to see what she had that people threw away. I think she sold rags as well. She'd pull out old clothes and she had those draped over. She was an elderly black woman and that big huge baby buggy was bigger than she was, but she pushed all day long. You'd see her all over town. The men who picked up scrap iron almost always had a pickup of some sort, a trash dump truck or an old jeep that was broken down, but the woman who pushed the baby buggy is the one I'll never forget.

There were so many more alley houses in other areas. Ours had thinned out a little, but when you went on the other side of Twenty-fifth Street in what was known as "the district," that was just solid alley dwellings. Big houses on the front and the alleys were just packed. And they were horrible . . . specifically behind the Post Office and Model Laundry. I never was in it until the later '60s, because I knew a couple of women who lived there that I worked with at the Jack Tar Hotel and they lived in the rear between Twenty-sixth and Twenty-seventh on Church [between Avenues F and G]. I remember it just dense and the noise that you would hear. The voices over-shouting the other. . . . It was in other blocks as well. You could see it. It was all black, maybe a few Mexicans, but I don't recall any whites at all. . . . It's so vacant now. There's not much there anymore. There was a lot of demolition in the early '70s.

It seems to me that there were various sections where the property was nicer and I don't know if it was because they actually owned it or if the slum landlord, quote unquote, just was a more responsible property owner and kept it better. It seemed to me more like a block basis because I can remember whole half blocks of houses that had not one scale of paint on them that looked like cardboard boxes.

After Hurricane Carla in 1961, a lot of sheds and outbuildings disappeared. It was just wrecked and damaged. People got rid of it. Still, it's amazing how long it persisted.

We Won't Have to Be Moving All the Time

There are many longtime alley residents still living along the alleys in Galveston. When Louis Martin and his wife Sarah moved to Galveston from Louisiana in 1945, jobs were plentiful but housing was tight. The Martins first lived with relatives in a house near the beach, then rented the alley house at 1505 Avenue F rear in Block 375 (figs. 109, 114, 115). They moved into the front house (fig. 177) once it was vacated and eventually bought the whole property. Martin worked for various cotton compress companies, including nineteen years for Moody's Compress, before retiring in 1977. His wife died in 1970. At the time of the interview, the alley house that Martin describes was occupied by Ethel Palmer (fig. 178).[6]

Fig. 177. Front house at 1505 Avenue F photographed from across the street on what was the Darragh property. Photographed 1995.

Fig. 178. Ethel Palmer and Louis Martin on the front porch of 1505 Avenue F rear. Photographed 1990.

When I come here in 1945, you could get a job anywhere. You walking up and down the street, they ask you if you want to work. . . . It was the end of the war. They had a lot of cotton coming in and they had plenty of work for people, and then they was using labor. They wasn't using no machines to operate.

I started renting when I come here in this very little house. That's it. And, I stayed on here. Damiani, he was the owner of the house. He was a lawyer and a judge on Market Street [Avenue D]. . . . So, I just stayed on here until he told me, he said, "Martin," he says, "since you pay your rent up so good, why don't you buy both those old houses? They don't cost much but the land." He was selling it for the land. He say, "You can get them and fix them up and then you come to own your own home." But, I said, I say, "Noooo, I don't want no house, no home. I don't want nothing like that." So, he say, "Yeah, I'll help you out. You won't have no problem. I'll pay the tax. All you have to do is just meet the note." So, I went and talk with my wife, and I tell her I didn't want to, but she say, "Yes, he right, buy your home. Something happen to me or you, we'll have one thing, we won't have to be moving all the time." She was right. But now, she left before I did and I don't have to be moving all the time.

When I came here, the house had the roofing on top—paper. I put this tin on now. It rain in here like it did outdoors. Just rain in here so I went on down and talk with Damiani. I told him, "It raining in that house like . . . it outdoors." He says, "Come here, Martin. You know what you do?" He say, "Can you fix it?" I said, "Yeah, I can do a little roof work." He say, "Fix it and I'll take it out on your rent." And, that's what I did. I got some kindling and stuff and fixed it.

The house didn't have no porch. It had a little shed over the door and it had a leak when you set on the steps and so I look up at it and I says, "I'm gonna put a porch here." There's a man tearing a house down over there and so I got some of the lumber, board and things, and put that porch on there. She [Ethel Palmer] says, "You don't know what you're doing." I says, "Don't tell me I don't know what I'm doing. I'm cutting, get these steps and put them there." Went and got me some concrete blocks, and I told her, I says, "Now, look how it is." "Oooh, yeah, that's all right. Don't have to sit out in the rain." We stay there when it's cool—out on the porch. But when it get cold, we can't hardly look out there.

Wood was easy to get when I first come here. See wood laying everywhere. Sometimes you had to buy it, but you walk in the alleys and go pick up a lot of wood. Enough to last you, I don't know how long. Can't do that now. Freeze to death if you go out there and fool around now.

I have a bicycle. Sometime I ride with people, but the way I used to do, I just get up and catch the Market [Avenue D] bus. When I catch the Market bus, I just ride right on to my work. When I quit riding the bus, then I got me a bicycle. I was riding a bicyle and so, I'm riding a bicycle yet. When I want to go somewhere, I get on and go.

If I didn't have a home, I wouldn't buy no house. Content where I'm at. I wouldn't fool around. It's too hard now.

They got a lot of little houses around in this town. . . . Got a lot of them torn down. They started tearing down houses. Of course, two used to be right over there [across the alley]. They tore them down. . . . Them houses that they tore down there was pretty good. They could have fixed them houses up. It was easy—wasn't too much the matter with them, but they tore them down.

When I come to Galveston, the colored had to live with the colored. Colored people couldn't live with the white then. You couldn't live like that. You could have colored live where the colored at. The white stay where the white was. Yeah, they had it different then because the civil rights come in where they change now. Lot of them say Dr. Martin Luther King, Kennedy [brought about civil rights], but that comes through God. That don't come through no person.

The Shade Comes Up

Painters Luanne and John Stovall, who live on Louis Martin's block but across the alley in a front house, are alley observers rather than alley dwellers. They converted their back building that was originally a carriage house and servants quarters into a workshop on the first floor and a studio on the second (figs. 179, 180).

John likes to credit himself—and he should—with improving alley life considerably. It's sort of a landmark in the alley because it's in the middle of the block and it's the only structure on this side of the alley now. The bottom part didn't have any cement slab and people would come in and out through those old rusted-out garage doors. . . . Then there was a lot of trash, all along, and no one had really paid much attention to it. So, John got rid of all the weeds on our side and put those new doors up and put siding on it and cleared a lot of the extra junk. . . . Then the other side started to clean up better because they felt, "Great, the alley is looking better." And now, it looks a lot better.

It's all black. Everybody's been there since we've been here, and I just get the impression that they've been there a lot longer. When I'm not working on a painting and I'm back in the house, I sort of forget about alley life, but then I go back to the alley. You hear a lot—you hear the radios, and the music, and a lot of the voices, and the people that come in back and forth. There's a guy called "Who-dat?" that lives in one place. I think that now they've closed one of those apartments down. They might have been, well, either evicted or else they can't live there because of the conditions.

There's a guy that fixes cars and there's a lot of odd jobs during the day. Like early evening, you hear the smashing of aluminum cans. They come down the alley and then they smash the cans down. A lot of them do the jobs outside themselves and you hear them fixing cars in the alley.

People come and you see the two white guys in the suits and briefcases coming up and knocking on the door and nobody answers, and they knock, knock, and nobody answers. Then they leave and everybody looks out the window in the alley.

There are always people at home during the day because they're older folks. . . . They are always there and notice everything. If I put my trash cans out, their window is right there and then, you know, the shade comes up. That's why I feel real secure here.

One lady decorated for Christmas. Those little bitty lights around the door and around the window. It was really sweet.

Fig. 179

Fig. 180

Renovation of back building at 1512 Avenue G. Photographs taken 1985 by John Stovall.
Fig. 179. Luanne and Matt Stovall in front of the building undergoing restoration by John Stovall.
Fig. 180. Yard view after the renovation was completed.

You always knew quite a bit about what "Who-dat?" and his sidekick were doing. They'd bring in some kind of car. They'd be working on it and philosophizing at the same time. I really enjoyed their philosophy. The homespun kind, funny, the humorous funny and I remember him telling his sidekick one day that all of his brain was in his left foot. He was mad. He started moving slower.

I've heard so many complaints about the alleys—most alleys, unfortunately—but this alley is really nice. We used to live on another block not far from here and there was a problem with alley life there because it was young, wild kids, a drug situation was going on, and cars going up and down the alley, and you couldn't trust it. You suspect prostitution in some of the places and definitely a low-life. This is not that way at all. So I think ours is special, really special that way.[7]

Fig. 181. Willie Mae Clay (left) and Chester Clay (right) with her granddaughter, Cheryl Dotson Lynch, and Kenneth Lynch, May 17, 1980.

They Were like Family

In 1951, Willie Mae Clay (fig. 181) moved from Beaumont to Galveston because "work was plentiful then." Separated from her first husband, Clay worked at various jobs, sometimes two at the same time. In the mid-1960s, Clay, her second husband, Chester Clay, and their young son moved into the second story of a carriage house and servants quarters located to the rear of 1703 Avenue J (figs. 182–184).

When I was working at St. Mary's, I lived in Bayview. It's a project-like. It was over on Market Street [Avenue D]. It's no longer there, but before they tore it down, I come out here to live. Dr. Drager, that owned this house, was a neurosurgeon, and I was working for her [Mrs. Drager]. . . . I would walk over in the mornings and then walk back in the afternoon because at the time, there wasn't a bus coming this direction and I wasn't driving. That's about fifteen blocks. And she told me, she say, "Why don't you move in that little house back there?" And I said, "Let me ask my husband." So, I talked to Chester about it. He said, "Well, it's left up to you. Do you want to move out there?" Well, all the children were grown and gone except two. The baby girl was in college over in Beaumont and I had only the little boy. So he said, "Well, okay." So we got rid of all the furniture because I had a three-bedroom house at the time. . . . I had a house full of children. Six—two girls and four boys.

But, anyway, we come out here and cleaned it up. Boy, it taken some work to clean it up. It always had to be two, a man and a woman, because the man would take care of the yard and the lady would work in the house. A servants quarters, that's what this was—a servants quarters, and he died and she moved out. So, the house was just setting here, but they were using the garage.

There was a bathroom just where it is now. There was a hot water heater in there, but it wasn't burning and we would have to heat the water on the stove. That was kind of terrible but, anyway, we didn't pay rent so there wasn't any complaining. If I had been paying rent, then you could have said something, but I wasn't paying any rent. And my husband was doing the yard and I worked over there and she paid me a salary. But he did the yard and no salary for that, but we didn't pay rent.

Chester worked for Schreiber and Miller Furniture Company. He worked there thirty-five years. Sure did. And he would walk to work and walk back, and in the afternoons he would work every day on the yard, and I would stop what I was doing and get out there and help, too. Tie my head up just as big and get out there and help him. When I would come from work, I would cook, and when we would come out of the yard and everybody take a bath, then we would sit down and eat our dinner and then everybody go to bed, we'd be so tired. And that's the way we lived in order that we could school children. We went through a lot trying to educate every one of them. But anyway, it paid off.

Fig. 182

Fig. 183

It was convenient living here, and I would not have to go back and forth over there to do things during the day. I would have my regular time. I would go in the morning—I guess around nine and around twelve or one I was through. I wasn't on call and I didn't work Saturdays and Sundays. They were like family. I did my washing there and it was just like family. . . . And Dr. Drager would always tell Junior, he said, "I want you to get an education," and he did and he's got his master's. I got two that got their master's. . . . I'm proud of all of them.

When Mrs. Drager moved away—six years I worked for her—she sold this place to Dr. Cavazos. Then Mrs. Cavazos rented it—I guess some two or three families lived there [in the main house] after she left. And then Mr. Rapp moved in and he stayed there for a good while before she would even sell it to him. He rented it before he bought it.

Now, the fixing up of it. Dr. Cavazos had these two rooms paneled, and to make room, I asked her could I take all the doors down. That would make more room. . . . Dr. Cavazos had a new commode put in and hot water heater. Now, she would pay Chester to do the yard and we would pay her rent—$50 a month rent.

When we first came here, sometime we would sit outside but not often. I go in and out any way I want. . . . Mr. Rapp has not told me one time which way to go in or go out. . . . Whenever the children come, they park on Broadway or they park in that little space on the side of the house. Sometimes they stop and park right in the alley, but they never stay too long.

I think since Mr. Rapp has been here, the alley's been in good shape. We all used to put our garbage out and they would come looking through the garbage for cans and they would just throw the garbage out. Whatever Mr. Rapp ask me to do, I do that, and he's so neat and clean, and I like that about him because I'm like that, too. He told me, he said, "Willie, let's put our garbage out on garbage day and that will keep the garbage off of the street." I don't know if he talked to the neighbors or not, but I notice they put their garbage out at certain times and it looks good now.

There's not too much traffic on the alley. Every now and then. Now, like when they have Mardi Gras or spring breaks and things like that, the children, you know, they be going, cutting

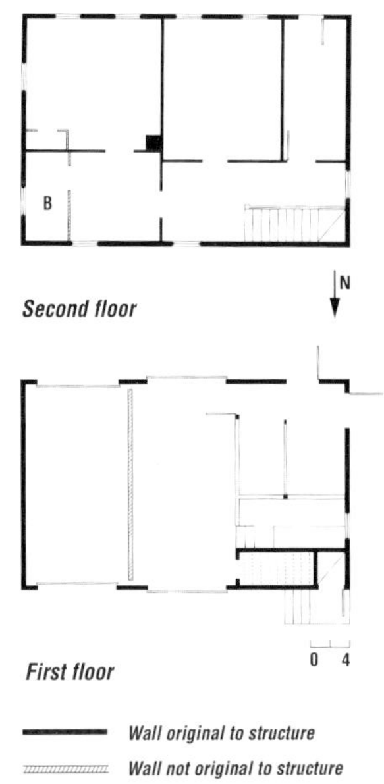

Fig. 184

Adriance house, 1703 Avenue J, rebuilt 1914. Photographed 1995.
Fig. 182. Main house with stable and servants quarters to the rear.
Fig. 183. Alley side of property, showing cistern and service building.
Fig. 184. Floor plans of the stable and servants quarters. The stalls and trough are intact on the first floor. Documented 1990.

corners, I guess. But, just to travel through there, I don't hear it too much. We don't have any problems with the alley, not in here, not in this block. I don't know about other alleys, but it's no problems.

I just make space. . . . Chester put that cabinet up for me to have to put my dishes in. He did a lot of work. He was handy with his hands, too. And then, I would suggest this or suggest that and then he would do it. . . . I had those ceiling fan blades taken down. I couldn't stand it. Every time I'd look up, I'd just see—it's too cluttered, too little up here. That was just too much.

I never did have a garden. I always had little flower pots, but Mike and Gary, when they lived over there, they had tomatoes, cucumbers, and lettuce—oh, they had some of everything. They even had the little—what kind of peas you call them?—snow peas. They had the fence just lined with those snow peas. And I would come home and they would have the porch full. I said, "Mike! Gary! I will never eat all of this." They left one weekend to go visiting, and Chester died while they were gone. And they come back, and they didn't know, and they come over to see how we were doing, and tell me about the good time they had, and I told them, and Gary and Mike was, oh, they were upset.

After Mrs. Drager's husband died and she decided to move, I wanted to move someplace else. I tried to find a place, but everywhere that I looked, it was too much for us. You know, the price, the rent was too high, and I didn't want to live in the projects. That was just too—and I had that boy. I didn't want to live there so I just made do here.[8]

My Kind of Style

Like Willie Mae Clay, alley dweller Margaret Dutton (fig. 185) also lives in what was originally a service building. When Dutton moved to Galveston in the mid-1970s, she quickly found a job at the University of Texas Medical Branch library. For three months she rented an apartment in an older front house in a nearby neighborhood, then moved to the back house on the same property. At the time of the interview, her landlady had died and the disposition of the estate was uncertain.

Fig. 185. Margaret Dutton at the entrance of her alley dwelling. Photographed 1995.

I like living back here. It's just my kind of style. I like things simple. Do I think that there is a stigma to being in the alley? A wonderful stigma! I'm not saying that for some people who didn't know who they were. There might be a problem with that. I can see where there might be. But, I love it because you don't get all the door-to-door salesmen. It's more private. If you want to come in and lock up your house and curl up and read a book, most people aren't going to bother you. I like the quietness of it, the sort of laid-awayness of it.

Living in an alley is a different life. . . . Like right in this neighborhood, there is an alley neighborhood and a front street neighborhood. In other words, I know my neighbors back in this area—right along the alley mainly and also into Market [Avenue D]—much better than I do the neighbors across the street from me on Postoffice [Avenue E]. Because I go to the University so often, I use my back door [on the alley] more than my front door, and I rarely come out the front way, so I may see all these people more than I do the people across the street from me on Postoffice.

My orientation is really to the alley, and that's how I came to be an alley cleaner. I started with my own alley because I had neighbors who used to think it was all right to just put the materials out in the alley in anything and they would lay on the ground, but after a while we got that cleaned up, so I moved from alley to alley on the East End. We built garbage racks and now, since the city has done some garbage-rack training, lots of people have racks that didn't used to have them.

The garbage men always carefully pick up my garbage because they know that they'll get calls if they don't. Like the other day, they didn't pick up some stuff down there that should have been picked up—wood, pieces of branches and stuff, a whole bunch of stuff. So, I tied it up and I called and told them and even the manager came out. . . . So, I never have any trouble with garbage pickup and if I think they're going to miss something, I stand at the back door.

I am debating that if I should stay here—that's in question because of the way the estate is done—I'm saying to myself, "Do I want the gravel and a little bit of grass in the alley to make an alley, or do I really want to get rid of the dust and have some pavement out there?" It's really something to consider. . . . And also, how much does the city charge? I am assuming that you pay for the material. I really don't want to do it. I like it in gravel, but within a month's time, you have so much dust, and of course, you have the track-in.

I feel free to do anything I want to in the alley, but with the yard, I've never felt that free with it, which is fine. I feel it belongs to the house, and my landlady used to keep some things out there sometimes that were, well, sort of trashy and she'd say to me, "Well," she said, "I just hate that. I know it's your front yard, but it's my backyard." I never worried about it. My friends never worried about it, so why should I worry about it?

I always think things ought to be fixed up rather than built new for economy reasons, but given that there are so many houses on the market in Galveston, maybe the alley houses aren't yet ready to come into the market, because they might not find people to live in them. On the other hand, I see a real need in Galveston for inexpensive living. The reason people are with me right now is because they could not find something that was inexpensive enough for them.

I don't feel anguish about the alleys. Quite a few people walk up and down the alley. I think some of them are on their way to the hospital to work. Others are just out walking and enjoying themselves. I walk alleys sometimes—that is, it has to be in pretty broad daylight. I can't think of any disadvantages to living in an alley. The fact that I'm looking for another alley house just in case I move from this one tells you something.

Conclusion: A Matter of Choice

The attitude changed toward alley houses when living in one of them was not just an economic factor and they became just another place to live.

Leon M. Banks Sr.

Ask a Galvestonian about the city's alleys and you will get an answer. In fact, you will probably get a story. Every Galvestonian—almost without exception—has an alley story, an alley memory, or, at the very least, an alley opinion.

No question but the alleys and back buildings of Galveston have a long and complicated history—one that belies the simplicity of the city plan and of the little back buildings, and one that is as much about the resourcefulness of people as it is about the alleys as a resource.[1] It is a history that began on the day in 1838 when the Galveston City Company accepted John Groesbeck's survey for the newly established city on the tip of Galveston Island.

It took little time for Galveston alleys to acquire a questionable reputation, as was also true for alleys in other cities. The services and activities relegated to the alleys and backyards meant that problems would inevitably develop, especially when a city was unable or unwilling to maintain its alleys. In Galveston, those problems were exacerbated even more by the swampy, sandy topography—"the mud and mire," as Matilda Houstoun had so aptly called it in 1844.[2]

The reluctance to maintain the alleys or, perhaps more correctly, the ofttimes indifference to their condition, also reflected the attitude shared by most Galvestonians toward many, if not all, alley dwellers. Undeniably, the history of Galveston alleys and back buildings is a history partly motivated by prejudice against the black population and the poor, the very poor, both black and white. That, too, was not confined to Galveston, nor was it limited to southern cities, as documented by the histories of such places as Washington, Cleveland, Philadelphia, and Detroit.[3]

As rich as the history of Galveston alleys and back buildings may be, researching it is not a tidy exercise. Standard historical sources are stingy, very stingy, when it comes to alley dwellers and alley buildings. There are few, if any, architects' drawings, mechanic's liens, probate and court records, or obituary notices for alley dwellers, and only scattered tax and insurance records.

The historical references that are found frequently do not match existing evidence about alley buildings and alley life in Galveston. Most nineteenth- and twentieth-century newspaper accounts describe the seedier side of alley life and the most decrepit alley buildings, but those are not the alleyscapes and alley buildings that have survived. As might be expected, little has been written about those that do remain because their stories, like the stories of most alley dwellers, have been much too quiet and much too ordinary for the local newspapers—which is why the oral histories that cross generational and decadal lines are so essential to any alley study.

Most alley residents in Galveston during the nineteenth and early twentieth centuries were like the majority of those who have always lived along the alleys. They were good and decent people who were "doing the best job they could,"[4] even though some of them lived under the most difficult and demeaning circumstances that Galveston had to offer. In many

Fig. 186. 1628 Avenue E, back building on Block 496, Kruger house, Nicholas J. Clayton, architect, built 1888. Looking northeast into the backyard. The main house is to the right. Photographed 1990.

respects, the childhood remembered by Bill Millican was like that of most children growing up in Galveston in the late 1930s and early 1940s. His neighborhood just happened to be the alley on which his family lived.

Saying that living on an alley did not make a difference is arguable, but certainly it made a greater difference to some alley dwellers than to others. For some, their alley house was a permanent home, perhaps one that they owned. For many, it was considered—hoped—to be a temporary residence. In most instances, living on an alley, like living anywhere in Galveston, was governed by an individual's or family's finances, an ever-tight housing market, and race.

Fig. 187. Looking west from the alley entrance at Forty-second Street between Avenues H and I. Photograph taken in August 1930 by the Southern Union Gas Co.

To some degree, alley dwellings have lost their stigma which, according to one Galvestonian, occurred in the 1960s when "the medical students made it feasible to live in them."[5] Actually, the attitudinal shift towards alley housing was far more gradual and complex than that. By the 1930s, the number of live-in servants was diminishing, ostensibly because fewer people could afford them. Given the always intense housing market in Galveston, especially after World War II, and the low wages paid domestic help, many people simply decided it was more profitable to rent their back building and hire domestic help as day workers (and it was). Technology, in the form of new and improved household appliances, also reduced the demand for full-time help at the same time that fewer people were willing to work as live-in domestics on twenty-four-hour call.

In the 1940s, new employment opportunities made it possible for more blacks to buy their homes. Many alley dwellers moved into government housing projects—sometimes located on the blocks where alley housing had been most dense. Demolition of the worst images of alley living, begun in the 1930s and peaking in the 1960s, removed some of the stigma of living on an alley, at least for some Galvestonians. For others, back buildings will never be an acceptable residence because of negative associations, a reminder, once again, that living on an alley in Galveston has meant many things to many people and what it meant, and means, has had a lot to do with choice.

Although Galveston's alleys are populated with fewer back buildings and people than in the past, the maintenance of the alley system is as imperative to the healthy functioning of the city today as it was in the nineteenth century. Fortunately, technology, public policy, and an evolving social consciousness have made that somewhat easier. But the present and future economics of scale, space, and material resources demand that Galveston and other older communities look beyond mere maintenance of their alleys and assess the physical and cultural value of the smaller streetscapes and buildings that complete their urban landscape.

Ironically, older communities like Galveston can look to the growing popularity of new residential projects across the country for inspiration to rejuvenate their aging alley system. Architects, planners, and developers are discovering (or is it rediscovering?) what many preservationists have always known: There is an efficiency to older city plans in which alleys serve as thoroughfares for vehicles, services, and utilities, and back buildings provide small-scale living units for family members, security or rental purposes, and office space for cottage industries. Regrettably, the fervor for alleyways in new developments is seldom transferred to advocating the maintenance of alleys and attendant services and benefits in older big-city neighborhoods or in smaller, less densely populated cities and towns.

Cities that are alley veterans, like Galveston, have something to offer the developers of new projects: a list of what has and has not worked, some of which is mentioned here. For starters, an alley system must be recognized for what it is—a permanent, secondary street network, one that will require perpetual care and will work well only if there is a mechanism ensuring long-term maintenance, such as a custodial civic or neighborhood entity, or deed restrictions that hold individual owners responsible for maintaining the alleyway adjacent to their property.

Alley surfacing and alley width are two of the most important physical and planning considerations. Galveston alleys have always been a maintenance problem and always will be, in part because surface drainage is a never-ending problem throughout the city. Paving an alley does seem to elevate its status and encourage better maintenance, as Galveston discovered with implementation of a program in which property owners share the cost of paving the alley on their block. However, an aggressive, never-ending effort is still required to keep the alleys clean.

When Galveston was established, a twenty-foot alley width was considered generous, but present-day users strongly recommend a wider alleyway— just ask Bill Millican and his sanitation crews. Twenty feet is a tight, sometimes impossible, dimension for maneuvering modern vehicles that range from private automobiles and pickup trucks to the city's fire and garbage trucks.

But Galveston alleys and Galvestonians have, for the most part, adjusted gracefully to the modern age. On a walk through the alleys today, there are many reminders—garages, cars, garbage cans, and gardens, laundry, doghouses, sheds, and plastic pools—that the motions of everyday life in most Galveston households have actually changed surprisingly little since the nineteenth century and are still conducted on the backside of the properties. What is missing are the odors—the effluvia—that would have been a strong accompaniment to the same walk not so many years ago.

The back buildings of Galveston have also proven their adaptability, although they are less secure than are the alleys as permanent fixtures on the Galveston landscape. The alleys in most blocks of the older neighborhoods still have at least one residential unit, if not more. The lessons in planning and design that the buildings offer also provide the rationale for rehabilitating the older ones and using them as prototypes for new ones. Many of them demonstrate that a small and simple building can establish a presence, even a formidable presence, in the most confined location. Generous light, cross-ventilation, and conservation practices are achievable in small buildings with proper siting and well-placed openings. Efficiency and livability can be accomplished through the careful arrangement of restricted space. And even the smallest buildings, if maintained, can have an astounding adaptability to change.

These qualities suggest that back buildings, new and old, are viable options in the

Fig. 188

Fig. 189

Garage and rental apartment unit built in the 1970s.
Fig. 188. View from the front street, showing a corner of the front house on the right and the neighbor's house on the left.
Fig. 189. Alley-side view, looking east. When built, the apartment served as the residence for the property owners while they restored the front house. The unit consists of a large multi-use space, with a kitchen on the east side, and a bedroom, bath, and sizeable closet on the west side. Photographed 1987.

search for affordable housing not only in Galveston but also in other communities. We must remember, however, that some of the characteristics that make the older back buildings so appealing today have not always existed. Stricter building codes, for example, have reduced the number of people who can live in individual units and thinned the number of structures that line the alleys—reminders that the maintenance of decent, affordable housing, like the maintenance of alleys, requires a long-term economic and social commitment by both the collective community and its individual residents.

Ultimately, this book, *The Alleys and Back Buildings of Galveston,* is a plea for smaller buildings and smaller places to be recognized as important to our urban landscapes and acknowledged in our urban and architectural studies. It is also a plea that our urban histories embrace the people for whom the alleys and the back buildings were and are the focus of their day. Finally, it is a plea to maintain and develop our resources in such a way that decent, affordable housing becomes a reality for all our citizens and that wherever we live becomes a matter of choice for everyone—for if it is truly a matter of choice, it will be a signal that we have made a greater use of all our resources, whether they be on a front street or an alley.

Fig. 190

Figs. 190 and 191. Signs at the Seventeenth Street entrance to the alley bordered by Sixteenth and Seventeenth Streets and Avenues G and H. When first photographed in 1992 (fig. 190), the sign read "Help Keep Our Alley Clean." The sign had been there for some time and remained tacked to the telephone pole until fall 1995, when it was replaced with the sign "Our Alley Is Katharo" (fig. 191)—*katharo* being the Greek word for "pure" or "cleansed." The signs, the sentiment, and the sense of humor belong to Riley S. Athanasiou, a BOI, who lives on the adjoining property.

Fig. 191

OUR
ALLEY
IS
KATHARO

Appendix A Listing of Interviewees

The quotations appearing throughout the book are excerpted from tape-recorded interviews conducted by the author with the following individuals. Interview dates are in italics. BOI indicates a native Galvestonian ("born on the island").

Irene Ayers: Visited grandmother in Galveston during early childhood; moved to Galveston in 1936 when entering first grade; community volunteer. *March 14, 1991.*

Leon M. Banks Sr. (1910–88): BOI, lifelong Galveston resident; businesses included real estate, insurance, and ownership of Margaret's Lounge; local historian. *March 1985.*

Annie Mae Charles: Moved to Galveston in 1936; domestic worker; officer, juvenile division, Galveston City Police Department, 1960–77; married in 1944; with her husband bought a house in 1947. *September 12, 1990.*

Willie Mae Clay: See chapter 11, page 128. *March 11, 1991.*

Ernest Z. Clouser: See chapter 11, page 117. *April 16, 1991.*

Gerald Z. Clouser Sr.: See chapter 11, page 119. *March 13, 1991.*

Izola Fedford Collins: BOI; music educator; member, Galveston Independent School District Board of Trustees; great-granddaughter of Horace Scull. *March 12, 1991.*

Pam Diamond: Writer; alley resident. *July 11, 1990.*

Margaret E. Dutton: See chapter 11, page 130. *April 24, 1990.*

Oscar T. Ekelund Jr.: BOI 1929; retired in 1992 after nearly forty years as Galveston City police officer; security chief, Moody Gardens. *March 19, 1991.*

E. Burke Evans: Began orthopedic residency at University of Texas Medical School, in Galveston, in 1950; chief, Orthopedic Division, University of Texas Medical Branch, in Galveston, 1965–92; lived at 717 Mechanic rear, 1953–62. *February 26, 1985; January 14, 1987; July 8, 1990.*

Alfreda Houston: Executive director, St. Vincent's Episcopal House; community organizer and activist. *February 21, 1991.*

Mavis P. Kelsey Sr.: See chapter 11, page 122. *February 6, 1991.*

Danny Lasell: See chapter 11, page 123. *February 7, 1991.*

Inez R. Lasell: See chapter 11, page 120. *February 19, 1991.*

Louis Martin: See chapter 11, page 126. *September 7, 1990.*

William H. (Bill) Millican: See Introduction, page 9. *November 19, 1990; February 21, 1991.*

George P. Mitchell: BOI 1919; parents were immigrants from Greece; president, Mitchell Energy & Development Corp. *April 13, 1991.*

Helen O'Rourke: BOI; pre–World War I recollections; retired employee, University of Texas Medical Branch. *June 28, 1991.*

Luanne L. Stovall: See chapter 11, page 127. *July 9, 1990.*

James B. Thomas: BOI 1924, fifth of eleven children; employee of United States Postal Service, 1949–80; pastor, Market Street Baptist Church; city councilman. *March 12, 19, 1991.*

Robert M. Tucker: BOI 1918; posted Sanborn insurance maps, 1939–41; employed in building trades; owner, Island City Woodworking Company, 1964–82. *April 18, 1985; February 22, 1991.*

The author also interviewed the following individuals:

Craig Bowie, Elbert Bradley, Jan Coggeshall, Manuel Corella, Barbara Davis, A. Filidei (telephone), Thomas Green, John Harris, Jim Havens, Jean Hosey, Carrie Jack, Gleaves James, Rusty Kattner, Adrian Levy, Harold Levy, John W. Lyons (telephone), Mary Richardson, David and Margaret Ritter, Mildred Robertson, Angelina Tropea, P. C. ("Pinky") Wallstein, and P. J. Zeigler.

Appendix B Reconstructing Alley Households

In June 1880, census taker Clinton Stone recorded the age, sex, race, household makeup, occupation, literacy, and birthplace of the 1,796 residents living in Ward Two, the ward in which Richard Johnson and Charles Wilkman and their families lived. The ward—bordered by Thirteenth and Seventeenth Streets, the north side of Avenue G, and Galveston Bay—was predominantly residential in character, with larger houses to the south, smaller residences and a greater mix of uses (including shops and industry) toward the bay, and several boardinghouses.

Like other census takers, Stone did not denote alley addresses, but it is possible, by matching the listings in the 1881–82 city directory and the 1880 census, to reconstruct, with some accuracy, the alley population on the Johnsons' and the Wilkmans' blocks.

The Johnsons' block, which was bordered by Avenues E and F and Sixteenth and Seventeenth Streets, was entirely residential, with the front houses primarily owner-occupied. Richard Johnson and two other individuals, Ed Davis and Alice Owens, were living at "rear 426 Church [Avenue F]," according to the 1881–82 Galveston city directory.

Johnson and Davis and their households were listed in the 1880 census as shown in table B.1. One asterisk after the name indicates that the person was listed in the 1881–82 directory. In all three tables, "Rel/hsld" indicates the person's relationship to the household. One asterisk following the birthplace indicates that the person could read but not write English; two asterisks indicate that the person could neither read nor write. Minor spelling adjustments have been made to some names because of differences between the census and the directory.

Table B.1
Listing of Alley Residents in Johnsons' Block

Name	Rel/hsld	Race[a]	Age	Occupation	Birthplace
Ed Davis*	Head	Mu	24	Laborer	Texas**
Emma Davis	Wife	B	19	Washing & I	Texas**
Richard Johnson*	Head	B	23	Laborer	Louisiana*
Nettie Johnson	Wife	B	20	Washing & I	Texas
Susie Johnson	Daughter	B	3	–	Texas
Alice Owens*	Black woman not listed in census	–	–	–	–

[a] Mu=mulatto, B=black, W=white.

The owner of 426 Church [Avenue F] was Kate Cherry, a fifty-year-old widow born in New York, who lived in the front house with her three unmarried Texas-born sons, all in their twenties, and a forty-year-old unemployed female boarder from Virginia.

The 1880 census lists thirteen individuals as working in servant positions in eight households in the same block. In table B.2, they are grouped by household. (George Early, the fourteenth name, was not listed as a servant.) The servants most likely to have lived in the main house were the three single white females. Only two (denoted by an asterisk after the name) of the thirteen individuals were listed in the same household in the 1881–82 city directory.

Some individuals listed as servants in the census—for example, eleven-year-old Francis Smith and two-and-a-half-year-old Henrietta Stamp—were children whose parents were servants. The assumption should not be made that the children, at least those of Francis Smith's age, were not servants also. There were instances (in other blocks) where the only servant in a household was a child, like Georgana [Raitler], a ten-year-old black girl who was the sole house servant for boatman John Anderson and his extended family of nine. Georgana could not write but had attended school during the previous year.

Table B.2
Listing of Servants in Johnsons' Block

Name	Rel/hsld	Race[a]	Age	Occupation	Birthplace	Mar/Sin
Josephine Heibling*	Servant	W	20	Cook	Germany	Single
Maggie West	Servant	B	24	–	Louisiana	Married
Henry Stamp	Servant	B	25	Laborer	Texas	Married
Henrietta Stamp	Servant	B	2 1/2	–	Texas	
Tom White	Servant	B	36	Cook	Texas**	Single
Henry Nichols	Servant	B	25	Laborer	Ohio**	Single
Dell Smith	Servant	B	28	Cook	Alabama**	Married
Francis Smith	Servant	Mu	11	Servant	Texas	
Herman Smith	Servant	B	35	Laborer	Texas	Married [b]
Lizzie Jackson	Servant	W	49	Servant	Louisiana	Single
Georgie Pennington*	House-keeper	W	30	House-keeper	Florida	Single
Marie Battie	Servant	B	27	Cook	N. Carolina	Single
George Early	–	B	27	Laborer	Tennessee**	Married
Mary Early	Servant	B	33	Cook	Texas**	Married

[a] Mu=mulatto, B=black, W=white.
[b] A Herman Smith was listed in the directory as a driver for a coalyard business, but no residential address was given. His employer did not live in Ward Two.

The Wilkmans lived on the block bordered by Avenues A and B and Fifteenth and Sixteenth Streets. In contrast to the Johnsons' block, it was nearer the bay and combined commercial and mostly rental residential uses. The residents of the Wilkmans' alley are listed in table B.3. Those included in the 1881–82 directory are indicated by an asterisk after their name. Again, some minor spelling adjustments have been made.

In contrast to the Johnsons' alley, the household heads were all immigrants in the Wilkmans' alley. There were no blacks, nor were there any listings for servants in either the census or the city directory. According to the census listings, none of the women in the Wilkmans' block worked, but it is highly probable that at least one of them took in laundry.

Table B.3
Listing of Alley Residents in Wilkmans' Block

Name	Rel/hsld	Race	Age	Occupation	Birthplace
Joseph Bouffa*	Head	W	40	Drayman	Italy
Annie Bouffa	Wife	W	41	Keeping house	Italy
Josephine Anella*	Sis-in-law	W	30	At home	Italy
Henry Steinhoff*	Head	W	44	Ship carpenter	Germany
Matilda	Wife	W	42	Keeping house	Germany
Annie	Daughter	W	4	At home	Texas
Margaret	Daughter	W	10 1/2	At home	Texas
Charles Smith*	Stepson	W	18	Laborer	Texas
John	Stepson	W	15	Laborer	Texas
Willie	Stepson	W	13	At'd school	Texas
Eddie	Stepson	W	13	At'd school	Texas
Agnes	Stepdau.	W	7	At home	Texas
Charles Wilkman*	Head	W	40	Laborer	Finland
Lena	Wife	W	39	Keeping house	Finland
Mary	Daughter	W	9	At'd school	Alabama
Charles	Son	W	6	At home	Texas
August	Son	W	4	At home	Texas
John	Son	W	2	At home	Texas

Appendix C Distribution of Alley Addressees Listed in 1881–82 and 1891–92 City Directories

The 260 people listed as living at an alley or rear address in the 1881–82 Galveston city directory were dispersed among ninety-five alleys in the city. Thirty-eight of those alleys had only a single listing, and twenty-one had two listings. It is unlikely that many—if any—alleys with a single listing in the directory actually had just one person or, for that matter, a single household living on the alley.

Three clusterings of alley listings are particularly notable. Ten blocks with alley listings are located on the northeast edge of town between Avenues A and D and Ninth and Thirteenth Streets. It was an area in which flooding was to be expected, land values were low, and houses were small, many on the front streets being indistinguishable in size from those along the alleys.

Ward Five—bordered by Twenty-fifth and Twenty-ninth Streets, Avenue J, and Galveston Bay—had the greatest concentration of inhabited alleys and alley residents. Originally, the ward had been predominantly residential. By 1881–82, the blocks nearer the bay were dominated by commercial activities associated with a transient, wharf-related workforce and some industrial use. The primary business district was east of Twenty-fifth Street.

With eleven listings, Fat Alley, the alley bordered by Twenty-eighth and Twenty-ninth Streets and Avenues D and E, was credited with the highest number of alley residents, not only in Ward Five but in the city as a whole. There were five black men, three black women, two white women, and one white man, a cook—the only person to have a listed occupation.

The block with the second highest density in the ward—and the city—was between Twenty-seventh and Twenty-eighth Streets and Avenues H and I. The ten listings for this block (five black men and five black women) actually represent seven households. Pastor and drayman Wiley Peterson, the only person on the alley with a listed occupation, and Wallace Seals lived in Martha Holloman's household, and two other listees also shared a house. Such arrangements, and the way in which they were included in the directory, were typical.

There was another concentration of alley listings to the south of Ward Five and in the blocks between Avenues J and N and Twenty-sixth and Thirty-first Streets, an area with strong associations for the black population. The first black Baptist church in Galveston, established during slavery, was located in the neighborhood, as were the black educational institutions. Three alleys in the area had six residents each: All the residents in two of those alleys were black.

Although the number of both alley addressees and inhabited alleys increased substantially between the 1881–82 and 1891–92 city directories, the same patterns continued. There was a high number of alleys with single listings (86) and two listings (37), but once again, those listings do not reflect actual household numbers.

Ward Five with its listing of 130 alley addressees, of whom 105 were black, had the highest concentration. The largest number of listings on a single alley both in Ward Five and in the city was 16: On the block bordered by Twenty-eighth and Twenty-ninth Streets and Avenues E and F (Block 448) were seven black men, eight black women, and one white male.

The fourteen people listed on Fat Alley were all blacks. They included seven women with no listed occupation, four laborers, a drayman, a harness cleaner, and a blind man named Jack Nelson. Nelson and two of the women lived in the household of Nancy Nelson who was a resident of Fat Alley in 1881–82. Neither of the Nelsons could be located in the 1880 census.

One of the alleys with the highest density and most even racial mix was bounded by Twenty-eighth and Twenty-ninth Streets and Avenues L and M. Its fifteen residents included seven whites—widow Cusack and her four sons accounting for five of them—and eight blacks—four men and four women. Three of the black men were dock workers; three of the Cusack boys were cotton press laborers and the fourth was an oyster opener. Two of the black women were domestic workers whose employers were specified.

Examples can be found of high-density alleys in which the listings were all white, such as the alley between Nineteenth and Twentieth Streets and Avenues C and D, an area that straddled the residential and central business district. Among the eleven addressees in three households on this alley were Rosina Millich and her four maiden daughters, all of whom worked at the bagging factory.

The growing population to the west, as evidenced in the 1891–92 city directory, is not surprising, but almost half of the 125 rear listings in Ward Six (as compared with just 13 ten years previously) are attributable to housing that gave new meaning to the term "rear" in Galveston. The Galveston Cotton and Woolen Mills, located on the north side of Avenue G between Fortieth and Forty-first Streets, built workers' housing on the block bounded by Forty-second and Forty-third Streets and Avenues G and H (Block 342). Fourteen one-story houses (seven pairs) fronted both Avenues G and H. A third row ran through the center of the block where an alley was usually located.

In the 1891–92 directory, 55 individuals were listed at thirteen "rear" addresses on Block 342. A typical household was that of millworker Walter K. Currin, who lived at "rear 4202 H" with five other Currins, all millworkers and probably his children. The company hired few, if any, blacks, so there were no blacks living on the block. Other blocks and alleys in the ward were more typical of Galveston in their racial makeup.

According to Gwendolyn Wright, families who rented company housing, such as that belonging to the Galveston Cotton and Woolen Mills, had to guarantee that the household would provide a prescribed number of mill workers—usually four or five. Boarders and extended family members could be counted, but if the number was not supplied, the family was evicted. See Wright, *Building the Dream: A Social History of Housing in America* (Cambridge: MIT Press, 1983 paperback edition), pp. 62, 66.

Appendix D Distribution of Alley Addressees Listed in 1901–2 and 1911–12 City Directories

The 1901–2 city directory was the first directory published after the 1900 hurricane. Listings for the 1911–12 directory were collected when the grade-raising project was nearing completion. As stated in chapter 6, a comparison of the listings in the two directories shows a slight reduction in both the number of alley addressees and the number of inhabited alleys, but a notable increase in the number of alleys in which there were twenty or more addressees: eleven alleys as compared with two in 1901–2.

Once again, Ward Five had, in 1911–12, the highest number of alley residents listed—317, of whom 276 were black. The ward also had eight of the alleys with twenty or more addressees. The residents on four of these alleys were all blacks, and two alleys had one white addressee. The two remaining alleys were Fat and Tin Can Alleys. Fat Alley was the most densely populated alley in the ward with twenty-eight addressees: twenty-two blacks (fifteen men and seven women) and six men whose names indicate that they were Hispanic. All the men worked as laborers except one black man, Henry T. Douglas, who was a musician. Tin Can Alley had twenty addressees: four black men, one white woman, and fifteen men whose names suggest that fourteen of them were Hispanic. All the men were laborers except one—Stephen Fisher, who was a delivery clerk for the Red Cross drugstore.

Wards Six and Eight were a distant second and third in alley listings—137 and 135 respectively—in the 1911–12 directory. In the years between the 1901–2 and 1911–12 directories, Wards One and Twelve showed a reduction in alley listings, probably because the blocks along the eastern edge of both wards were within the canal right-of-way and near the Seawall, and required the temporary and sometimes permanant relocation of some residents. Wards Three, Four, and Six, which, like Ward Five, were not in the primary grade-raising area, also showed a drop in listings. In part, this may reflect the flooding problems that these wards experienced as a result of the raising of adjacent areas, especially those immediately north of Avenue J. At the time the 1911–12 directory was assembled, portions of Ward Seven were being raised, which may account for the reduction in alley listings in that ward. The remaining wards—Two, Nine, Ten, and Eleven—showed relatively little change.

Appendix E Supplemental Tables Based on City Directory Listings: 1881–82, 1891–92, 1901–2, 1911–12

The tables that follow are based on the listings of alley addressees in four Galveston city directories: 1881–82, 1891–92, 1901–2, 1911–12.

There are specific reasons why the four editions were selected. The 1881–82 edition was the first directory to make a deliberate effort to list, in any substantial numbers, both alley addressees and blacks. The 1891–92 directory, the first to list addresses according to the house-numbering system still used today, provided a convenient ten-year period. The 1901–2 directory was the first citywide listing after the 1900 hurricane and predated the grade-raising project. The 1911–12 directory was assembled when the grade-raising project was nearing completion.

The tabulations reflect only those listings for which an alley location is definite. The "wks" [works] entries are not included. Although many individuals listed in the directories as "wks" were domestic employees living on their employer's property—and probably in a back building—the exact location of their living quarters is uncertain.

As stated in the text, the directory editors multiplied each entry by three to estimate the city's population.

Table E.1
Number of Inhabited Alleys, Alley Addressees, and Directory Listings

	1881–82	1891–92	1901–2	1911–12
No. of alleys with addressees	95	221	290	271
Total alley addressees	260	765	1,284	1,221
Total directory listings	9,052	16,074	17,695	22,194

Table E.2
Number of Alley Addressees by Ward and Race

	1881–82		1891–92		1901–2		1911–12		
Ward	Black	White	Black	White	Black	White	Black	White	Chinese
1	13	8	48	10	51	12	38	8	
2	5	10	35	14	88	17	93	20	
3	10	3	10	20	78	10	53	16	
4	24	8	70	8	119	11	79	5	3
5	55	24	105	25	232	39	276	41	
6	7	6	31	94	98	77	82	55	
7	13	4	63	10	109	11	85	7	
8	29	3	65	10	82	3	130	5	
9	4	1	31	5	45	7	43	9	
10	8	2	13	15	75	9	82	4	
11	7	3	24	14	50	14	59	3	
12	9	1	35	10	36	7	16	9	
? [a]	1	2			3	1			
TOTAL	**185**	**75**	**530**	**235**	**1,066**	**218**	**1,036**	**182**	**3**

[a] The specific alley, and therefore the ward, are not clear.

Table E.3
Number of Blocks in Each Ward with Alley Addressees

Ward	1881–82	1891–92	1901–2	1911–12
1	11	19	21	18
2	4	18	20	22
3	5	12	26	22
4	8	17	20	17
5	19	24	28	26
6	4	24	43	38
7	7	22 [a]	38	31 [b]
8	12	18	19	17
9	4	14	18	23
10	6	15	18	22
11	9	17	21	21
12	6	21	18	14
TOTAL	**95**	**221**	**290**	**271**

[a] One block is outside the map area shown in fig. 52 (p. 53).
[b] Two blocks are not on the map area in fig. 90 (p. 78).

Table E.4
Number of Directory Entries per Alley

No. of Entries Per Alley	Number of Alleys			
	1881–82	1891–92	1901–2	1911–12
1	38	86	75	83
2	21	37	55	50
3	13	30	34	33
4	6	15	21	21
5	5	11	27	16
6	6	9	20	13
7	2	8	11	10
8		10	8	9
9	2	5	6	2
10	1	1	9	7
11	1	4	7	3
12		1	1	4
13			3	4
14		1	2	2
15		1	2	1
16		1	2	
17			1	
18			3	2
19			1	
20				(Ward 5) 3
21				(Ward 5) 2
23				(Ward 5) 1
25				(Wards 5, 8) 2
26				(Ward 4) 1
27				(Ward 2) 1
28				(Ward 5) 1
29			(Ward 5) 1	
32			(Ward 5) 1	
55		(Ward 6) 1		

NOTE: Three addressees were not in a specific block in 1881–82, and four were not in a specific block in 1901–2.

Appendix F Alphabetical Listing of Alley Dwellers Mentioned in the Book

Listed below are the names of individuals who are definitely known to have lived or had a business in a back building along a Galveston alley and are mentioned in the book. The names appear in the text unless otherwise noted: ap=appendix; n=note. The asterisk denotes either an interviewee or an alley dweller mentioned in an interview conducted by the author. For page numbers, consult the index under the specific name.

Ackermann, Christina Schmish
Ackermann, Hermann
Adam, William
Adams, John
Alexander, Julius (coffee roasting and spice mill)
Allen, Mary
Anella, Josephine (ap)
Ash[e], Hannah
Ash[e], Tena
Baker, Mrs. (n)
Bennett, Sarah
Bouffa, Annie (ap)
Bouffa, Joseph (ap)
Brantigan, Francisca Hendel
Brantigan, Peter
Caldwell, Sarah
Charles, Annie Mae (née Fiedler) *
"Chicken Brain, Miss"*
Clark, James
Clay, Chester *
Clay, Willie Mae *
Coffey, John
Coffey, Kate
Cole, Esther
Cole, Lewis
Coleman, Jennie
Collins, Arthur *
Compton, Winnie
Cullen and Gleich (horseshoers and farriers)
Cunningham, Walter *
Currin, Walter K. (ap)
Cusack, Johanna (ap)
Davis, Ed (ap)
Davis, Emma
Day, Matilda
Diamond, Pam *
Douglas, Henry T. (ap)
Drave, Adolph (n)
Dutton, Margaret
Eggert, Friedrich
Ennis, Robert
Ernest, Mr. (operated policy shop) *
Evans, E. Burke *
Fisher, Stephen (ap)
Frank, L. (n)
Gains, Jane
Green, Mrs. (n)
Green, William (Bill)
Griffin, Louis
Griffin, Mina
Grimes, Lucy
Harris, Pat
Hawkins, Rachel
Hertz, Pauline (pseudonym) *
Holloman, Martha (ap)
Hornsberry, Matilda Johnson
Hornsberry, Nathaniel
Hudson, Henry
Jackson, Alf
Jackson, Amelia
Jackson, James
Jackson, Jane
Jackson, Mitchell
Jalousey, Mariano
James, Alford
James, Penny
Johnson, Henry
Johnson, Jack
Johnson, Nettie
Johnson, P. (n)
Johnson, Richard
Johnson, Susie
Lohmann, Johanna Wedemeyer (later Johanna Toebleman)
Lohmann, Teodor

Lynn, Eva (née Scott)
Martin, Louis *
Martin, Sarah *
Millican, Bill *
Millich, Rosina (ap)
Mitchell, Elsie
Mitchell, George
Mosely, Mrs.
Neal, Henry (n)
Nelson, Jack (ap)
Nelson, Nancy (ap)
Newberry, John
Newberry, Stella
Ort, Johann
Owens, Alice (ap)
Owens, William
Palmer, Ethel *
Peterson, Wiley
Pettit, Charles
Pettit, Ophelia
Ramsey, Ella Belle
Richardson, Mary
Robinson, India
Robinson, Isaac
Robinson, Linda
Robinson, Manuel
Scott, Eva (née Lynn)
Scurry, Elzina *
Scurry, Mitchell *
Seals, Wallace (ap)
Sims, Amos
Smith, Agnes (ap)
Smith, Charles (ap)
Smith, Eddie (ap)
Smith, John (ap)
Smith, Willie (ap)
Stanley, Maude
Steinhoff, Annie (ap)
Steinhoff, Henry (ap)
Steinhoff, Margaret (ap)
Steinhoff, Matilda (ap)
Strawberry, Mr. (operated policy shop) *
Thompson, Andrew
Thompson, Pearley (n)
Thompson, Sarah (n)
Toebleman, Conrad
Toebleman, Johanna
Trave, Joseph
Walker, Mary
Walls family *
Washington, Becky
Washington, Ella
Washington, Lucinda
Wentzel, A. E.
White, Amanda
"Who-dat?"*
Wilkman, August (ap)
Wilkman, Charles (father)
Wilkman, Charles (son, ap)
Wilkman, John (ap)
Wilkman, Lena
Wilkman, Mary
Wooden, Kate

Last name unknown:
Becky (laundress, Hanna family)
Eveline (servant, Kempner family)
Isabel (servant, Kempner family)

Notes

The following abbreviations appear in the notes for frequently cited sources:

CAH	Center for American History, University of Texas, Austin, Texas
CGL	Clayton Genealogical Library, Houston, Texas
GCCO	Galveston County Clerk's Office
GCPC	Galveston County Probate Court
GDN	*Galveston Daily News*
RL	Rosenberg Library, Galveston, Texas

Introduction: Views and Interviews

1. The primary depository of Sanborn fire-insurance maps of Galveston used by the author was the Rosenberg Library. The library has original maps for the years 1889, 1899, and 1912. It does not have original maps for 1876 and 1885. Original maps of all years are available at the Center for American History, University of Texas, Austin; the Library of Congress; and the Sanborn Mapping and Geographic Information Service, Pelham, New York. The Rosenberg Library has a photostat copy of the 1885 map. There can be minor variations in the annotations or pasteover additions to maps for the same year, so it is advisable to use the same set.

2. *Morrison & Fourmy's Galveston City Directory, 1936–37* (Dallas: Morrison & Fourmy, 1936).

3. George P. Rawick, ed., *The American Slave: A Composite Autobiography,* suppl., ser. 2 (Westport, Conn.: Greenwood Press, 1979), vol. 9, *Texas Narratives,* pt. 8:3580–83.

4. *Morrison & Fourmy's General Directory of the City of Galveston, 1901–02* (Galveston: Morrison and Fourmy, 1901); *Directory of the City of Galveston 1909–10* (Galveston: Morrison & Fourmy, 1909); *Morrison & Fourmy Directory Co.'s Galveston City Directory, 1919* (Houston: Morrison & Fourmy, 1919); *Morrison & Fourmy's Galveston City Directory 1930* (Dallas: Morrison & Fourmy, 1930).

5. Taped interviews with Bill Millican, November 19, 1990, and February 21, 1991.

6. At the time Bill Millican's family and the Antones lived at the property, the house number was 2616. It is now number 2620. The Antone family bought the property in 1901. According to the 1910 census, Peter Antone was a forty-five-year-old mulatto and a "So.Am. Portuguese" who had immigrated to the United States in 1880. He is listed for the first time at the address—2616 Avenue M rear—in the 1901–2 Galveston city directory. The 1910 census lists Antone as a cotton runner on the wharf; city directories list him as a screwman. U.S. Census records for Galveston County, 1910, microfilm, CGL; Galveston County Assessor's Abstracts for Galveston City Lots, 1898–1903, RL.

7. Galveston Island is two miles across at its widest point and thirty-two miles long.

8. The property is still owned by the family.

Chapter 1
In View . . . on the Backside: The Pre–Civil War Years

1. Charles W. Hayes, *Galveston: History of the Island and the City* (1879; reprint, Austin: Jenkins Garrett Press, 1974), 1:260.

2. Major streets had other names besides their numerical or alphabetical designations. Avenue J, the major east-west thoroughfare, for instance, was also called Broadway, and the major north-south street, Twenty-fifth Street, was also known as Bath Avenue. To avoid confusion, only numerical and alphabetical street names are used here, except for street names appearing in quotations.

3. Matilda C. Houstoun, *Texas and the Gulf of Mexico; or, Yachting in the New World* (Philadelphia: G. B. Zieber & Co., 1845), p. 128.

Alleys were integral to the Galveston plan from the early stages of the city's development. In 1837, before any survey was conducted, the Galveston City Company published a plan of the proposed city. There are no alleys in the five-mile grid, but grandiosity, not practicality, was the theme of the promotional publication. The 1845 Sandusky plan, the first to be published after Groesbeck made his survey, shows the alley system. See John W. Reps, *Cities of the American West: A History of Frontier Urban Planning* (Princeton: Princeton University Press, 1979), pp. 129–34, 709 (nn. 34–38).

Alleys quickly became a reference on the Galveston landscape. Hayes relates that Andrew Baldinger erected a bakery "on the corner of the alley and Twenty-third street" in late 1839. Hayes, *Galveston,* 1:309.

4. German traveler Dr. Ferdinand Roemer claimed that when he saw Galveston for the first time in 1838, there were only one or two houses. When he

returned in 1845, the city had "expanded to include five thousand inhabitants, a number of wholesale mercantile houses, three churches and several hotels." Ferdinand Roemer, *Texas with Particular Reference to German Immigration and the Physical Appearance of the Country*, trans. Oswald Mueller (San Antonio: Standard Printing Co., 1935), p. 40.

5. Lucy Weston Shaw to Jane N. Weston, February 24, 1839, typescript, Mrs. Lucy Parker Weston Shaw Letters, RL.

6. Ibid., September 29, 1839.

7. Ibid., January 13, 1839.

8. Ibid., January 13, 1839; February 24, 1839.

9. Houstoun, *Texas and the Gulf*, pp. 123, 217.

10. *Civilian and Galveston City Gazette*, April 22, 1843; March 16, 1844; GCCO, Real Property Records, Book D, pp. 265–66.

11. *Civilian and Galveston City Gazette*, December 11, 1847; December 2, 1843.

12. Ibid., December 11, 1847.

13. 1846–1855 Cash Account Book, John L. Darragh Papers, p. 156, RL.

14. *Civilian and Galveston City Gazette*, July 22, 1851. Galveston's first ordinances levied a $75 monthly tax on any black who rented or owned property in the city. After 1846, slaveholders were allowed to rent a building for their slaves if they posted bond guaranteeing good conduct. See Paul Dean Lack, "Urban Slavery in the Southwest" (Ph.D. dissertation, Texas Tech University, 1973), pp. 73–74.

15. Ibid., pp. 74–75; *Charter Amendments and Revised Ordinances of the City of Galveston* (Galveston: Printed at the "Civilian" Book & Job Office, 1855), p. 52; *Charter and Revised Code of Ordinances of the City of Galveston, Passed in the Years 1856–7* (Galveston: Printed at the Civilian Book and Job Office, 1857), pp. 89–91. Both charter references RL.

16. See Richard C. Wade, *Slavery in the Cities: The South 1820–1860* (London: Oxford University Press, 1964); Earl Wesley Fornell, *The Galveston Era: The Texas Crescent on the Eve of Secession* (Austin: University of Texas Press, 1961); and Lack, "Urban Slavery in the Southwest."

Wade's book is required reading for anyone interested in the subject of urban slavery. The cities that serve as Wade's case studies (Savannah, Charleston, Mobile, Louisville, New Orleans, St. Louis, Richmond, Washington, Norfolk, and Baltimore) are all older and most considerably larger than Galveston. Still, there are many similarities in their histories. The author disagrees with Wade's statements (p. 61) that "urban housing in the South . . . omitted alleys" and that "unlike the thinly sliced commercial and residential areas elsewhere, the city blocks in the South remained solid" as a way to control slave activity. Galveston is just one of many Southern cities and towns in which alleys existed during slavery.

Fornell's description of Galveston prior to the Civil War is helpful in a general way but very limited in its interpretation of the slave population. Lack's dissertation is a more useful source. He selected four cities for a comparative study: Galveston, Austin, Little Rock (Arkansas), and Shreveport (Louisiana). Unfortunately, Lack's dissertation has not been refined and published.

17. Rawick, *American Slave*, vol. 9, *Texas Narratives*, pt. 8:3403–4; *Civilian and Gazette*, July 14, 1857. The precise years to which Josephine Ryles was referring in her interview are uncertain. The interviewers were not very exacting in recording and checking names or in identifying people like slaveholders Sultry and Schwoebel. Neither name is listed in the 1860 census or in the early city directories. Sultry may have been James Sorley who was, according to the 1859–60 city directory, a cotton factor and commission merchant. He is listed in the 1860 Slave Schedule as owning five slaves, but none of the slaves is a close match in age to Ryles. According to the 1900 census, Ryles was born in 1849 and therefore would have been old enough to have clear recollections of the years before the Civil War. W. & D. Richardson, *Galveston Directory for 1859–60* (Galveston: Printed at the "News" Book and Job Office, 1859); U.S. Census, Galveston County Free and Slave Schedules, 1860, microfilm, Houston Public Library and CGL; U.S. Census records for Galveston County, 1900, microfilm, Houston Public Library and CGL.

18. Lack, "Urban Slavery in the Southwest," pp. 109–11. Free black sailors, for example, were not allowed to disembark from ships that docked in the Galveston harbor.

19. Shaw to Weston, December 3, 1839.

20. A. DeLano, *Galveston Directory for 1856–7* (Galveston: Printed at the News Book and Job Office, 1856); *Galveston Directory for 1859–60*; GCCO, Real Property Records, Book G, p. 361. L. Frank, carpenter, and P. Johnson, occupation unidentified, lived on the alley between Avenues B and C and Seventeenth and Eighteenth Streets. Adolph Drave, carpenter, owned his property on the alley bordered by Avenues F and G and Twenty-eighth and Twenty-ninth Streets.

21. Shaw to Weston, January 31, 184[1]; April 25, 1841. Lucy Shaw dated the January 31 letter as 1840, but it was written in 1841.

22. "Running the Blockade," letter 38, January 12, 1930, typescript, Margaret Sealy Burton Papers, CAH; "The Frosch House," initialed and dated "K.V.P./1935," typescript, Ratchford Collection, Texas State Archives. In the Burton papers, the McLeod name is spelled McCloud.

23. J. D. B. DeBow, *Statistical View of the United States . . . Being a Compendium of the Seventh Census* (Washington: Gideon and Company, 1852), p. 397; Joseph C. G. Kennedy, *Population of the United States in 1860; Compiled from the Original Returns of the Eighth Census* (Washington: Government Printing Office, 1864), pp. 486–87.

24. U.S. Census, Galveston County Free and Slave Schedules, 1860. In Wards One and Two, which covered the area east of Twenty-third Street, there were 141 slaveholders, 624 slaves, and 172 slave houses. Most slaveholders—108—had between 1 and 5 slaves and only 1 slave house. Some owners with 6 slaves had more than 1 slave house, although there were others who had only 1 house for 6, 7, or 8 slaves. Owners with 9 or more slaves always had at least 2 slave houses, but space was never generous—two slaveholders, for example, had 15 slaves in 2 houses, and another had 28 slaves in 3 houses.

The census taker in Ward Three did not count the slave houses, but given the standards that existed in Wards One and Two, 149 would be a conservative estimate. In the area between Twenty-third and Thirty- first Streets, there were 120 slaveholders and 554 slaves. Of these, 96 slaveholders owned between 1 and 5 slaves, and the remaining 24 had between 6 and 29 slaves.

The number of slave houses may sound excessive, but a map drawn sometime during the Civil War, and showing the footprint of both front and back buildings throughout the city, easily supports that number. *Map of Galveston, Texas, Showing the Rebel Line of Works. Surveyed and Drawn by Order of G. L. Gillespie, Brevet Major and Chief Engr., Mil. Div. of the Gulf, Under the Direction of Lt. S. E. McGregory, Comdg. Topl. Party, by Pl. St. Vignes, Asst.*, Cartographic Division, National Archives. The map could not be reproduced to a legible size for the book.

25. Historic American Buildings Survey [HABS], Photograph–Data Book Report, Henry Rosenberg House (TEX-260), 1967, Library of Congress; U.S. Census, Galveston County Free and Slave Schedules, 1860. The Rosenberg Library has photocopies of the HABS data sheets.

26. Eugene Marshall's Diary 1859–1860, Eugene Marshall Papers, William R. Perkins Library, Duke University.

27. Hayes, *Galveston*, 1:387; Houstoun, *Texas and the Gulf*, p. 128.

28. Hayes, *Galveston*, 1:340–41, 361–62.

29. *Charter and Revised Code, 1856–57*, pp. 71–72, 74.

30. Ibid., pp. 74–75.

31. Ibid., pp. 102–4.

Chapter 2
Independent of the Front House: The Post–Civil War Years

1. Hayes, *Galveston*, 2:661; 2:738; 2:643; *GDN*, June 13, 1865.

2. *GDN*, July 15, 1865; Hayes, *Galveston*, 2:661; Francis A. Walker, *A Compendium of the Ninth Census* (Washington: Government Printing Office, 1872), p. 343. The racial breakdown was 10,810 whites, 3,007 blacks, and 1 Indian.

3. "Life and History of Tim Finn, 1854–1896," handwritten manuscript, Finn Papers, p. 66, CAH; Hayes, *Galveston*, 2:661; *GDN*, July 4, 1865.

4. *GDN*, August 29, 1865.

5. Ibid., June 8, 29, 1865; August 30, 1865; July 15, 1865.

6. Ibid., July 27, 1865; September 19, 1865.

7. "Black Galveston: A personal view of Community History in many Categories of Life," handwritten manuscript, Ralph Albert Scull Papers, pp. 5, 75, 77, RL.

8. Dr. Greensville Dowell, "Medical Topography of Galveston," in W. Richardson & Co., *Galveston Directory, 1866–67* (Galveston: Printed at the "News" Book and Job Office, 1866), p. 62.

9. Mrs. Rebecca McLeod to Jonathan Sturges Beers, June 12, 1867, and November 17, 1867, Beers Family Papers, RL. Rebecca McLeod was the widow of Hugh McLeod, attorney and general in the Confederate army. The family had left Galveston and moved to Savannah at the beginning of the war; Hugh McLeod died in Richmond in 186[2] while in command of his regiment. *GDN*, July 4, 1869.

10. "Black Galveston," p. 7; Lucian Minor to H. M. Trueheart, August 25, 1870, H. M. Trueheart Papers, RL.

11. GCCO, Real Property Records, Book X, Bill of Sale, filed August 26, 1867, pp. 67–68.

12. U.S. Census records for Galveston County, 1870, microfilm, CGL.

13. Amelia E. Barr, *All the Days of My Life: An Autobiography* (New York: D. Appleton, 1913), pp. 261–66; Amelia Barr to Jennie [Alexander], March 3, 18[67], and June 3, 18[67], Barr Papers, CAH.

14. McLeod to Beers, February [n.d.], 1866, and February 2, 1867.

15. *GDN*, July 10, 1869; November 2, 1870.

16. Minor to Trueheart, October 3, 1870; U.S. Census records for Galveston County, 1870.

17. John Burbank to H. P. Hervey, February 5, 1928, in "Reminiscences of Galveston, 1865–1868," typescript copy, CAH.

18. *GDN*, May 4, 1866; Dowell, "Medical Topography," p. 63.

19. *GDN*, April 13, 1867; Dowell, "Medical Topography," p. 62; *GDN*, July 4, 5, 1867.

20. "Life and History of Tim Finn," p. 67.

21. Hayes, *Galveston*, 2:738; Barr, *All the Days*, pp. 278–85; Burbank to Hervey, February 5, 1928. It is just happenstance that the author found such a disparate set of documents representing such a disparate group of people all referring to the epidemic, but it shows how deadly and all-pervading the fever was. The number of deaths varies slightly by source; the number used here is quoted in Hayes.

22. "Life and History of Tim Finn," p. 67; "Black Galveston," p. 5; Burbank to Hervey, February 5, 1928.

23. *The Galveston Republican*, March 16, 1868; June 1, 1868.

24. *GDN*, July 11, 9, 1869; March 20, 1870; April 3, 17, 1870.

Chapter 3
From Privies to Prostitution: The 1870s and 1880s

1. I. H. Kempner, *Recalled Recollections* (Dallas: The Egan Company, 1961), pp. 2–3.

2. *Fayman & Reilly's Galveston City Directory, for 1875–6* (Galveston: Strickland & Clarke, 1875).

The eighteen black men included seven laborers, three draymen, a porter, and a preacher. Five of the eighteen had no occupation, and that of another, Henry Neal, was not specified. Neal's business, Patterson & Neal, was neither identified nor listed elsewhere in the directory. There were no black women listed with an alley address.

The occupations of the twenty-four white men were more varied. They included four laborers, three carpenters, three vegetable-stand vendors, two fruit-stand vendors, and one each of the following occupations: tinner, cook, mattressmaker, cigarmaker, baker, coffee-stand waiter, butcher, shoemaker, blacksmith, and coffee-stand proprietor. Two white men did not list an occupation. Two white women, Mrs. Green and Mrs. Baker, were listed with alley addresses but no occupation.

Twenty-one whites and six blacks were concentrated in the blocks between Eighth and Twenty-fifth Streets and north of Avenue J. One alley between Avenues B and C and Sixteenth and Seventeenth Streets had five residents, all white: a cook, a baker, a carpenter, a laborer, and Mrs. Green. There were eight blacks and three whites in the area south of Avenue J and between Thirteenth and Twenty-fifth Streets. Five of the blacks—three laborers, the preacher, and one man without a specified occupation—lived on the alley between Avenues J and K and Thirteenth and Fourteenth Streets. In the area between Twenty-fifth and Thirty-second Streets and north of Avenue H, there were three blacks and two whites.

The coffee-stand proprietor, the waiter, and two of the produce vendors lived on alleys close to their city market businesses. The blacksmith and draymen may have been operating businesses from their alley locations, but the distinction is not always clear between those who worked for themselves and those who worked for others.

In some cases, it is difficult to determine the exact alley to which a listing refers, one example being Robert Ennis's residence in the "alley, near cor. av. L and 25th." Listings like "alley bet. 16th and 17th nr Strand [Avenue B]" have been grouped with specific alleys in the vicinity, such as the "alley bet 16th and 17th, Strand and Mechanic [Avenues B and C]," because a number of people were listed in the latter and it was, obviously, an inhabited alley.

3. The 1880 census records partially corroborate Kempner's recollections. At that time, the household consisted of Mr. and Mrs. Kempner, their two sons, a nephew, and four black female servants—a house servant, a cook, and two nurses, one of whom was Eveline. Eveline's last name is indecipherable. U.S. Census records for Galveston County, 1880, microfilm, CGL.

4. *GDN*, April 2, 3, 1870; May 5, 1867; May 29, 1870.

5. Ibid., May 19, 1875; *Fayman & Reilly's Galveston City Directory, for 1875–6*.

6. *GDN*, April 25, 27, 1880.

7. Ibid., October 29, 1880; February 10, 1886.

8. Ibid., October 20, 1885; November 5, 1885; City of Galveston Mortuary Record No. 1, January 1, 1875–December 31, 1886, pp. 261, 263, RL.

9. *GDN*, June 28, 29, 1887; *Morrison & Fourmy's General Directory of the City of Galveston 1886–87* (Galveston: Morrison & Fourmy, 1886); *Morrison & Fourmy's General Directory of the City of Galveston 1888–89* (Galveston: Morrison & Fourmy, 1888).

Local law officials were given generous leeway in enforcing vagrancy laws, which covered such activities as loitering, drunkenness, homelessness, and prostitution. Following the Civil War, vagrancy laws were widely and often arbitrarily used to control the black population in Southern cities and towns. See Leon F. Litwack, *Been in the Storm So Long: The Aftermath of Slavery* (New York: Knopf, 1979), pp. 318–22.

10. *GDN*, May 31, 1899.

11. Ibid., September 13–17, 23, 1885.

12. Ibid., May 30, 1880.

13. Ibid., May 23, 7, 1875; May 18, 1880; November 10, 1885. Through a typographical error, Fannie Miller's last name appears as "Millie" in the article.

George Harris was also on the Criminal Court docket on November 25 for keeping "a disorderly house, failure to pay occupation [tax] and exhibiting gaming." *GDN*, November 10, 1885.

14. Ibid., November 14, 1880.

15. Ibid., August 15, 1875; April 18, 1875.

16. Ibid., August 15, 1875.

17. Ibid., July 9, 1875; May 27, 1880; June 15, 16, 1875; [City of Galveston] Index to Interment Record 1866–1881, p. 203, RL.

18. *GDN*, September 2, 1885.

19. Ibid., May 29, 1880.

20. Ibid., September 16–19, 1875.

21. Ibid., September 25, 1875.

22. Ibid., October 10, 1875; September 24, 25, 1875; October 24, 1875.

23. Ibid., November 13, 14, 1885.

24. Kempner, *Recalled Recollections*, p. 7; Rawick, *American Slave*, vol. 10, *Texas Narratives*, pt. 9:3974–75. When Washington was interviewed in 1937, she was living at 2714 Avenue H rear with her daughter, who supported the two women by taking in washing.

25. *GDN*, November 17, 15, 14, 1885.

26. Ibid., November 14, 26, 1885.

27. Ibid., November 20, 1885; December 3–5, 18, 1885; April 4, 1886; Galveston County Assessor's Abstracts for City Lots, 1880–1890, RL.

28. *GDN*, October 3, 1885.

29. Ibid., June 11, 1875; May 22, 1875.

30. Ibid., April 1, 4, 14, 16, 20, 1875; March 21, 1880.

31. Ibid., May 15, 1880; June 5, 1880.

32. Ibid., May 23, 1880.

33. Ibid., June 30, 1887; July 1, 1887.

Chapter 4
Living "in the Rear"

1. U.S. Census records for Galveston County, 1880. Wilkman's name was spelled various ways, including Velkman, Welkman, and Weltman. The family apparently adopted—or accepted—the Wilkman spelling in the early 1880s. It is the spelling most often used.

2. *Morrison and Fourmy's Directory, 1881–82* (Galveston: M. Strickland & Co., 1880).

3. C. W. Marston, compiler, *Galveston City Directory, for 1868–1869* (Galveston: Shaw & Blaylock, 1868), p. vii.

4. John H. Heller, *Galveston City Directory, 1872* (Galveston: Printed at the "News" Steam Job Printing Office, 1872); *Galveston City Directory, for 1875–6*. If the directories had started listing blacks at an earlier date, it would be easier to determine the blacks who stayed in Galveston, those who continued living with their former owners, and those who migrated to the city in the years immediately after the Civil War.

5. Of the 260 alley addressees in the 1881–82 city directory, 120 can be identified in the 1880 census: 78 people are probably living at the same address; another 42 are living at different locations, which means they moved to their alley address sometime after June, when the census was taken, and by early December, when the directory was tabulated.

6. The individuals and families described in the chapter were selected as representative alley dwellers. Using the 1881–82 city directory as the initial source, the author first checked the 260 names of alley addressees against the 1880 census. The names of the 120 people who were identified in both documents were then checked in other census records and city directories, as well as mortuary and marriage records, tax assessment abstracts, and deed and probate records. Some names yielded no additional information beyond the listings in the 1881–82 city directory and the 1880 census. In some instances there were minor discrepancies in such details as dates, the spelling of names, and ages. After working with the sources over a period of time and becoming familiar with the personalities, the author found it easier to detect inaccuracies.

In researching the profiles, the following documents were used repeatedly and are not cited separately for each individual:

Galveston city directories, 1856–57 through 1915, RL

Galveston city directories on microfiche and microfilm for the years 1856–57 through 1902, Houston Public Library

U.S. Census, Galveston County Population Schedules, 1860, 1870, 1880, 1900, and 1910, microfilm, CGL

Sanborn insurance maps, 1885 (photostat copy), 1889 with 1891 and 1894 updates, 1899 with 1906 update, and 1912 with multiple updates, RL.

City of Galveston Mortuary Records are located in the Rosenberg Library. They are cited according to book number:

No. 1, January 1, 1875–December 31, 1886
No. 2, January 1, 1887–August 9, 1894
No. 3, August 10, 1894–March 30, 1900

No. 4, March 30, 1900–December 31, 1903
No. 5, January 1, 1904–January 31, 1910
No. 6, February 1, 1910–May 31, 1918
(index only)
No. 7, June 1, 1918–December 30, 1926
Index to Interment Record 1866–1881

The same information was not recorded in every mortuary book. For example, Book 5 was the first to record how long a person had resided in Galveston. Occasionally, the recorder did not enter all the requested information such as burial location.

7. One all-inclusive footnote is given at the conclusion of each profile. (Hornsberry and Cole) Index to Galveston Marriages, Book D, pp. 152, 407, microfilm, Houston Public Library; Mortuary Record No. 1, pp. 52, 242; Mortuary Record No. 2, p. 2; Mortuary Record No. 5, p. 38; Interment Book, p. 223, line 414. Nat Hornsberry's name was listed in the mortuary report of the *Galveston Daily News*, December 28, 1884. When Lewis Cole died, there was a short notice in "The City" column, *GDN*, January 15, 1887.

8. (Bennett) Mortuary Record No. 7, p. 5. Mortuary records state that Bennett was born in Selma, Alabama, but the birthplaces of her parents are unknown.

9. (Pettits) Actually, the Pettits lived on the Hance property for a very short period of time. They had married in November 1879. Charles Pettit died of hepatitis in October 1881, after which Ophelia lived in a succession of locations, including the alley of a block on which Charles had lived when a bachelor. Index to Galveston Marriages, Book F, p. 499; Mortuary Record No. 1, p. 167.

10. The Jalousey spelling appears only in the 1881–82 city directory. Thereafter, it was Gelussick.

11. In the nineteenth century, "washerwoman" was one of the labels given women who were prostitutes. This was probably true for some women listed as "washerwoman" in the Galveston census, but this is not to suggest that all washerwomen were prostitutes. It was difficult enough for a woman to earn a living if she was white and could read and write; it was even more difficult if she was black and could not read or write. In order to survive, many women, black and white, combined working as prostitutes with other service jobs or resorted to prostitution when no other income was available. See Timothy J. Gilfoyle, *City of Eros: New York City, Prostitution, and the Commercialization of Sex, 1790–1920* (New York: W. W. Norton, 1992), pp. 59–61.

12. (Ackermann) *Ships Passenger Lists Port of Galveston, Texas 1846–1871* (Easley, S.C.: Southern Historical Press, 1984), p. 116; Index to Galveston Marriages, Book D, p. 409; Galveston County Assessor's Abstracts for Galveston City Out-Lots, 1880–1903; Clarence Ousley, *Galveston in Nineteen Hundred* (Atlanta: William C. Chase, 1900), p. 291. Ackermann must have bought the Fortieth Street property in 1900 because, in that year, he was still listed in the abstracts as owner of the Sixteenth Street property but not the Fortieth Street lot.

13. (Jackson) *GDN*, June 26, 1875; Galveston County Assessor's Abstracts, City Lots, 1880–1899; Mortuary Record No. 3, p. 56. In *Morrison & Fourmy's General Directory of the City of Galveston, 1895–96* (Galveston: Morrison & Fourmy, 1895), Amelia Jackson is listed as a laundress, and Mitchell Jackson is a janitor at a downtown building fifteen blocks away.

14. (Coffey) Index to Galveston Marriages, Book C, p. 298; *GDN*, August 1, 1877; May 7, 1881; Mortuary Record No. 1, p. 155. Thomas Coffey's birthplace, according to the 1870 census, was South Carolina, and both his parents were Irish. The mortuary record states that he was born in England.

15. The Thompsons lived on both Tin Can and Fat Alleys. According to the 1900 census, Thompson, born in North Carolina and sixty years old, was a day laborer who had been unemployed for six months of the year. His forty-five-year-old wife, Sarah, was born in Texas. Four of their fifteen children were living, two of whom lived with them, as did a grandson. Their fourteen-year-old daughter, Pearley, worked as a nurse, and the boys, ages eight and nine, attended school. At one point, Amos Sims (see Introduction) was among those living on the same property with the Thompson family. Thompson died of heart failure on October 29, 1901, and was buried in Old Potter's Field. Sometime during the next few years, his grandson, Henry Hudson, moved to another alley to live with his aunt, Sarah Bennett. Sarah Thompson and her son stayed in Ward Five. Mortuary Record No. 4, p. 48.

16. *GDN*, July 31, 1877; August 1, 2, 1877.

17. Ibid., August 4, 1877.

18. Ibid., August 4, 2, 1877.

19. (Griffin) Mortuary Record No. 2, p. 66. Griffin's death record states that he was born in Washington, D.C. The 1880 census recorded that both Griffins were from Virginia. Their four children, the eldest twelve, were all born in Texas.

20. (Robinson) *GDN*, October 29, 1880; November 13, 1880; Galveston County Assessor's Abstracts, City Lots, 1885-1895; Index to Marriages, Book H, p. 58; Mortuary Record No. 5, p. 91.

21. *Morrison & Fourmy's General Directory of the City of Galveston, 1891–92* (Galveston: Morrison & Fourmy, 1890). The tripling of alley addressees between 1881–82 and 1891–92 may reflect, to a minor degree, an effort to better record the alley population. The numbers, however, do not seem excessive given the growth of the city and the dwindling housing options available to poor residents.

22. Most of the 1890 census burned.

23. Of the 72 white women with alley addresses, 37—including 25 widows—did not list an occupation. The cotton mill employed 19 women, and another 10 worked in the bagging and rope factories. Three women were seamstresses, 2 were domestics who listed their employer, and 1 was a fruit peddlar. In addition to the 198 black women with no listed occupation and the 17 listed as working for a specific employer, 2 were listed as cooks and 1 was listed as a porter.

24. The listing for Priscilla Parks is typical: "Parks Priscilla (c), wks Mrs. Lucy Sandall, r. same."

25. Mortuary Record No. 2, p. 101; Galveston County Assessor's Abstracts, City Lots, 1891–1903.

26. Mortuary Record No. 2, pp. 63, 132.

Chapter 5
Owning Alley Property

1. Although the number of property owners living on the alleys was small, the exact number is virtually impossible to determine. Of the 260 alley dwellers listed in the 1881–82 directory, only 11 names appear in the Galveston County Assessor's Abstracts as property owners, a number that does not account for those whose property was in another name or for those who lived on an alley but were not listed as such in the directory.

The following documents were used repeatedly in researching this chapter and are not cited separately for each property:

Galveston city directories, 1856–57 through 1915, RL
Galveston city directories on microfiche and microfilm for the years 1856–57 through 1902, Houston Public Library
Galveston County Assessor's Abstracts for Galveston City Lots and Out-Lots, 1880–1914, RL
U.S. Census, Galveston County Population Schedules, 1860, 1870, 1880, 1900, and 1910, microfilm, CGL
Sanborn insurance maps, 1885 (photostat copy), 1889 with 1891 and 1894 updates, 1899 with 1906 update, and 1912 with multiple updates, RL
Index to Galveston County Deed Records, Stewart Title Company.

Other documents that are specific to a property, such as deeds and probate, marriage, and death records, are cited individually.

2. One all-inclusive footnote is given at the conclusion of each profile. (Brantigan) GCCO, Real Property Records, Book N, p. 696; Book 124, p. 392; Index to Galveston Marriages, Book D, p. 389, microfilm, Houston Public Library; *GDN*, November 14, 15, 1885; December 5, 1885.

3. (Eggert) *Ships Passenger Lists*, p. 57; GCCO, Real Property Records, Book 3, p. 352; Index to Galveston Marriages, Book E, p. 109. The first year that Eggert was listed at the Avenue K address was 1871, the year in which he married.

4. (Toebleman) GCCO, Real Property Records, Book 10, pp. 556–59; Book 27, pp. 545–48; Book 29, pp. 430–31; Book 35, pp. 324–28; Book 57, pp. 501–2; Book 72, pp. 602–5; Book 216, p. 62; Index to Galveston Marriages, Book E, p. 359, and Book F, p. 414; Index to Mortuary Record No. 6; Galveston Insurance Board Records, RL. The insurance records note that the back house was "moved & added to front bldg 1921."

5. (Allen) GCCO, Real Property Records, Book 43, p. 614; Mortuary Record No. 1, p. 279; *GDN*, June 12, 1914. Mary Allen's obituary described her as a longtime Galveston resident who was "much interested in work among the poor, having been identified with church societies for many years."

6. (Wooden) GCCO, Real Property Records, Book R, p. 282; Book V, pp. 246–47, 503; Book W, pp. 180–81, 510–11; GCPC Minutes Book 33, pp. 146–49, 243–44; Index to Galveston Marriages, Book C, p. 320; Mortuary Record No. 1, p. 11; Mortuary Record No. 3, p. 45. The many variations and spellings of Kate Wooden's name in the city directories, tax records, and other documents illustrate the difficulties in tracing many black residents in Galveston. She appears as Catharine Kansberry, Kitty Canterberry, Kittie Canteberry, Katie Canterbury, Katie Wooden, Kate Woods, Katie Wood, and Kate Wootens. To complicate matters further, there was another black woman named Kate or Katie Woods living in Galveston, although she was considerably younger.

7. GCPC Minutes Book 51, pp. 29, 269–70; Book 91, pp. 336–37, 587–88.

8. Houstoun, *Texas and the Gulf*, p. 123; *Flake's Bulletin*, July 14, 1869; *GDN*, July 13, 14, 1869; August 27, 28, 1875.

9. Ibid., November 3, 1885; *Galveston Tribune*, April 3, 1915.

10. (Trave) GCCO, Real Property Records, Book 48, pp. 16–18. In the 1880 census, Trave is Trava, but his name is Anglicized in other documents.

11. (Adam) GCCO, Real Property Records, Book 82, pp. 215–16; Galveston Insurance Board Records; GCPC Minutes Book 54, pp. 469–471; J. P. Alvey to "the Honorable Mayor and Board of City Commissioners," February 18, 1904, Papers of Edmund R. Cheesborough, 1867–1961, Grade-Raising Letterpress Book 2, p. 215, RL; Mortuary Record No. 5, p. 129. Adam's name was not spelled Adams.

12. Day, née Matilda Young, married James Day in February 1868, but the city directories never listed a Matilda Day and a James Day at the same location. She appeared in Recorder's Court in July 1869, when a bedstead she owned, valued at $5, was stolen. She died

in 1901. Index to Galveston Marriages, Book D, p. 48; *GDN*, July 15, 1869; Mortuary Record No. 4, p. 31.

13. (Jackson) *GDN*, September 24, 1875; Mortuary Record No. 3, p. 112. James Jackson, like Matilda Day, was buried in Potter's Field.

14. GCPC Records, Inventories Book 2, pp. 223–24.

15. (Cross) GCCO, Real Property Records, Book 5, pp. 352–53; Book 6, p. 449; Book 43, pp. 533–34. After the fire, Cross moved to the corner of Avenue C and Fourteenth Street, where he had bought two more lots; on them were a second grocery and feed store operated by his family and at least four more residential units that added to his rental income.

16. (Cunningham) Ibid., Book 32, pp. 193–94.

17. (Burnett) U.S. Census records for Houston County, 1870, microfilm, CGL; *GDN*, October 5, 1875; GCPC Minutes Book 17, pp. 587–92, 607–12; GCCO, Real Property Records, Book 181, p. 107; Book 156, pp. 633–34; Book 146, p. 601; *GDN*, December 5, 1908; *Galveston Tribune*, December 5, 1908.

18. (Palliser) GCCO, Real Property Records, Filing Index No. 6, beginning date January 2, 1883; Book 208, p. 462; Book 251, p. 56; GCPC Minutes Book 79, pp. 519–23. No connection has been established between this Robert Palliser and Palliser Palliser & Co., a New York architectural firm and publisher of popular plan books.

19. Ort is an enigmatic personality. The 1900 census and his 1907 death record disclose that he was born in Germany in 1825 and migrated to the United States and to Texas in 1851. His name does not appear in earlier census records for either Galveston or Texas, but the transferral of his body to Fayetteville, Texas, as noted in the mortuary records, suggests that he first settled elsewhere in the state. Mortuary Record No. 5, p. 74.

20. In 1900, both Ort and Burnett were living with their children. Ort's son was a "landlord" in Galveston, and given the amount of property for which they were assessed, this must have kept him busy. Burnett had moved to Houston with his daughter and son-in-law, a realtor whose management of family investments still included Galveston holdings. U.S. Census records for Harris County and Galveston County, 1900, microfilm, CGL.

21. Index to Galveston Marriages, Book O, p. 33.

Chapter 6
Devastation and Reconstruction: The 1900 Hurricane

1. U.S. Census for Galveston County, 1900; *Morrison & Fourmy's General Directory of the City of Galveston, 1899–1900* (Galveston: Morrison & Fourmy, 1899).

2. Ousley, *Galveston in Nineteen Hundred*, pp. 291–305.

3. Rawick, *American Slave*, vol. 6, *Texas Narratives*, pt. 5:2010–12.

4. *Report of the Central Relief Committee for Galveston Storm Sufferers. Galveston, Texas, May 2, 1902* (Galveston: Clarke & Courts, 1902), p. 1, RL.

5. Ibid., p. 9; Edmund R. Cheesborough to Peter Kleyn, February 2, 1904, Cheesborough Papers, Letterpress Book 2, p. 122.

6. *Report of the Central Relief Committee*, pp. 9–10. Committee funds also were used to repair 42 cotton mill cottages, and to build and set 1,432 water closets and cesspools.

7. H. M. Trueheart to Arthur J. Burns, Yonkers, New York, October 12, 1900, Trueheart Papers, Letterpress Book 286, p. 434.

8. Trueheart to Mississippi Valley Trust Co., St. Louis, September 27, 1900, p. 115; Trueheart to A. O. Slaughter, Chicago, September 26, 1900, p. 93. Both Letterpress Book 286. According to the 1900 Galveston County Assessor's Abstracts, Slaughter owned lot 8 in Block 507, which was valued at $2,000 with improvements valued at $1,500.

9. Trueheart to Slaughter, September 26, 1900, Letterpress Book 286, p. 93.

10. David G. McComb, *Galveston, A History* (Austin: University of Texas Press, 1986), p. 122.

11. Galveston city directories, 1899–1900 and 1901–2.

Following the storm, Ward Five continued to have the highest alley population with 271 listings. Ward Six, with 175 alley entries, was second highest. Ward Six was the only part of town where individuals were listed as living in tents at a rear address: There were 9, all white, 2 of whom were women.

There were 106 individuals at the same alley address in both directories, as well as another 22 people who were probably at the same alley location. Another 133 individuals had moved to a different alley. These numbers do not reflect servants who may have been living in back buildings on their employer's property. In both directories there were two businesses at rear addresses; one of them, a kindergarten, was at the same address both years.

12. Lynn M. Alperin, *Custodians of the Coast: History of the United States Army Engineers at Galveston* (Galveston: Galveston District United States Army Corps of Engineers, 1977), pp. 242–44; *GDN*, January 27, 1902; December 28, 1904; July 20, 23, 1904; August 11, 1910.

There is not a precise date when the filling began. On July 2, 1904, the *Galveston Daily News* reported that "the inauguration of dredging," begun on July 1, "was not made a demonstrative event," because the sand was not, as yet, being deposited in the fill area. On

July 20, the paper declared that "residents of Galveston may now consider the work of raising the city as practically commenced." Three days later, a headline read: "NOW FILLING IN AVENUE A."

The primary printed sources for the grade-raising project are two sets of scrapbooks containing newspaper clippings, which are in the Rosenberg Library. The Cheesborough Papers include six "Grade-Raising" scrapbooks that were kept by Edmund R. Cheesborough, the Secretary of the Grade Raising Board. In 1913, the library staff assembled three volumes of clippings pertaining to the Seawall and the grade-raising. There is duplication in the two sets, but there are also differences: Cheesborough tended to clip more articles about personal anecdotes than did the library staff. The newspaper articles cited in this chapter are contained in the two sets of scrapbooks, both of which are arranged chronologically.

The primary grade-raising area was everything east of Thirteenth Street, and south of the north line of Avenue J to Forty-fifth Street. This excluded the downtown commercial district; Ward Five, which had the highest alley population in the city; and Ward Six. Engineers calculated that these areas were not sufficiently below grade to justify jacking up the buildings, which would have been particularly difficult, if not impossible, in the commercial district. In those areas, it was left to individual property owners to raise their properties to a specified grade at their own expense. *GDN*, June 4, 1903; December 12, 1903.

Both the Seawall and the raising of the island have been extended well beyond the boundaries of the original projects.

13. McComb, *Galveston*, pp. 134–43. McComb provides a good summary of both the Seawall and the grade-raising projects and the politics involved. See also T. Lindsay Baker, "Galveston Graderaising Was a Big Engineering Project," *GDN*, May 11, 1974; Don Walden, "Raising Galveston," *American Heritage of Technology and Invention*, Winter 1990, pp. 8–18.

14. *GDN*, February 21, 1904; September 20, 1903; December 17, 1903; December 12, 1903. The number of houses that were raised was adjusted to 2,156 in an article in the *Galveston Daily News*, January 1, 1905. This was also the number used in a final project report published in the *News* on September 1, 1910.

15. *GDN*, February 21, 1904; October 31, 1907. Raising a house on fifteen-foot supports was the highest reference noted. Most buildings were raised less than ten feet.

16. Various locations were considered for obtaining fill material. Dredging from the bay was believed to be the safest and most economically feasible solution and had the added appeal of deepening the harbor.

17. *GDN*, April 14, 1905; *The Galveston New Idea*, July 30, 1904; Rawick, *American Slave*, vol. 8, *Texas Narratives*, pt. 7:3234–37. Ramsey was listed intermittently in the city directories at 1228 Avenue I from 1909–10 through the 1920s. Her interviewer in 1937 noted that "she now lives at 1228 Ave. I (rear)." Rawick, *American Slave*, p. 3227.

18. *Galveston Tribune*, November 18, 1904.

19. Cheesborough to "Mrs. Mosely (Col'd)," June 13, 1904, Letterpress Book 2, p. 459.

20. Cheesborough to Messrs. Goedhart & Bates, June 13, 1904, Letterpress Book 2, pp. 464–65. Many of Cheesborough's letters written to the Galveston office of Goedhart & Bates were not directed to a specific individual. In his letter regarding Rachel Hawkins's lot, Cheesborough stated that the owners of the lot were "a family by the name of Stone." Fannie Stone owned the north, or front, half of the lot. In the February 21, 1904, issue of the *Galveston Daily News*, a listing of houses that had to be raised included "Mrs. R. Hawkins," not Stone, as owner of lot 4. Cheesborough probably considered Stone and Hawkins to be a single family unit.

21. Cheesborough to Goedhart & Bates, June 13, 1904, Letterpress Book 2, pp. 464–65; *Galveston Tribune*, November 18, 1904; *GDN*, January 1, 1905. Leaving the lots unfilled caused havoc to adjoining lots once the bulkheads were removed, but property owners who could not afford to raise their houses certainly could not afford to fill their lots, which was the policy. Just how this was resolved remains unclear.

22. *GDN*, December 12, 17, 1903; *Map of the City of Galveston, Texas*, compiled by C. G. Wells, C.E., January, 1904, with pencil overlay showing grade-raising canal, RL (Map 466-A). This is the map that was used to make the schematic maps in figs. 43, 52, 89, and 90.

23. Cheesborough to Kleyn, March 21, 1904, pp. 344–45; Cheesborough to Judge William T. Austin, Mayor of Galveston, April 27, 1904, p. 389; Cheesborough to Goedhart & Bates, May 12, 1904, p. 420 (all Letterpress Book 2); *Directory of the City of Galveston 1903–1904* (Galveston: Morrison & Fourmy Directory Co., 1903); *Directory of the City of Galveston 1906–07* (Galveston: Morrison & Fourmy Directory Co., 1906). Peter Kleyn was an engineer with Goedhart & Bates.

24. Cheesborough to Kleyn, February 13, 1904, Letterpress Book 2, p. 162; Cheesborough to Goedhart & Bates, March 8, 1905, Letterpress Book 3, p. 324; Galveston city directory, 1903–4 and 1906–7. In the 1903–4 directory, Wentzel's address was "rear 618 Winnie"; in the 1906–7 directory, it was "613 7th" and his household had added an eighth member.

25. *Galveston Tribune*, [November 30] 1905; *GDN*, March 7, 1905; Cheesborough to V. E. Austin, January 30, 1905, Letterpress Book 3, p. 270; *GDN*, April 12, 1905; February 24, 1905.

26. Cheesborough to Judge M. E. Kleberg, May 18, 1905, Letterpress Book 3, pp. 417–18. Kleberg was the

City Attorney. On October 9, 1909, Cheesborough sent a similar request to Commissioner I. H. Kempner on behalf of "Clara Cooper, a negro woman" who leased her property to the city for the canal. Cheesborough noted that "this negress was very fair with the city" and that it will be "necessary for her to make a sacrifice" to pay all her back taxes, asking Kempner to be "as liberal as you can in the way of a rebate." Letterpress Book 5, p. 359.

27. *GDN*, January 1, 1905; November 1, 1907; April 22, 1908.

28. *GDN*, April 14, 1905; *Galveston Tribune*, May 18, 1905; *GDN*, February 22, 1905.

29. Cheesborough to Kleyn, March 21, 1904, Letterpress Book 2, p. 345; Cheesborough to Goedhart & Bates, April 6, 1908, Letterpress Book 5, p. 113.

30. *GDN*, October 15, 1908.

31. Cheesborough to Mrs. L. M. Clayton, September 26, 1905, Letterpress Book 4, pp. 68–69; Cheesborough to Miles Crowley, July 2, 1910, p. 451; Cheesborough to A. T. Dickey, July 26, 1910, p. 459; Cheeseborough to Oswald Killi, July 29, 1910, p. 461. Last three letters in Letterpress Book 5.

32. Galveston city directory, 1901–2; *Directory of the City of Galveston, 1911–12* (Galveston: Morrison & Fourmy Directory Co., 1911).

Of the 1,221 alley residents listed in the 1911–12 directory, only 18 people can be identified as definitely living at the same address as in the 1901–2 directory, a very small number proportionate to the number of people listed on the alleys. Another 100 individuals had moved to a different alley location.

Chapter 7
Change along the Alley: Technology and Housing Reform

1. James S. Hanna, *What Life Was Like When I Was a Kid* (San Antonio: The Naylor Company, 1973), pp. 46–47.

2. Ibid., p. 20.

3. Ibid., pp. 27–28, 44. Becky, whose last name was never mentioned by Hanna, was among those women who lived on their employer's property and whose primary responsibility was laundering. Other women took in laundry rather than working for a single family. The 1910 Galveston census lists 1,121 laundresses, second in number to the 1,138 female servants, the largest occupational category for women. There were also 30 male launderers, and 79 women and 19 men who worked in commercial laundries. *Thirteenth Census of the United States, Population 1910, Population Statistics* (Washington: Government Printing Office, 1914), 4:236.

4. U.S. Census for Galveston County, 1900 and 1910. Becky was not listed in the Hanna household in either the 1900 or 1910 census. This suggests that she lived on the property sometime between those years. Not knowing Becky's last name makes a simple check in the city directories impossible. No one with the first name of Becky is listed as working for the Hannas in the 1901–2, 1903–4, or 1905 directories.

5. Hanna, *What Life Was Like*, pp. 59–60.

6. Interview with Adrian Levy on February 12, 1991; *GDN*, June 16, 18, 20, 1915; *Galveston Tribune*, April 3, 1915.

7. *GDN*, June 19, 1915; May 28, 1914; *Abstract of the Fourteenth Census of the United States, 1920* (Washington: Government Printing Office, 1923), p. 782.

8. Both the July 27, 1904, issue of the *Galveston Daily News* and the July 30, 1904, issue of *The Galveston New Idea,* a black newspaper, reported the incident. The *Daily News* printed the inquest testimony at length, but it was the *New Idea* that embellished the story, describing Singleton as an "embryo Baptist preacher" and a "Dr. Jekyl and Mr. Hyde" who "carried himself sanctimoniously and wore a silent churchy bearing," and who, "as a minister . . . was making fast strides, as a devil still faster." Few issues of black newspapers published in Galveston are extant.

9. *Negro Population in the United States, 1790–1915* (New York: Arno Press and The New York Times, 1968), pp. 472–73; *Thirteenth Census of the United States, Population 1910, General Report and Analysis* (Washington: Government Printing Office, 1913), 1:1365.

According to the 1910 census, the total population in Galveston was 36,981. The city's 8,036 black residents lived in 2,023 "Negro homes." Of these, 1,752 (87 percent) were rented, 169 (8.4 percent) were owned, and 102 were not reported. In contrast, of the 6,235 houses occupied by whites, 3,730 (60 percent) were rented, 2,253 (36 percent) were owned, and 252 were not reported.

On a statewide basis, Galveston was one of sixteen Texas cities with a black population of 2,500 or more in 1910. It was fifth in population—behind Houston, Dallas, Fort Worth, and San Antonio— but fifteenth in the number of homes owned by blacks. Only Temple, with a black population of 2,814, had fewer black-owned homes (141). On a national level, there were 188 cities with a black population of 2,500 or more. Only eighteen cities had a smaller percentage than Galveston of blacks who owned their houses. *Negro Population*, pp. 472–74.

10. Larry James Wygant, "Medicine and Public Health in Galveston, Texas: The First Century" (Ph.D. dissertation, University of Texas Medical Branch at Galveston, 1992), p. 263; *GDN*, September 1, 1913.

11. George Waverly Briggs, *The Housing Problem in Texas: A Study of Physical Conditions under which the Other Half Lives*, reprinted from *The Galveston-Dallas News*, November–December, 1911, p. 45.

12. Ibid., pp. 40–41, 44.

13. Ibid., pp. 45–47.

14. Ibid., pp. 17, 20–21, 24–25, 41, 69–70, 83.

15. Ibid., p. 49.

16. Ibid., pp. 94, 96. Veiller considered the alley "both a blessing and a curse" but "a distinct sanitary evil." See Lawrence Veiller, "Buildings in Relation to Street and Site" in *Proceedings of the Third National Conference on City Planning, Philadelphia, Pennsylvania, May 15–17, 1911* (Boston: 1911), pp. 80–96.

17. Briggs, *Housing Problem*, pp. 90–91; City of Galveston Minutes, April 13, 1911, through April 19, 1913, Book No. 6, City Hall.

18. Ibid., February 20, 1913, Minutes, Book 6, p. 430; *GDN*, February 21, 1913.

19. James Persons Simonds, *Report of a Sanitary Survey of the City of Galveston, Texas* (Galveston: Galveston Commercial Association, 1913), p. 2.

20. Ibid., pp. 4–5, 14–15.

21. Ibid., pp. 15–16. Twelve shotgun houses were built on lots 9 through 12 by owner Gustav Schultz, manager of the Western Union Telegraph Office. Four of the houses were parallel to the alley and the entrances reoriented. Seven houses, including six modified shotgun houses, were built on lots 13 and 14 by realtor William F. Ort, son of Johann Ort. A notation on the block diagram in the tax assessor's abstracts states that new improvements were built on these two lots in 1910. Three houses were built on lot 8 by George H. Nicholls, who was a partner in a freight transfer and warehouse business. The north half of the block was occupied by residences and the black high school. The family of J. H. Burnett owned lot 4. Sanborn maps, 1899 and 1912; Galveston County Assessor's Abstracts, 1898–1914; Galveston city directories.

22. Simonds, *Sanitary Survey*, pp. 30, 16.

23. Minutes, City of Galveston, February 12, 1914, Book 7, p. 222.

24. Ibid., April 2, 1914, Book 7, p. 274; *GDN*, April 3, 1914. The minutes for the April 2, 1914, meeting of the city commissioners recorded that Judge Robert G. Street of the 56th District Court submitted a report, but the minutes did not disclose the contents. That information was printed in the newspaper.

25. Ibid., May 28, 1914. Briggs began his journalism career in Austin in 1905 and became editor of the *GDN* sometime in 1913-14, a position he held for "several years" before resigning in 1918 to become state banking commissioner. He later accepted a position as an official in a Dallas bank. *GDN*, December 28, 1928.

26. Ibid., May 28, 1914.

27. Minutes, City of Galveston, June 4, 1914, Book 7, p. 322; ibid., June 11, 1914, Book 7, pp. 326–27; ibid., July 23, 1914, Book 7, p. 373; *GDN*, June 5, 11, 12, 1914.

28. *Building Code, City of Galveston*, adopted October 29, 1914, p. 86, RL.

29. Simonds, *Sanitary Survey*, p. 15; Wygant, "Medicine and Public Health," pp. 284–86.

30. Ibid., p. 283.

31. The ordinance was published in the *Galveston Tribune*, October 4, 1920.

Chapter 8
Alleyscapes

1. See chapter 1, note 24, page 150, for a description of the Civil War map.

2. Thomas Barns to Iola Barns Beers, September 22, 1894, Beers Family Papers.

3. GCCO, Real Property Records, Book V, pp. 166–68; Book X, p. 77. The James Codling mentioned here is the same James Codling who was carpenter John Burbank's cousin and who died in the 1867 yellow fever epidemic (see chapter 2, pp. 25, 26).

4. McLeod to Beers, February 18, 1867, and June 12, 1867; Simonds, *Sanitary Survey*, p. 14.

Chapter 9
Stepping into the Yard: Service Buildings and Back Houses

1. *GDN*, November 22, 1885.

2. Building specifications, W. S. Deats and Bros. for William H. Williams, Samuel May Williams Papers, RL. Photocopy document 23-4163.

3. HABS, Photograph–Data Book Report, Henry Rosenberg House.

4. Eleanor H. Gustafson, "The Open Gates: the George Sealy house in Galveston," *The Magazine Antiques* (September 1975): 508–14; N. J. Clayton & Co., Architects, to George Sealy, Statement of Expenditures, March 9, 1892, Clayton Papers, RL.

5. George Sealy Stable, Drawings and Floor Plans, 1889–1891, Clayton Papers, RL; U.S. Census records for Galveston County, 1900.

6. (Sonnentheil house) Galveston Insurance Board Records. The insurance board records are valuable documents in studying Galveston buildings, but they must be used with care. Inspectors from the late nine-

teenth century until the 1960s frequently used the same worksheets, and it is not always easy to decipher notations nor to determine when they were written. The worksheets are arranged by block number.

7. (Smith house) *GDN,* August 4, 1884; Galveston Insurance Board Records; U.S. Census records for Galveston County, 1900.

8. (Landes house) Paul Goeldner, *Texas Catalog: Historic American Buildings Survey* (San Antonio, Tex.: Trinity University Press, 1974), pp. 105–6; HABS, Photograph–Data Book Report, March 17, 1967, TEX-2102, photocopy, RL; Galveston Insurance Board Records; U.S. Census records for Galveston County, 1900.

9. (Clarke house) *GDN*, September 1, 1899; Galveston Insurance Board Records; *GDN*, June 6, 1900; W. W. Dexter, *Picturesque Galveston* (Galveston: Clarke & Courts, [1900?]), p. 78; U.S. Census records for Galveston County, 1900. The photograph in *Picturesque Galveston* is a corner view and does not show the carriage-house side of the property. The closets mentioned in the insurance records were not water closets. The insurance form made a clear distinction between closets and bathrooms.

10. See notes 7–9 above.

11. (Henck house) Galveston Insurance Board Records; U.S. Census records for Galveston County, 1900.

12. (2020 Avenue J) The Galveston Insurance Board sheet for this property offers no help in dating the rear building.

13. (Kruger house) U.S. Census records for Galveston County, 1900.

14. Minor to Truehart, October 3, 1870; Galveston Insurance Board Records.

Chapter 10
Stepping into the Alley: Alley Houses

1. Taped interview with Inez R. Lasell, February 19, 1991.

2. *GDN*, October 20, 1885; City of Galveston Minutes, Book 11, December 4, 1899, p. 387, City Secretary's Office, City Hall; *GDN*, May 28, 1914.

3. *Galveston Daily Mercury*, March 20, 1875.

4. (1112 Twenty-second Street) Galveston Insurance Board Records; Galveston County Assessor's Abstracts. By 1901, Mrs. Rudolph (Lena) Kruger had become the owner of the property. This is the same Kruger family that owned the house at 1628 Avenue E. (See chapter 9, pp. 104–5.)

5. (1505 Avenue F rear) Galveston Insurance Board records; taped interview with Louis Martin, September 7, 1990. Sarah Bennett was listed in the city directories as living in this block on the Avenue G side of the alley from 1901–2 through 1909–10. (See chapter 4, pp. 44–5.)

6. *Civilian and Galveston City Gazette,* December 11, 1847.

7. (1515 Avenue L rear) Galveston Insurance Board Records; Galveston city directory, 1901–2; Galveston County Assessor's Abstracts.

8. For a discussion of the shotgun house and its origins, see John Michael Vlach, "The Shotgun House: An African Architectural Legacy," in *Common Places: Readings in American Vernacular Architecture*, ed. by Dell Upton and John Michael Vlach (Athens: The University of Georgia Press, 1986), pp. 58–78. Vlach has authored numerous publications about the shotgun house, but this article is cited because the book includes other essays of interest to students of vernacular architecture.

9. *GDN*, November 20, 1885; *Report of the Central Relief Committee*, p. 10.

10. (2810 and 2818 Avenue L rear) Galveston Insurance Board Records; Galveston County Assessor's Abstracts; Galveston city directory for 1911–12.

11. *Building Code, City of Galveston*, adopted October 29, 1914, pp. 12, 14–15.

12. *GDN*, April 2, 1880.

13. Ibid., April 4, 1885.

14. Eugene Marshall's Diary.

15. *GDN*, October 3, 1875. The paper published a short list of additional building improvements on October 5, 1875.

16. *Civilian and Gazette*, January 13, 1857; U.S. Census, Galveston County Free and Slave Schedules, 1860; "Black Galveston," pp. 7, 11, 77.

17. *GDN*, July 11, 1865.

Chapter 11
Speaking of Alleys and Back Buildings . . .

1. Interview with Margaret and David Ritter, February 20, 1991.

2. All the interviews in the chapter, except those with Mavis P. Kelsey Sr. and Danny Lasell, were conducted in Galveston; Kelsey and Lasell were interviewed in Houston. The interviews were taped.

3. The middle name of all three Clouser boys is Zachary, their mother's maiden name.

4. Kelsey is a founder of Kelsey-Seybold Clinics in Houston.

5. Pauline Hertz is a pseudonym.

6. Ethel Palmer died in 1994.

7. Since the interview, the Stovalls have moved to another location.

8. Willie Mae Clay has also moved. The living quarters in the service building have been adapted to office use.

Conclusion: A Matter of Choice

1. Any reference to the alleys as a resource must acknowledge the publication written by Grady Clay, *Alleys: A Hidden Resource* (Louisville: Grady Clay and Company, 1978). Clay has had a long-standing interest in alleys as well as being a promoter of their benefits. This publication was a planning document for alleys in Louisville.

2. Houstoun, *Texas and the Gulf*, p. 128.

3. Thus far, there is only one book devoted exclusively to the alleys of a specific American city—James Borchert's seminal study, *Alley Life in Washington: Family, Community, Religion, and Folklife in the City, 1850-1970* (Urbana: University of Illinois Press, 1980). Documents, particularly photographs, are probably much more extensive for Washington alleys than for alleys in most other places. The condition of Washington alleys became a national concern because of their proximity to the Capitol.

See also David M. Katzman, *Before the Ghetto: Black Detroit in the Nineteenth Century* (Urbana: University of Illinois Press, 1973).

There are many books that discuss alleys, albeit briefly, but even then the subject frequently is not indexed. Hopefully, this oversight will be corrected as more writers and scholars in a variety of disciplines conduct research into alleys, alley dwellers, and alley buildings and as the subject acquires greater acceptance as being worthy of attention.

4. Taped interview with Oscar T. Ekelund Jr., March 19, 1991.

5. Interview with Leon M. Banks Sr., March 1985.

Illustration Credits

The author wishes to express her appreciation to the institutions and individuals who provided illustrations.

Courtesy Rosenberg Library: Figs. 1, 13, 16, 17, 19, 20, 23, 25, 27, 28, 30, 32, 35, 36, 39, 40, 41, 54, 71, 75, 76, 81, 82, 83, 84, 91, 92, 93, 94, 95, 99, 101, 107, 108, 116, 118, 123, 132, 168, 169, 174, 175, 187. In addition, all photographs of Sanborn insurance maps were made from the holdings of Rosenberg Library. Photographs of the 1885 Sanborn insurance map were made from a photostat produced by the Library of Congress: Figs. 4, 14, 26, 29, 31, 33, 69, 70, 105. Photographs of the 1912 Sanborn insurance map with later pasteovers are courtesy Rosenberg Library and Sanborn Mapping and Geographic Information Service: Figs. 11, 96 (bottom). Photographs of the 1889 and 1899 Sanborn insurance maps, and of the 1912 map with no pasteovers are courtesy Rosenberg Library: Figs. 45, 47, 50, 53, 56, 57, 61, 67, 72, 73, 96 (top), 100, 110, 111, 119, 124, 138, 152, 157, 161.

Photographs by author: Frontispiece, figs. 2, 3, 7, 8, 9, 24, 37, 42, 48, 51, 55, 59, 62, 63, 74, 78, 104, 112, 113, 114, 115, 117, 120, 121, 125, 128, 131, 134, 135, 137, 139, 140, 141, 144, 146, 147, 148, 149, 151, 153, 154, 158, 159, 162, 163, 165, 177, 178, 182, 183, 185, 186, 188, 189, 190, 191.

Courtesy H. Kempner Trust Association: Figs. 5, 46, 66, 68. The close-ups in figs. 5, 46, and 66 were made from the association's print of the 1885 Koch bird's-eye view. The close-up in fig. 68 was made from another bird's-eye view published by the Galveston printer M. Strickland & Co. after the 1885 fire and demarcating the area burned. Clearly based on the Koch view, the Strickland view is easier to read for some sections of the city because it does not have the shading of the Koch view. The sometimes shaky lines of the Strickland view suggest that it was a tracing of the Koch view.

Courtesy Texas and Local History Department, Houston Metropolitan Research Center, Houston Public Library: Fig. 6.

Architectural drawings by Longoria/Peters: Figs. 10, 38, 60, 106, 109, 122, 127, 129, 130, 133, 136, 142, 143, 150, 155, 156, 160, 184.

Courtesy Bill Millican: Fig. 12.

Courtesy Library of Congress: Figs. 15, 18, 21, 22, 77.

Maps by Minor Design: Figs. 34, 43, 52, 80, 89, 90.

Collection of Douglas R. Zwiener Jr., and Allison Z. Parsley: Fig. 44.

Courtesy Blocker History of Medicine Collections, Moody Medical Library, University of Texas Medical Branch, Galveston: Figs. 49, 102.

Author's collection: Figs. 58, 145, 171, 172. (The Bunjes drawings were reproduced for sale.)

Courtesy Robert M. Tucker: Figs. 64, 65.

Courtesy The Center for American History, University of Texas at Austin: Fig. 79.

Courtesy Billy Phillips: Figs. 85, 86, 87, 88, 126.

From *Survey*: Figs. 97, 98.

Courtesy Leon M. Banks Jr.: Fig. 103.

Courtesy Annie Mae Charles: Fig. 164.

Courtesy Gerald Z. Clouser Sr.: Figs. 166, 167.

Courtesy Inez R. Lasell: Figs. 170, 176.

Courtesy Mavis P. Kelsey Sr.: Fig. 173.

Courtesy John and Luanne Stovall: Figs. 179, 180.

Courtesy Willie Mae Clay: Fig. 181.

Index

Page references in italics refer to illustrations. References in boldface type refer to excerpts from interviews.

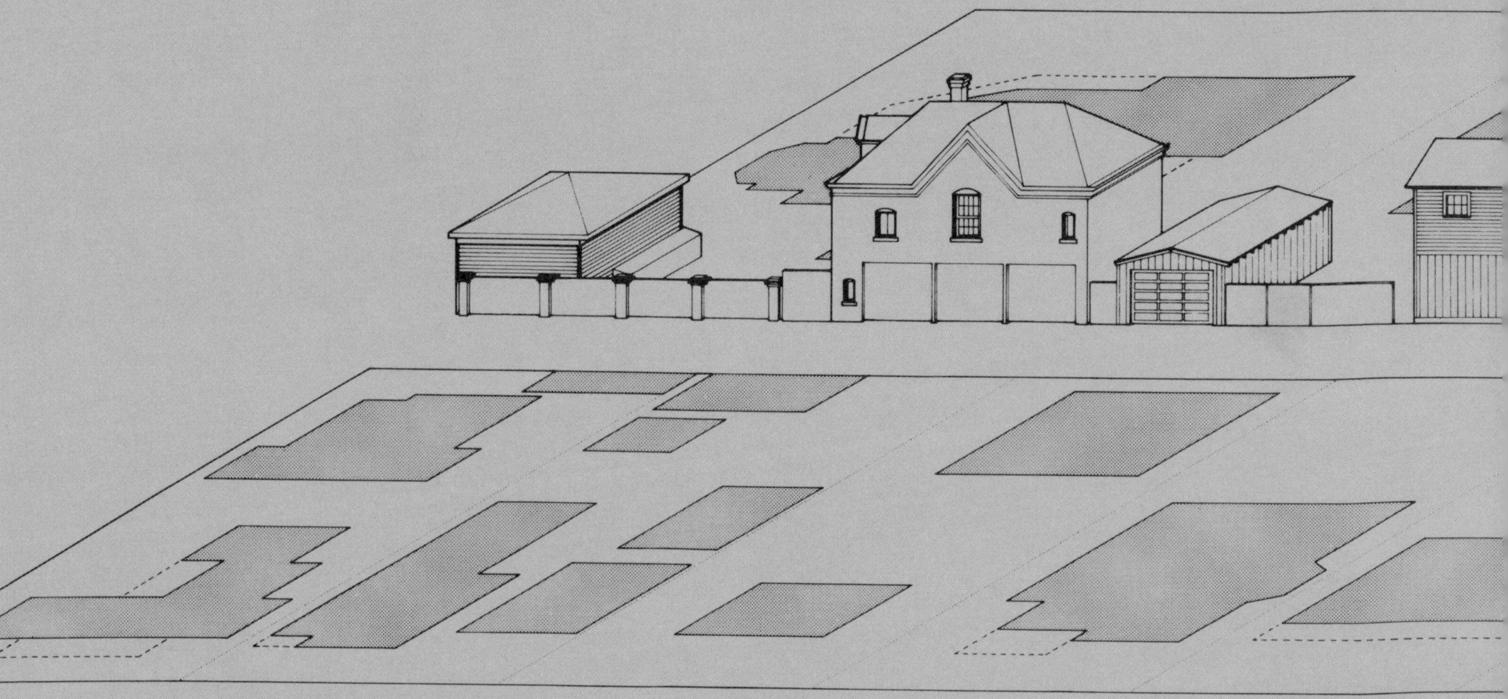